D 14

Cyril Fox
Archaeologist Extraordinary

SIR CYRIL FOX
From a drawing by Evan Walters 1937 presented to the National Museum of Wales by Lady Fox 1948
(By courtesy of the National Museums and Galleries of Wales)

Cyril Fox
Archaeologist Extraordinary

by

Charles Scott-Fox

with a Preface by

Christopher Chippindale

Oxbow Books

Published by
Oxbow Books
Park End Place, Oxford

ISBN 1 84217 080 5

A CIP Record of this book is available from the British Library

This book is available from

Oxbow Books, Park End Place, Oxford OX1 1HN
Tel: 01865–241249; Fax: 01865–794449
Email: oxbow@oxbowbooks.com

and

The David Brown Book Co.
PO Box 511, Oakville, CT 06779
Tel: (860) 945–9329; Fax: (860) 945–9468
Email: david.brown.bk.co@snet.net

and via the website

www.oxbowbooks.com

Printed in England at
The Short Run Press
Exeter

To Cyril Fox

A companion volume
to your Festschrift
from your children
with affection

Abbreviations

Ant.J.	*Antiquaries Journal* (Society of Antiquaries)
Arch.	*Archaeologia* (Society of Antiquaries)
Arch.Camb.	*Archaeologia Cambrensis* (Cambrian Archaeological Association)
Arch.J.	*Archaeological Journal* (Royal Archaeological Institute)
Beds.Hist.	*Bedfordshire History* (Bedfordshire Historical Society)
BBCS	*Bulletin for the Board of Celtic Studies*
Br.Acad.	*Proceedings of the British Academy*
Camb.Ant.	*Communications of the Cambridge Antiquarian Society*
Cardiff Nat.	*Cardiff Naturalist Society*
CPRW	The Council for the Preservation of Rural Wales
Mus.Journ.	*Museums Association Journal* (Museums Association)
NMGW	National Museums and Galleries of Wales
NMW	National Museum of Wales
Path.Bact.	*Journal of Pathology and Bacteriology* (The Pathological Society of Great Britain and Ireland)
Prehist.Soc.	*Proceedings of the Prehistoric Society*
Proc.Pre.E.Ang.	*Proceedings of the Prehistoric Society of East Anglia*
Records of Bucks	(Buckinghamshire Archaeological Society)
Soc.Cym.	*Y Cymmrodor, Transactions of the Honourable Society of Cymmrodorion*
Som.Arch.	*Somerset Archaeology*
Times Lit.Sup.	*The Times Literary Supplement*

Contents

List of Illustrations

Although most of the illustrations in this book came from Cyril Fox's pen or camera, the majority were destroyed shortly after his death. They only survive as illustrations for his books, or in the publications of the learned societies to which he contributed. I am most grateful to those Societies, the Cambridge University Press and to the National Museums and Galleries of Wales for permission to reproduce from their publications. The publication from which these illustrations have been taken is shown below. I also gratefully acknowledge the assistance of the National Library of Wales and Western Mail & Echo Ltd for four photographs taken from the Western Mail and South Wales Echo. Despite an extensive search the origins of four illustrations from the family archive cannot be traced.

Colour Plates *(between pages 141–142)*

Note
1. Illustrations of *Offa's Dyke* were reprinted by the British Academy.
2. Some illustrations for *Pattern and Purpose* can be found in earlier proceedings of several Societies. Acknowledgement of first publication is given in the footnotes.
3. Unattributed illustrations are from the family archives.
4. Most illustrations in the Routledge publication *Life and Death in the Bronze Age* were first published in Society journals. Attribution is given to those Societies but the author wishes to acknowledge Routledge's permission for the use of some photographs from that book.

Preface

Archaeologists, like historians, think the past matters; that is why we spend our lives exploring archaeology and history. We can only study those subjects because the materials survive from the past to tell the story. If we are to have any consistency, then we jolly well should create the materials about ourselves for people in the future in turn to use when we are past. In our modern lives, fortunately, we create garbage and rubbish in terrifying quantity, enough to create artificial mountains of refuse tips. On our deaths, some of us behave less well. The duty at that moment is to do the right thing with our physical selves, for burials are a prime source of archaeological evidence, especially when they are richly furnished with artefacts. At the other extreme, if a human body is cremated, if the fragments of burnt bone – especially when ground to powder as crematoria nowadays always do – are then scattered, it leaves practically no archaeological trace; indeed, the unhappy archaeological trace, a diffuse and ill-defined spread of phosphate in the soil, is dismayingly similar to what is created by manuring. As archaeologists are more self-consciously professionals guided by correct ethics, I have often thought we should declare it unprofessional conduct to be burnt and scattered; instead we must require all of us properly to be inhumed with artefacts usefully informative and diagnostic of ourselves – from which successor archaeologists in some distant future may try to learn from if they wish.

Alongside that right way of leaving our material traces, honoured or not, it is good there is a healthy tradition of archaeologists writing autobiographies, a task in which we are helped by so many archaeologists living to a grand age. One of us who has recently done so is Aileen Fox, with her *Aileen – A Pioneering Archaeologist* (Leominster: Gracewing, 2000). Aileen is Cyril Fox's widow as well as a distinguished and strikingly original archaeologist in her own right. More of us neglect that autobiographical duty, rightly believing that our lives are too plain to be worth reporting, or the things we spend years doing are too technically obscure. Glyn Daniel, one of us who did the right thing by publishing an autobiography (but his body was cremated and may, I fear, have then been scattered), illustrated in it the billboard for the London *Evening Standard* which said 'Famous Archaeologist Dies.' Who was the 'Famous Archaeologist'? In

Daniel's era, it could only be, and duly was Sir Mortimer Wheeler: none of the rest was so famous they needed no name. Wheeler became famous through television, like Glyn Daniel, and in some remote years in the early 1950s the two friends were declared successively TV Personalities of the Year for their performances on 'Animal, Vegetable, Mineral'. Looking at the few minutes of peculiar black-and-white film, which is all that survives, one may think TV must have been even odder then than it is now – if such is possible. Our subject, Cyril Fox, did at least do part of the right thing by writing just a few autobiographical notes, but they were not published.

Fewer archaeologists have biographies written by others, and when they do, it is usually other archaeologists who write them: Wheeler's life was written by Jacquetta Hawks, Grahame Clark's by Brian Fagan – of the trade, by the trade, for the trade. Myself an archaeologist immersed within the little world of archaeologists, even I find this habit seems closed and even incestuous. But perhaps the same is true of all the world, and in each little compartment, chemists write biographies of chemists which only chemists read, and so on in a thousand separate little worlds.

This is the first way in which the present biography stands out: a biography of an archaeologist written not by an archaeologist, but by an author who lives in a different and more real world, and frankly states that the technical obscurities in which its archaeological subject was immersed are beyond his ken. The book is the better and the fresher for that. And there is a personal aspect to it, which catches my interest: Charles Scott-Fox was born son to Cyril Fox, his subject, when his father was 51 years old. Like many a child of an old father, his own knowledge and memories are of the older man, and so an impulse to his writing this book has been the discovery of his own father: who was this man, when a child? when young? when in (the younger parts of) middle age? this man who the author knew only in his older years? what were the things done or not done, suppressed or forgotten or left behind – the things which lay behind what was visible or acknowledged in the adult world the author was born into?

* * *

Archaeology is a capricious business. Many a promising site disappoints or turns into a nonsense: a singular feature called 'Peter's Mound' was briefly a key element in the ancient astronomy of Stonehenge at many hundreds of years BC – until its exploration proved it to be a couple of cart-loads of rubbish reliably datable (by the diagnostic artefacts contained therein) to years during or around the First World War. Contrarily many an unpromising site when explored proves a golden asset.

The same is true of the ideas and methods archaeologists work with, although it is less obvious. A key concern of Cyril Fox's generation was the patient working-out of a chronology for prehistoric Britain, a slow and painstaking affair in which careful deduction from ambiguous evidence could – astonishingly – compose an overall scheme in which all could at that time have confidence. In the *Archaeology of the*

Cambridge Region, Cyril Fox concluded that the first metal objects that reached Britain during the 'Copper Age' will have arrived about 2000 BC. In taking this sensible view, he reported and set aside the long chronology of the European archaeologist Oscar Montelius, which would have had the Copper Age beginning at 2500 BC. Late in Fox's life, the invention of radiocarbon dating for the first time made possible the direct determination of the age of ancient organic materials. The old basis of the relative chronology was abandoned – and it was Montelius's long chronology rather than Fox's short chronology or the even shorter one preferred by his contemporary Stuart Piggott which turned out to be right. Importantly, with radiocarbon many of the specific skills and observations on which that way of working depended were ditched also – just as the craft and skills of hot-metal typesetting, the means by which all Cyril Fox's books were printed, were many of them immediately worthless relics when the hot metal was scrapped and computer-based composition, the means by which the present volume is typeset, took their place. Equally importantly, though, is the truth that many aspects to the craft and skills of hot-metal printing survive; good editing is as central to the making of good books as it ever was.

The easy, and the useless, way to write intellectual history is as a story of winners and losers. Some brilliant and precocious pioneers glimpsed the truth far before its accepted time – the winners; the rest of the dolts didn't – the losers. But research, and certainly archaeological research in the 20th century, is not like that. Montelius was not a perceptive visionary who acutely grasped the insights the others overlooked; he was one of a group of researchers working in much the same framework with much the same body of evidence and observations and each coming to a slightly different conclusion. (The difference between short and long chronologies is only 500 years in 4000, not large potatoes.) In time, new approaches – specifically radiocarbon – swept the whole edifice of reasoning away. With hindsight, one can say 'Montelius right, the others wrong' but it is not therefore the case 'Montelius competent, the others less so'.

* * *

Many a good academic thesis, and many a good book later made from a thesis, hides behind some broad title '*The general story of something large*' a sub-title saying how and where the actual work was actually accomplished '*as illustrated "by the examples within the county of Oxford" or "by the collections in the Fitzwilliam Museum, Cambridge"*': the point being that the work is practically confined to a convenient travelling distance from (or even within) whichever university it chanced to be done from. The approach, a perfectly reasonable one in terms of practical efficiency, echoes the long-standing rule of Cambridge University that its students must live within three miles of Great St Mary's, the University church hard by the Senate House which is the ceremonial centre of University business. Sometimes, one may think when the University is being parochially minded, it is as if *everything* that matters is, or jolly well should be, within three miles of Great St Mary's. (To this day, Cambridge University requires its academic staff not just to attend there to work, but to reside no further away than a stated number of miles; they may not, for instance, commute from London, perfectly feasible though that is in daily travelling time and although thousands commute daily the other direction from Cambridge to jobs in London.)

Cyril Fox's Ph.D. thesis *Archaeology of the Cambridge Region* (1923) is of this genre in an extreme form, and more openly stated. Its scope is a square of land with sides of 44 miles, Cambridge at its centre. It is a case-study within a grand and expansive topic, the relationship between human settlement and the topography of a landscape, as that is conveniently explored by a worked example confined to a distance from Cambridge chosen as sufficiently small to be coverable, sufficiently large to provide a generous number of examples to work with. In his reflections on the book written nearly quarter of a century later,[1] Fox explained its scope as a 'manageable region, not too large to be covered by bicycle with occasional expeditions by car' for its boundaries except at the corners were only 20–25 miles from Cambridge.

*   *   *

In one sense this first book, *Archaeology of the Cambridge Region*, is the test-case for the larger picture and pattern of its successor, the *Personality of Britain* of 1932, in which the same approach of the human response to topography is set out for the British Isles as a whole.

One can explore this series of nesting scales, both of the physical evidence and of the frame of thinking, in several directions both up and down from the declared focus of *Archaeology of the Cambridge Region*.

Going up in scale of the frame of thinking, it belongs not just alongside the *Personality of Britain*, but as another within a whole series of studies concerned with combining a mass of long-recognized evidence relating to human culture with the then-new possibilities of the environmental sciences. The great contemporary to Fox in this approach was O. G. S. Crawford, whose inspiration Fox duly acknowledged especially for Crawford's *Man and his Past*, published in 1921 when the typescript of *Archaeology of the Cambridge Region* was well advanced towards completion. But this was not only a British interest, for the great exemplars of the approach were the French historical geographers, such as Vidal de la Blanche. Unacknowledged though they are, surely they must have been the inspiration to Crawford, Fox and the rest. Yet, as the record of their published writings and private papers shows, the British group were unaware of the simultaneous and parallel interests of their colleagues across the Channel – just as Charles Darwin and Alfred Russell Wallace, in the most famous

---

[1] Reflections on *The Archaeology of the Cambridge Region*, first published in *Cambridge Historical Journal* 9(1) for 1947, and reprinted as Appendix IV to the reissue of *The Archaeology of the Cambridge Region* in 1948.

example of simultaneous and independent discovery, developed identical theories of evolution in isolation each from the other.

Going down in scale of the physical evidence and its material, the work was indeed largely done with bicycle and map to that certain number of miles from the county town, but it was also largely done from the collections of the Cambridge Antiquarian Society. Like many of the English counties, Cambridgeshire had seen a lively and growing interest in its archaeology and history in the Victorian period. The Cambridge Antiquarian Society (CAS) was the Cambridgeshire outcome, founded 1840 three years after Victoria's accession, and the local cousin to, for instance, the Wiltshire Archaeological and Natural History Society (founded 1853) and the Yorkshire Philosophical Society, whose even broader agenda expressed in its title has a wonderfully Yorkshire arrogance to it. In a county dominated by its county town, and with that county town dominated by its university, the CAS was very much a venture of university colleagues. Like the other county societies, its membership organised meetings and lectures, went off on exploring field trips – and began to accumulate a collection. This collection was largely given to the university in 1883, and became the founding collection of a new University Museum of Archaeology & Anthropology whose own substantial building opened in 1919 after delays caused by the Great War. That founding collection was all – bar a small handful of items – from Europe, and then within Europe 94% from England, 76% from East Anglia, 68% from Cambridgeshire, 24% from Cambridge. It was this accumulation, with many additions made between 1883 and when Fox used it for his Ph.D. work, which was the heart of Fox's study, together with the records of just where it all came from – the physical scale of the study in this way reduced down from the 44-mile square to the contents of a single building. The present writer, who chances to be curator of that same collection today, is every day aware of how vague and unsatisfactory the record is of where its things come from, often just by parish with ('from Thriplow') or without ('said to be from Ely') certainty, and of course nowhere approaching the modern standards of systematic record when we expect location of an individual archaeological site to the nearest 100 metres of an Ordnance Survey map reference and of individual sites to strata and deposits within that site recorded at least an order of magnitude more exactly.

* * *

The characteristic illustration to the *Personality of Britain*, even more than to *Archaeology of the Cambridge Region*, is the distribution map, in which a scatter of dots mark where examples of this or that object were found. Approached in the right way, those patterns will show where ancient people were and were not; from that can be deduced what they were and were not doing. The central way this is used by Fox is in deciding where the impenetrable and uninhabited archaic forest was, and where was the more open country which people actually occupied – open because it naturally was heath or marsh country, or open because the wildwood had been humanly cleared. The voids without finds mark the woodland, and the settled area corresponds to the presences.

This is the heart of Fox's approach, and it is instructive to see how it has fared since – in the way research knowledge develops, which should have no regard for the care and diligence with which work is done, but only with whether it turns out enduringly to be correct. The essence of the problem is survival and sampling. In one store of our Cambridge museum today, on our modern high metal racking, are the collected materials for Roman Cambridgeshire. This is not *all* the materials for Roman Cambridgeshire by any means, but it is a major portion of that, and it includes most of what Fox himself had to work with, on which to build his distribution maps for the Roman period. Its boxes, arranged by parish, occupy perhaps half the volume within a space 2 metres by 3 metres by 20 metres, or about 60 cubic metres. It is a sufficiently large quantity of stuff that, in a decade of my being responsible for it, I still have not seen every single little object in every single little box within every one of the larger boxes. Yet, Roman Cambridgeshire had a population of several tens of thousands of human beings, who lived their lives over a period of more than three centuries; and the Roman period is distinctive – as is our own age in an extreme form – in the sheer quantity of material objects, brooches and pins and red-slipped pots and quern-stones and mosaic tesserae and bricks and tiles and who else knows what, which its people possessed, discarded and lost. All this has been winnowed down to a handful of cubic metres. The number of actual objects in those cubic metres is several thousand, but that several thousand is far fewer than the total population of the region in the Roman era. The typical trace in the established Museum, then, of the life spent over some decades of human existence by an average inhabitant of Dvraliponte (the Roman name for Cambridge) is nothing whatsoever.

Alongside Fox's exploration of artefact distributions and – with Miss Lily Chitty – of presenting them in coloured maps, O. G. S. Crawford simultaneously explored and developed the potential of air photography. It was this that turned out to be the key to new knowledge, across all Britain and with that across the Cambridge region. Unsuspected from the pattern of surface finds are complex sequences of substantial archaeological traces of all periods, which year-by-year aerial reconnaissance has slowly pieced together. Every season is different, and many reticent in what they reveal; but now that we have, for much of England, more than seventy years of systematic aerial photography, the combined record makes a palimpsest of extraordinary refinement and detail. The air photographic record has also been helpful for the equivalent history of the natural environment. The Cambridgeshire rivers, for example, turn out to have an intricate sequence of complex change; in this nearly flat landscape, the meandering rivers choke their own courses with silt and mud, then abruptly break out into new routes or take once more to a channel previously abandoned. Most recently, on a grand scale only in the last ten years, the ever-growing gravel pits that feed the building boom in Cambridgeshire are often being explored archaeologically before the gravel is dug. The remains in the gravels turn out also to be rich and complex, very often, as well as – usually – partly visible in the air photographic archives. And a final contribution to the burgeoning archaeology of the Cambridge has come from the most simple kind of field observation, simply walking the fields when they are in plough and picking up every artefact seen on the surface, as the most recent cultivation has chanced to throw it; astonishingly, most of the thousands of hectares of the Cambridgeshire Fenland has been systematically surveyed that way by the persistent patience of one man, David Hall.

In these several ways, the knowledge we have of the Cambridge region has been enormously magnified, and the patterns that Fox identified turn out to be in large part a simple consequence of the smaller sample he had to deal with, and the particular way that sample came about, as reports of field studies in the published literature, and as elements in the collections in Cambridge and in the hands of key private collectors. Distribution maps, it turns out, are in large part maps of where the *archaeologists* were, of the places they went to look and of the places where objects found by others were then conveyed to the archaeologist – rather than maps of the *archaeology*. That central way of Fox's reasoning, beginning in *Archaeology of the Cambridge Region* and strong in both the *Personality of Britain* and in his great survey of Offa's Dyke in the Welsh borderlands, was in deducing the locations of the unbroken woodland from the distribution maps: where there were no or few artefacts, there will have been the impenetrable forests largely empty of a human presence. Reasonably enough, the distributions of the artefacts and of the woodland then corresponded. But this can be a circular reasoning, in which they match largely or only because the woodland has been deduced from the artefacts. The research generations after Fox, blessed by improved methods and technical devices, benefiting from the accumulated knowledge of Fox's own generation, have rather been empowered to deduce a rather different story because our several strands of evidence are both more varied and more independent each of the other.

* * *

In these prefatory remarks, I have sketched some ways in which this archaeologist looks back on Fox's works, in a spirit both of a deserved respect and of a recognition that our knowledge has far moved forward. Good archaeological research, especially when it is well and persuasively published, carries its own destruction. That is part of the joy and the sadness of it. If genuinely taken to its limit, then any research approach can be taken forward no further (though it may productively be applied in other contexts). And when taken towards or to its limit, the weaknesses are conspicuous to the acute critic alongside the strengths. This reality is consistent with how archaeologists treat the sites that are the focus of their material evidence; an archaeological excavation itself destroys the site it studies, so that labour of love both celebrates and brings to an end that thing to which it pays its fullest attention. Good research takes far forward, even to the limit, the potential of any given approach; in this respect, Fox's work perhaps takes to the limit, and therefore to the end, what one can do with that effective approach to be invented and advanced.

It chances that some of my own work, half a world away from Cambridge, concerns the archaeology of a region which has been haphazardly and incompletely explored. One maps what is reported to be there, from scattered and patchy reports or one's own incomplete knowledge, without knowing whether the gaps in the maps are real absences or whether they also or more reflect where the archaeologists have been, or – before the archaeologist – whether it is the capricious variability of climate and landscape that shapes the evidence through the vagaries of what survives, rather than through real differences in what was actually there in ancient times. One tries to deduce from the maps, as Fox did, and – through a kind of optimistic duty – I find myself having more confidence in the approach, and more confidence in what it tells me, than I know I should. Such is research. Chancing to work – decades later – under conditions which resemble what Fox faced in addressing Cambridge archaeology immediately after the First World War, I find myself recapitulating much of his approach; and that recapitulation means recapitulating both the strengths and the weaknesses in what he did.

Looking myself at Fox's collected work, there seems a distinct pattern in what he did. It seems to me to start well and then to get better. The St Fagans museum, though not an absolute novelty for it built on Scandinavian experience, has been an enduring success: only the other day there were newspaper reports on the astonishing number of visitors St Fagans has recently been receiving, now it has been liberated from government-imposed admission charges. From the middle years, then, remarkable innovations. Fox's study of Monmouthshire houses – 'medieval', 'sub-medieval' and 'renaissance' – is an astonishing achievement, and one which is respected as a foundation stone in the modern study of vernacular architecture. From the later years, then, a study of surpassing novelty and imagination – alongside, as always with Fox, a painstaking interest in and respect for the ambiguous details of the material evidence. By comparison, the early work seems limited in what it achieves. In this I see time in its usual role as the great leveller, along with the integrity and merit of research knowledge as having an existence separate and autonomous from the individual human beings who create it; that knowledge has its own life which moves forward at a pace careless of the human individuals who create it. Cyril Fox was a remarkable researcher who did remarkable work – and whose story is here told in a remarkable book – but like all archaeological researchers he was encased in his own time, as all humans beings must be and always are.

Christopher Chippindale
Curator for British collections
Cambridge University Museum
*   of Archaeology & Anthropology*
7 January 2002

Cyril Fox
Archaeologist Extraordinary 1882–1967

Introduction

This is the tale of a remarkable man, who came from obscurity as a 36-year-old undergraduate to a pinnacle of academe in less then seven years and whose interests ranged from archaeology to architecture and from the environment to heritage. In parallel with this extraordinary tale is the story of a museum with pretensions of serving a nation but which at the end of the First World War was bankrupt and, except for the natural science departments, little better than the Cardiff Municipal Museum it had replaced. By the end of his term as Director in 1948 it was a truly Welsh national museum with an international reputation and with a daughter museum at St. Fagans to house the 'folk' collection that he had so ardently nurtured and supported throughout his period in office.

It is only natural that children should be interested in the achievements of their father, especially one who had gained fame and international recognition in his lifetime. The unfortunate death of Cyril Fox's first wife in 1932 and his remarriage the following year provided him with two families. For those of us in the 'second batch' he was an old man by the time we had all reached maturity and there was little opportunity to get to know him as a friend as well as a father or to discuss with him his life and achievements. I have therefore had to recourse to the traditional biographer's path of his written words and the memories of those who knew him. My parent's life together has been vividly recorded in my mother's autobiography, *Aileen – A Pioneering Archaeologist*, but there are now unfortunately few others who survive from that golden age of British archaeology. I was fortunate to have been able to interview some of them between 1985 and 1987, and their contributions have been invaluable. I am also grateful to my two half-sisters for their memories of the early years before I came onto the scene. Having completed the first draft of a manuscript I was very conscious of the need for professional evaluation. The contributions and encouragement of the late George C. Boon, Lord Raglan and Dr Peter Smith were much appreciated. However it is to Dr Christopher Chippindale and Dr Douglas Bassett that I owe most of all; not least for the Preface and Appendix written under their own names but especially for the time spent reading my manuscript and providing me with editorial criticisms and amendments. I am also indebted to Douglas Bassett for drawing my attention to Dr Iorwerth C. Peate's writings in Welsh and for arranging translations of parts of Peate's autobiography. This was an essential contribution to the chapters that cover my father's work at the National Museum and the establishment of the Welsh Folk Museum at St Fagans.

Throughout my researches I have been struck by the number of requests put to my father to produce a record of his own life. He did indeed attempt to put pen to paper on this topic but found the task beyond him as his memory failed in the last few years of his life. My opening chapters make free use of the few biographical notes that he made and provides some insight into these formative years. It is British archaeology's loss that he found it impossible to do more than this. His own life summary was enclosed in a letter written in 1960 to his friend Sir Mortimer (Rik) Wheeler concerning his own biographical (obituary) notes as a Fellow of the British Academy.

"My dear Rik,
I send you typescript for my 'file' (if it is a file) at the Academy, having noted with appreciation the careful record provided for deceased Fellows and being in my 78th year. A brief comment is perhaps permissible. The favourable home and school circumstances which produced an 'intellectual success' at the age of 12 (1894) in the entrance exam for Christ's Hospital, followed by misfortunes, which inhibited intellectuality for 27 years, and thereafter by a spate of output of research and new thought (embodied in books, and papers in journals) for 37 years (1921–1958) present perhaps an unusual life pattern, and if so worth defining for posterity. The spate begins with 'Anglo-Saxon Monumental Sculpture' at Cambridge and ends with 'The siting of the Monastery of St Mary's' at Exeter. I am now finished: the well is dry again; but I am happy.
Your friend, Cyril"

This volume is an attempt to define for posterity this unusual life pattern, to fill the gaps between those two published works and to give a little insight to the man behind the written word.

C. S-F.
Ayshford 2002

I

The Formative Years 1882–1910
Childhood and Horticulture

> If you can fill the unforgiving minute
> With sixty seconds worth of distance run
> Yours is the earth and everything that's in it
> And – which is more – you'll be a Man my son.
> *Rudyard Kipling*

A deep love and knowledge of English literature and above all a particular fondness for the works of Rudyard Kipling was a hallmark of Cyril Fox well known to his friends and relations. Both in his writing and his speech an apposite quotation was always to hand, declaimed with sheer pleasure in the glory of the language and admiration for the writer's ability to convey his intent and meaning in verse or prose. This verse from 'If' was one of his favourites and singularly appropriate; if ever a man filled the unforgiving minute it was him, and he it was, who certainly became a Man.

But it was not always so, for his was a strange career shrouded in anonymity for almost forty years that then burst upon the Cambridge archaeological scene like an incendiary device forcing this subject into the twentieth century. That this talent was latent waiting only for a suitable catalyst was clearly apparent from his earliest writings as a member of the Literary Society at Stansted in the early 1900s. However he himself was clearly uncertain of his future or indeed of the way ahead. Writing to his brother Norman in 1904 he expressed this uncertainty in explicit terms:

'I do not know why I am not happy here, I ought to be as I keep telling myself, with a good friend and interesting work, and yet I feel as though the best part of my life were behind me, and hope and energy for what lies before me are dead within me. My feelings are those of a man whose work is accomplished, whose position is gained, and yet I am a young fellow of one and twenty, who ought to be full of buoyant energy and hope for the future. What worries me most in this connection is the thought of dear old Father, proud of the son who is going to make a name for himself, the son who bids fair to be a nonentity all his life.'

It was to be nearly twenty years before his father's hopes started to be realised but it was these years that were the foundation of his art and craftsmanship and an apparently necessary apprenticeship for his chosen career.

Cyril Fred Fox was born at Chippenham, Wiltshire, on 16 December 1882, the eldest of four children of Charles Frederick Fox and his wife Henrietta Maria (nee Paul). Charles Fox (1859–1953) was at that time the senior clerk in the Capital and Counties Bank in Chippenham. Subsequently he was manager of its branches in Sandown and Newport on the Isle of Wight and finally at Winchester, Hampshire. The Fox family had for two centuries been property owners in the parish of St. Mary's, Southampton – Teague's Orchard is a recurrent local name in their wills – and there were a dozen tombstones of the clan to be seen in the churchyard before the blitz of 1940.[1] Charles Fox's father, Frederick Fox (1825–1911), inherited enough capital to build a country house in Bursledon on the edge of the Solent. A keen yachtsman he was a frequent winner of prestigious races at the Southampton Yacht Club, which was subsequently given 'Royal' status. A massive bearded figure, whose portrait and trophies are still in the family's possession, unfortunately he was also an inveterate gambler. His four unmarried daughters inherited his depleted wealth leaving little for the two sons.

Figure 1: Charles Frederick Fox – Newport, Isle of Wight 1900

Figure 2: The Fox family with their Governess Laura Barnes taken by Cyril at The Lawn, Bursledon 1904. From left to right: Norman, Charles and Henrietta Fox, Dorothy, Laura and Mary (Babs)

Cyril's mother Henrietta was descended from the Paul's, a Liverpool family of merchants and the Crackenthorpe's, a long-established group of farmers, maltsters and parsons in north Cambridgeshire, whose origins can also be traced back to the mid-seventeenth century. He was very proud of this pedigree and would often pronounce that he was of 'good yeoman stock'.

Together with his brother Norman and sisters Dorothy and Mary, Cyril was brought up in a typical middle-class Victorian household where father's word was law and mother's influence might be felt but not heard (Figs 1 and 2). Charles Fox was a well-educated man, who had joined the bank from school and had an abiding interest in the local geology and in archaeology. He was a Fellow of the Society of Antiquaries and a frequent letter-writer on his pet subjects to local newspapers. As Cyril recalled[2] 'the highlights of my childhood were all associated with my father and with the Isle of Wight. In his capacity as Bank Manager he visited clients – farmers mostly, who had borrowed or wished to borrow money – on Saturday afternoons; a stroll round the fields, assessing crop prospects, was followed by dinner at the farm at about 5.30 pm. At this time on the Island the farm workers sat with the family for this principal meal of the day. The long table had the master and mistress with their guests and children at the top end – and what a grand joint of meat my brother Norman and I saw in progress from kitchen to table. Each labourer touched his forelock as he came in, before sitting down, which I thought very strange. On Bank Holidays and some Saturdays we went on the Downs. I loved the country and put up with the chalk pits where father searched for fossils. He fortunately knew something about barrows and defensive earthworks, which aroused my childish interest, but it was long afterwards that I came to grips with Early Man and his work'.

Perhaps somewhat unusually for a Victorian parent, Charles Fox tried to imbue some of his own interest in the countryside and its origins to his children but, Cyril excepted, met with very limited success. Mary the youngest and Cyril's favourite sister, who was born in 1891 and was always known to the family as Babs, remembered 'having little love for my father fearing him and his gruff ways but worshipping my poor mother, who was treated more like a servant than a wife.' Her brother Norman had had similar memories. Cyril himself felt deprived of love and affection from his mother. 'She never let me kiss her you know', he confided to his daughter Penelope in his later years. Yet this shrinking tiny little person adored him; as he achieved success, she was in awe of him, marvelling that she could have produced such a remarkable son. The unfortunate truth was that she was so terrified of passing on her consumption to her children that she never allowed herself to display her natural feelings of affection for them.

Cyril was sent to a Preparatory School in Sandown becoming Head Boy at the age of 12 in September 1894 (Fig. 3). The principal Mr Etches was a good teacher and did well by his pupils. Charles Fox was offered a nomination for Christ's Hospital, the Blue Coat School in Newgate Street, London, and arranged for his son to sit the entrance examination in December. He was placed second out of 98 candidates and early in 1895 at the age of 13 entered the school (Fig. 4). An unhappy period followed. With no family or friends in London he never left the walled, asphalted, treeless compound for the twelve weeks of each term. His most vivid memories of those days were of bullying in the dormitories; the name 'Fox' providing boundless opportunities for taunting and torment. Unchecked and unsupervised by the masters this made his life a misery. In February 1896 he contracted diphtheria. Following a long convalescence he was always behind his fellow pupils in his work, and finally left in December 1896 on reaching the age of sixteen.

Figure 3: Cyril Fox aged 12 at Newport 1895

His father, not unreasonably, con-

Figure 4: Christ's Hospital Newgate 1895 (Fox back row 2nd from right)

sidered that Cyril needed an open-air life. He therefore placed both of his sons with Mr Ernest Gaye who ran a nursery near Lowestoft, Cyril was put in charge of the office while Norman worked outdoors. Norman remembered it as being a 'busy job for the business was maintained by advertisements in a large range of journals. *Buy sturdy plants from the most easterly nursery in Britain* was the constant theme, but all the more expensive produce, which we advertised, was from nurseries elsewhere in Britain sent to customers at our order and with our labels. Wrathful letters were occasionally in our post bag from people who studied the rail charges: of course we offered to return the money but few dissatisfied customers wanted to go as far as this – they just wanted to blow off steam. If we couldn't fulfil an order, letters explaining that business was so active that we had sold out temporarily of that particular plant were in routine use when necessary. These shady methods sometimes resulted in visits from the local policeman,' which presumably had to be diverted by Cyril the office boy.

Still, the job had its bright side. Mr Gaye was a keen yachtsman and the boys spent the weekends for nine months of the year sailing on the Norfolk Broads and rivers – often getting as far as Norwich. Cyril grew to love these reed-fringed expanses of water, and he became a competent sailor. But after two years Charles Fox thought that to finish their training a 'better class affair' should be tried and another employer was found with a grape and tomato nursery near Worthing on the Sussex coast.

An ulterior motive may well have been that his father did not approve of Cyril's fiancée Maisie Barnes, daughter of the Reverend B. G. Barnes, Vicar of Naughton near Ipswich. Babs, then aged 10, remembered the occasion well and the furore it caused at home in Sandown. Cyril had seen a picture of Maisie in the magazine 'Studio' and wrote to the editor for her address. A true romantic, he courted this magazine belle with letters and poems. He was invited to call on her at her home in Naughton whilst working at Lowestoft and proposed during the summer of 1901. Several years later he told Babs of his experiences in that Vicarage which had 'nearly put him off Reverends for life'. The house was unheated and freezing in the East Coast winter; it had no sanitation except for one outside lavatory that was never available when he wanted to use it. The only place he could ever find to relieve himself was a nearby hedge that was well used. Despite these inauspicious surroundings the relationship flourished and Maisie's father had no objections. Their engagement continued throughout Cyril's temporary stay at Worthing. It was finally broken off amicably in September 1903 although they continued to exchange letters for several months.

The boy's new employer was always thought by them to be an unfrocked parson. His organisation, barely solvent in 1902, was failing rapidly. His foreman was competent but Cyril was uninterested not having been consulted in any way about the choice or the move itself. Within twelve months the nursery was declared bankrupt and sold. For want of any betters ideas he returned to Ernest Gaye at Lowestoft. As he subsequently discovered, both employers had charged their father a substantial fee for this 'training', which required full-time working for a ten-hour day with pay of less than a standard labourer's wages. However it was whilst he was at Worthing that chance provided Cyril with the opportunity for a meeting with the man, who was to be the major influence on his future career, Dr Louis Cobbett of Cambridge.

* * *

This meeting in a shelter on Worthing sea-front in early 1902 was a vivid and oft-recalled memory. Without doubt it was the turning-point in his life. Dr Cobbett (Fig. 5) was a well-known pathologist, who was expecting to take up an appointment at Stansted as scientific investigator to a Royal Commission investigating Bovine Tuberculosis with particular responsibility for experimental farms. He was an enthusiastic cyclist and historian, two interests which, when combined with his professional investigative instincts, had led him into the fields of archaeology and anthropology. He had been at Cambridge since 1893, taking a special interest in the prehistoric earthworks and other evidence of early occupation and cultivation of the surrounding countryside. A life-long bachelor, nevertheless deeply interested in the younger generation and well known in Cambridge for helping to pay for University

Figure 5: Dr. Louis Cobbett (The Pathological Society of Great Britain & Ireland)

education of talented young men who could not afford the fees. At this critical juncture Cyril had also taken an interest in early history, reviving boyhood memories of exploring earthworks with his father on the Isle of Wight, by cycling around the local area and recording local sites of archaeological interest. He had recently been to Cissbury Hill Fort and drawn a scale plan with notes on the features of particular interest.

A thunderstorm provided the opportunity for Dr Cobbett, on holiday in Worthing, to strike up a conversation with the young market-garden trainee. There are several versions of this conversation, the earliest written one being that recorded in Fox's contribution to Louis Cobbett's obituary.[3] Cyril's own notes record that 'when asked by Cobbett about the antiquities of the chalk downlands, I produced from my bicycle basket a scaled sketch plan of Cissbury, which surprised him. The subsequent conversation also made it clear that I was looking for a job. A few weeks later he wrote to tell me that he had been appointed a bacteriologist to a Royal Commission investigating Bovine Tuberculosis. The body had been offered the home farm of a wealthy London merchant at Stansted in Essex for their experimental work and a clerk was needed to keep the records – would I like the job?' Unfortunately the contract with the Sussex market garden and his own concern for financial independence prevented him from accepting, but he kept in touch with Dr Cobbett during his remaining time at Worthing and following his return to Lowestoft.

A year later on 16 February 1903 Dr Cobbett wrote again. 'The clerk we engaged is leaving and I am again able to offer you the post at Two Guineas a week. I want you to come … I honestly think it will be for your best interest in the future to take it.' Dr Cobbett was obviously well aware that his young protégé was likely to reject the offer, primarily on financial grounds. Cyril was obviously doing extremely well at Lowestoft and had a happy relationship with his employer. Cobbett's letter therefore continued with his ideas for a future career in an academic field rather than the horticultural one that might seem to be offering the more secure financial future.

'I have been much struck by the keen interest which you have taken in literature, history and archaeology and with the critical power you have shown in writing and talking of these things … During the existence of the Commission you would be comfortably off. While working here you would gain insight into a number of things scientific and you could not help absorbing a good deal in the atmosphere of a laboratory. You moreover would have your evenings free and be able to put in a good deal of work on your own account … thus the time spent here might be excellent training for something after. Now with regard to that something after I have been thinking for some time that you ought to go to University and I am anxious to help you to do so. I don't want to suggest that I am able to offer you an allowance sufficient for one of the expensive colleges at Oxford or Cambridge, but provided of course that I think you have made sufficient use of your opportunities in the meantime, I will make it possible for you to go somewhere. Perhaps London or Birmingham, or if I am then resident at Cambridge you might be a non-collegiate student there. It will depend on circumstances; but anyhow you can rely upon me to make some sort of university career possible for you.'

This letter, which continued in a similar vein urging careful consideration of his future, has been quoted at length since it provides an extraordinary insight into the generosity and concern of Dr Cobbett as well as his ability to detect the potential of a young man for high academic success despite his lack of schooling. The reply has not survived but the dazzling prospect held out by Dr Cobbett clearly failed to impress. Six days later he wrote again. 'I am by no means convinced by your reasoning… that you feel too old and settled to recommence your education. Interest in the subject matter and a desire to know the truth and the faculties necessary to succeed are industry and a critical turn of mind to sift evidence. Now these I think you have and it is for this reason that I think you are the kind of person to take advantage of University training. …Do you care nothing to meet educated people who can discuss with you the subjects in which you are interested. … It is the intellectual environment, which makes life worth living, where will you find it in your present life?'

Perhaps aware that his lengthy 'tour de force' might not be quite sufficient Cobbett wrote at the same time to Mr Gaye to enlist his support for his employee's future. He also wished to ensure that Cyril would be released if he should decide to accept the appointment to join the Royal Commission staff. Clearly this attack on two fronts was successful for on 26 February Dr Cobbett wrote to Cyril to say 'so glad you will come for I feel sure you ought to. Mr Gaye wrote very kindly about it to me and seemed quite anxious that you should though very sorry to lose you'. Mr Gaye's letter to Dr Cobbett was, in the circumstances, kind and concerned for Cyril's future but also pointed out what he was losing by the move. 'I shall be able to let you have Cyril in a month's time. Our agreement was *for three months* but I am willing to waive this. Yes! You owe me more than you think. You would never have got him without my help. It will be a cruel wrench to me as I shall never be able to replace him. I hope his distinguished career will be a *profitable* one also with something hanging to it (sic). I was going to take him into partnership shortly and could have guaranteed him within ten years an income of £1000 a year. I am clearing this myself altho' I have only been in the business ten years. But cash is not everything and I am anxious that Cyril should have a chance of displaying his fine abilities and making a name for himself.'

The decision to exchange a profitable career – £1000 a year in 1903 was a very considerable income and nearly ten times the salary being offered by the Royal Commission – for a potentially distinguished one was obviously not taken lightly nor without some persuasion from Ernest Gaye. However once the decision was made it started Cyril Fox along a road to great distinction – though little financial reward. He did not match the £1000 a year until the late 1930s but there were other compensations. There is no doubt that he never regretted his move to Stansted and was always grateful to Louis Cobbett for all that he had done. In Cobbett's obituary he wrote. 'Being thus for the first time brought into direct and continuous contact with University people and

Fox's Office and Administration Block

Hospital Boxes for Tuberculosis patients

Figure 6: Blythwood Farm 1905

scientific humanism I feel I owe my happy life of congenial work to him.' The official letter confirming his appointment and requiring him to 'devote the whole of your time to the work and to reside in the neighbourhood' at a salary of two guineas a week arrived by the first post on the following day. Dr Cobbett had got his man; he was clearly determined not to give him time to change his mind. Mr Fox duly started his duties at the laboratory at Blythwood (Fig. 6) on 23 March 1903 and remained there until 1910; by then the Commission had completed its work, submitted its report and was disbanded.

* * *

Work for the Royal Commission and life in the village was infinitely better than anything that Fox had previously experienced, and the months passed happily enough for 'my experiences hitherto had not led me to expect much out of life'. Clearly his father still had great, almost prescient, expectations of his eldest son writing to him from the Bank in Newport in 1903 on the eve of his 21st birthday (Fig. 7).

Figure 7: Cyril Fox aged 21. The Buckle Ring was a 21st Birthday gift from his parents

'My dearest Laddie, I might have proudly and fondly hoped twenty-one years ago to-day that the morrow would bring me a son for my first born but I could, even in my wildest and most fervent dreams, have hardly anticipated that he would grow up such a good laddie and be such a comfort to his dad. ... That you are taking up the course of scientific study you are, with the intercourse of intellectual men, unfortunately denied me, I am indeed delighted and I look, dearest boy, confidently forward to the day when you will be found in the forefront of scientists. It is a father's proud dream, but I *know* you will be there for with your determination and attainments no obstacle will stifle your ambition. You will only have yourself to thank; I have done nothing towards your progress. With fondest love and many happy and prosperous returns of tomorrow from your ever affectionate and proud, Dad'.

The tasks that Fox was required to do for the Royal Commission were mainly routine and well within his capacity; clearly his standards were extremely high, earning him public commendation. In late 1903 only eight months after he had joined the Commission the Secretary wrote. 'The two reports recently drawn up for Blythwood and Walpole Farms were presented to the Commission. ... I informed the Commission that the greater part of the work involved in the preparation these two reports had been done by you... I was directed by the Commissioners to convey to you their thanks and to inform you that they appreciated the manner in which it had been carried out.' The hours were not arduous and there was, as Cobbett had promised, ample free time to devote to his hobbies of cycling, studying the local countryside and its relics of earlier occupations and improving his education. He studied assiduously reading widely and commenting both verbally and in writing, mostly to Cobbett, on all he saw.

His own recollection of this period is brief. It makes no reference to other members

Figure 8: The Royal Commission Staff at Blythwood Farm, Stansted 1905. Dr Cobbett and Fox seated right

of staff (Fig. 8) or his job but dwells on the role that Cobbett played in his academic development. 'For five years I lived in lodgings at Stansted, spending most winter evenings talking in the house that Cobbett rented, his sister (Effie) being in charge.[4] I applied his attitude of mind and method of dealing with the unknown to my own interest – archaeology – but had at this time no thought of writing on the subject. Cobbett was a delightful companion, treating youngsters as though they were his equals and laying before them the riches of his mind without stint. He taught me by inference and indirectly the importance of exact statement and to avoid emotionalism in expression.'

Although his principal interest was archaeology, the time at Stansted was one of consolidation and general education. From his few surviving papers of this period, including some essays and a literary diary for April to July 1907, it is clear that he joined a local Literary Society that studied the classics and submitted essays for mutual criticism on a wide variety of historical and literary subjects. Without doubt these were later discussed with Cobbett over an evening meal or a weekend walk and pub lunch or just a glass of beer. He also retained a collection of poems written between 1905 and 1908 at least two of which were published in the *Lowestoft Journal*.

Mostly these were for his own amusement; but some were private Valentine dedications to a succession of girl friends. Other poems and essays have a religious connotation. The Christian aspects of his upbringing were clearly in the course of severe personal examination during this formative period of his life. Often writings, in a lighter vein, indicate his preoccupation with creation, life and death. His poem 'Autumn' written 10 October 1906 is typical:

> The autumn sky is deckt with billowy cloud
> The sunbeams chequer the broad vale below
> And paint the woods with gold: The wind sings loud
> O'er field and copse. Yet this fair outward show
> Is false as in a dream
>
> For in the woodlands dark the tall trees sway
> The leaves are falling, fallen and they drift
> Before the sudden gusts of wind that stray
> Adown the glades; here too the shadows swift
> Follow the sunlight gleam
>
> The shrivelled leaf, rotting upon the ground
> The shadowed sunshine, and the moaning sound
> Of many winds, recalled th'eternal strife
> O Death, I wondered
> Art thou the Lord of Life?

He read the Bible in great detail and could in later life quote freely from it as he could from most of the classics of English Literature. He liked to be able to relate these studies of literature and the scriptures to the commercial morals of the day. In an essay on the writings of the Prophet Habbakuk he wrote, 'Are there not individuals who lay up wealth for themselves and their children that they may live securely, wealth obtained by means of underpaid labour and questionable commercial morality?' That eventually he found the answers to this spiritual questioning of his beliefs and so obtained peace of mind was clear. He became a dedicated Christian with a profound understanding of the Almighty. Above all this manifested itself in a love of his fellow man and their achievements and an ability to make those who met him reciprocate.

From his own admission much of this self-examination had been conducted in discussions with Dr Cobbett, an admitted atheist but a man who clearly had the ability to allow a 'pupil's' true convictions to emerge rather than impose his own. In concert with this spiritual development Fox's writings had begun to show the hallmarks of his later work – clarity of thought and expression and an ability to identify himself with his reader (or listener). Thus what might, on the face of it, appear to be a dry and uninteresting subject could, under his guidance, become alive and absorbing. As is clear from Dr Cobbett's letters, the development of these innate abilities had to have come from within but it is equally plain that they only achieved their potential by

Figure 9: Essex Imperial Yeomanry Camp, Sudbury 1909. Fox standing third from left

being nurtured at his fireside. However as their friendship developed over the months and years there were clearly times when the pupil outpaced the master. ' I don't know whether to advise you to read Herbert Spencer', Cobbett wrote; 'I never could read him myself but then you seem able to read all sorts of stuff I can't manage.'

Towards the end of 1907 Fox joined the Essex Imperial Yeomanry (Volunteer Force) as a Trooper. Apart from the immediate benefit of learning to ride and of owning his own pony which he was allowed to keep free of charge at the Research Farm, he was given a virtually free 14 day holiday every year when he took part in the annual camp (Fig. 9). Through the Yeomanry he developed an intense interest in map reading, scouting and in the use of land formation to the soldier. This too was to have a major influence on his life. His passion for archaeology and man's cultural development over the ages could now be put into geographical perspective when the lie of the land and pre-historic or historic remains were brought together. This way of thinking was later to express itself in the distribution maps of '*Archaeology of the Cambridge Region*' and '*Personality of Britain*'.

* * *

By 1910 the Royal Commission had been in existence for eight years, Fox had been with it for seven, and its task was complete. In March Fox wrote to his father, who had now been moved from the Isle of Wight to manage the much larger Winchester branch of the Capital and Counties Bank, to inform him that after nearly two years of threatened closure the Commission was to be wound up in June. In a letter dated 18 March 1910 his father replied 'I am very sorry to hear that at last a definite date has been fixed for closing up the R.C. on T. as it unfortunately means the termination of your happy period of office. …few young fellows at such an impressionable age have had such unique opportunities of which you have made good use storing up material which you will well know how to reap the goodly print of in God's good time. Well it is the future we have now to look for and what is in store for you and how to secure the competence to enable you to live. Your work, your large circle, all in like work, should be able to give you something. Secretaryship to a Scientific Institution or professional man would be the ideal berth, preferably the former. It is your University men and London professional men of the Scientific Cult [sic], who have the opportunities and hear of the berths. Still dear boy you must not be downhearted for you have a home to come to until the appointment does turn up. Your credentials and the work done well for the R.C. should stand for something and will! I have no fears. Your fond Dad.'

This letter was clearly well founded and well informed. Shortly afterwards Dr Cobbett, and the other scientists who had been undertaking the Commission's research, decided to approach the Cambridge School of Agriculture with a view to setting up a laboratory to continue research into animal-borne diseases. This proposal found favour with the University, and it was agreed that the laboratory should be established in Milton Road. A Superintendent would be appointed to supervise the staff, to oversee the care and maintenance of the animal quarters and to run the accounts. Having had such a happy relationship with Dr. Cobbett and his colleagues at Stansted Fox was invited to fill the post at a slightly reduced salary of £200 per annum. In addition to his routine responsibilities the Superintendent was to act as Secretary for the Field Laboratories Committee, which met two or three times a year under the chairmanship of a Professor appointed by the Agricultural Department and was responsible to that department for its tasking and efficiency. The minute books of this committee, all in Fox's familiar hand, only survive from May 1912 although it is clear that he had recorded their transactions from the beginning. This move completed the third part of a triangle of influences that were to mould his character and set him on the road to academic success.

Notes

[1] Fox family tree – Appendix 1.
[2] Draft biographical notes for the British Academy 1958
[3] *Path.Bact.* LIX, No. 4 pp. 695–706
[4] Actually seven years – one of many examples of his condensing time in his recollections of this time of his life.

II

The Formative Years 1910–1919
Cambridge in Peace and War

Cambridge, with its ancient University and two well-established and well-stocked museums, ensured a truly academic environment covering a wide range of disciplines that interested Fox; it gave him easy access to the archaeological and anthropological studies and finds of experts in those fields. Additionally the area around Cambridge had a wealth of pre-historic and historic remains; all were within easy cycling distance of the City and provided ample material for investigative study. Cobbett was very familiar with the area, but it was mostly new to Fox. Their common interests extended to all things historic, from earthworks to cathedrals and farmhouses to ancient dykes and causeways. As at Stansted, the day's work of the Superintendent of the Milton Road Laboratory was essentially routine, leaving ample time in the summer evenings and at weekends for exploration and in the winter evenings for research and discussion. Recalling this period Cyril wrote 'I readily agreed to the proposal [his appointment as Superintendent] for I had been in village isolation long enough. I got rooms nearby and began to study the antiquities of the 'Cambridge Region' in my spare time, sometimes in the company of Cobbett. Gothic architecture, particularly Church architecture, interested him greatly and I owe my interest therein mainly to his teaching. His archaeological and architectural leanings were just part of the good life as he conceived it giving point and interest to his expeditions into the Cambridgeshire countryside…'

It is evident at this stage that Fox's relationship with Dr Cobbett became much closer; he believed that, in the accordance with the practice of the time, that this might be recognised by a more familiar form of address than the formal 'Doctor' he had always used. The subject was broached in the course of a business letter concerning the laboratory and evoked the reply 'Dear Fox … Call me Cobbett by all means. I got so used to being called 'Doctor' by you that I never noticed it. Perhaps it was as well while I was at Stansted, but it is quite unnecessary now.' With the passage of time and deepening friendship it was to become 'My dear Fox' and 'My dear Cobbett' but never a hint of Louis or Cyril or even Sir Cyril. This vignette of a bygone era recalls forms of address that are forgotten in this age of pressing familiarity with the inveterate use of the 'first' (no longer Christian) name.

Although his move to Cambridge had taken him out of the catchment area of the Essex Imperial Yeomanry, by transferring to the Essex Yeomanry Territorial Forces Trooper Fox was able to continue his service with them until 1913 when his five-year 'engagement' was complete. He was taught 'the importance of forest cover as a screen for horsemen' and became an expert in scouting techniques and map-reading; skills that were to prove invaluable during the 1914–18 War. They were now combined with his studies of the origins of man in the Cambridge area, providing him with a framework for his theories on the relationship between settlement and movement of man through the ages and the soil. He wrote, 'I had absorbed (as a child) the basic elements of geology in its secondary and tertiary phases and when in 1912–14 ... I had begun work on the archaeology of the region I plotted distributions on a geological map and so learnt not only that the distribution of man (in the Cambridge region) was profoundly influenced by the nature of the soil and subsoil, but that this distribution of finds, changing as it did in the course of centuries, could be explained as representing a growing control over environment.'

The use of maps to illustrate distribution was not novel. O. G. S. Crawford in his book *Archaeology in the Field* describes the archaeological origins of this method of presentation: 'The marking on the Ordnance Maps of a large number of ancient sites is the essential preliminary to the publication of special period maps such as those of Roman Britain and of the Dark Ages. It also greatly facilitates the compilation of distribution maps of certain types of sites and objects. [These] should be capable of being so marshalled spatially, that is to say geographically, as to yield new knowledge comparable with that which ensued when they were marshalled temporarily. As one whose interest in geography has always been as great as his interest in archaeology and history, this possibility intrigued me at an early date. Forty years ago [1913] I was much mixed up with the early developments. Abercromby had published a distribution map of beakers in Great Britain[1] ...I took the Early Bronze Age and mapped the distribution of certain selected types of object – flat bronze axes and beakers – and found that they not only roughly coincided, but that there was a very obvious geographical explanation of the grouping of the sites. It was not quite the first time this had been done. Schlitz had done it for the *Band-keramik* of Central Europe, pointing out how its distribution coincided with loess formation. Lissauer had also published distribution maps of selected bronze objects of the Bronze Age, but he had not gone on to suggest any geographical explanation – nor had Abercomby, whose lists and maps of beakers had inspired my own.'

This application of geography to archaeology was not new in 1912. Indeed it is almost certain that Fox and Cobbett would have been familiar with the work of Abercromby as well as Professors Herbertson at Oxford and Myres at Cambridge, who were all experimenting with this technique. What was novel was the extension of simple distribution to the environment and it was this that was to be one of cornerstones of his work at Cambridge. It was at this very early stage that Fox first started to put down his ideas on paper although, unfortunately, none of these early drafts survive and research on this topic has to rely on his article for a military paper called 'Buzz' in 1918 and his final Cambridge Region thesis. Commenting in later life on his initial attempts, and on the unique style of prose that he had developed, he gave particular credit to the benefits obtained from his literary studies of the previous nine years. Describing his own style of writing, he said, 'the pains I took in early life by study of the "masters" and to increase my vocabulary to write straightforward lucid prose – good English in short. I have always taken care to write good readable English and when occasion demands to heighten or emphasise it by the various devices developed in the late 18th and early 19th centuries devices for lengthy sentences, often broken by colons and semi-colons. I avoid the short sentence except for unusual occasions.'

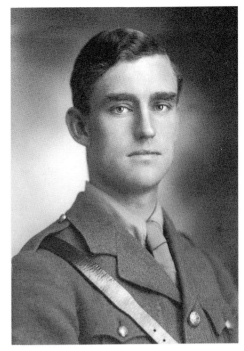

Figure 10: 2nd Lieutenant Fox 1915

Whether his studies would have taken Fox to University before 1919, when he was eventually enrolled at Magdalene College, Cambridge, will never be known for, in his words, in 1914 war came 'to interrupt this pleasant routine of convivial work and archaeological research'. Life for all became dictated by the need for service manpower and the national effort to support the army in the field. All immediate thoughts of academic study were swept away by the turmoil and fever of war – since everyone thought it would probably all be over by Christmas, it was merely a short postponement of whatever life had in store.

Having completed his period of service in the Yeomanry, Fox was not called up and did not immediately volunteer but, 'realising the seriousness of the situation I applied, as my Yeomanry experience and present position justified, for a Commission at Cambridge. This I obtained in late October 1914 with the Cambridge University OTC being gazetted 2nd Lieutenant 28 January 1915 (Fig. 10). So drained of trained officers was the Cambridge HQ (all regulars having been transferred into front line units) that I was sent to Aldershot for a short training course for newly appointed officers. On my return to Cambridge my Commanding Officer told me that I had headed the list and the shortage of trained officers was such that he asked me for a time to help him in teaching the new recruits. Thus instead of being sent overseas I was set to work in the classroom and countryside teaching map reading to dozens of young newly commissioned officers a few weeks junior to myself. I was necessarily overworked – like everybody else then at this HQ – it was a wet winter and in early spring I became seriously ill with pneumonia. On recovery I was graded "Home Service only" and when at length I returned to duty I was seconded as an instructor to No. 2 Officer Cadet Battalion.'

This assignment almost certainly saved his life. The chance of survival of young officers in the trenches in 1915 was less than 20% and even if he had escaped the German bullet his bronchial weakness – he had never truly recovered from his childhood diphtheria – would almost certainly have killed him. So the remainder of his war was spent teaching young officer recruits the elements of map reading and the arts of scouting and reconnaissance. He was promoted to Temporary Lieutenant on 15 February 1915 to give him the necessary authority for his instructional post, and was confirmed in the rank and transferred to No.2 Cambridge University Officers Cadet Battalion in February 1916 (Fig. 11). On 11 November 1917 he was promoted to Acting Captain, and in February 1918 sent to the Instructor's course at the Senior

Figure 11: No. 2 Cambridge University Cadet Battalion 1916

Officers' School at Aldershot. The Commandant was clearly impressed with his capabilities and by his personality, reporting that Acting Captain C. F. Fox was 'cheerful, determined, reliable, with much energy and drive. Tactful and hard working. Very keen. He was a particularly good instructor with excellent methods of imparting knowledge. Very sound ideas in spite of lack of experience on Active Service. He has done excellent work in all subjects. The best all round in the syndicate.' (Fig. 12).

* * *

Throughout this period Fox had continued with his duties as Superintendent of the University Field Laboratories. On 15 December 1915, the Field Laboratories Committee minutes record that, because of his war duties, the Board of Agriculture

Figure 12: Acting Captain Fox, December 1917

had reduced the Superintendent's salary to £150 in October. The Board was also questioning what time he was able to give to his work or indeed whether there was any need for his services at all until the war was over. Fox reported 'his military duties occupied his whole time during the week and that the only day he was able to utilise for work at the Field Laboratory was Sunday. He had however been able to get a day off occasionally when there was an extra amount of work needing attention, and so had been able during the past year to carry out all the financial and administrative work which could not be delegated, and he felt able to continue to do this in future.' He also pointed out 'if the Field Laboratory was to be considered to be in a position to provide at any time facilities for research in conexion [sic] with the war an administrative head was necessary.' He offered to relinquish his post for the period of the war, if the Committee could find someone who could give more time, or to accept a further reduction in salary. However the Committee were totally satisfied and agreed that 'so long as the Institution was satisfactorily administered the amount of time that the Superintendent gave to the work was of very little importance.'

Nine months later the subject was raised again, this time outside Committee by the Board's Deputy Chairman Professor Wood, who wrote on 21 October 1916 to clarify: 'Dear Fox, I finally succeeded in getting hold of Professor Hopkins [Chairman Agriculture Board Finance Committee] last night. After full consideration we think that you may continue to draw your £150 for the next twelve months…if the war goes on we think we ought to reduce you to £100 from October 1917.' When his reduction in salary was put into effect Fox, who had been drawing £155 a year as a Lieutenant, found it was balanced out by his increase in service pay on promotion to Captain. In any case it only lasted for a year for by the summer of 1918 it became apparent that the war was almost over with Haig being recalled for armistice discussions with the Cabinet and the newspapers full of stories of the impending 'peace'. The work of the OTC eased off and Fox was able to resume almost full time work at the Laboratory.

Following the German surrender to Marshal Foch on 11 November 1918 the war was officially declared to be over and his army career effectively came to an end. In his final report Colonel Edwards, Commandant of the Cambridge University OTC wrote, 'Captain C. F. Fox has been engaged in training officers and cadets since the beginning of the war. He has shown remarkable skill as an instructor, not only in his special subjects, map reading and reconnaissance reports, but also in ordinary duties: and by his keenness and good example as an officer and leader he has never failed to win and keep the interest of all for whose training he has been responsible. I set a very high value on the work he has done during the war.' In a letter dated 20 November 1918 replying to an enquiry regarding release from the service, Colonel Edwards said: 'I have written something about you but I don't think I have done you justice for I do value exceedingly the work you have done. Yes your name is in the list prepared by me for the WO [War Office] of members of staff of University Departments… but I cannot say how rapidly the WO will be able to carry out the release.' In fact it was to be 19 January 1919 before he was released from service and over a year later before the War Office finally approved his application to resign his commission.and at the same time gazetted his promotion to Substantive Lieutenant. In 1921 he received his 1914–1918 General Service Medal, inscribed with his Acting rank, but for some unexplained bureaucratic reason it seems that he was never issued with the 1914–1919 Victory Medal. The only other medal that he was entitled to wear was to be issued nearly twenty years later for the Coronation of King George VI.

It had been an interesting war, spared as he was the horrifying experiences of trench warfare, but as for so many others who had survived the slaughter, they were wasted years and it was now time to try to resume the normal peacetime pattern of life. There were of course advantages for the survivors. Many years later Cobbett remarked, 'You know Fox, I always cite you as the best example of a man made by the War. Your generation, in your field of interest (as in others) was mostly killed in the War, so there was no competition for vacant posts when it ended, and you just walked in where you liked.' This comment, which hardly does justice to the remarkable ability of his protégé, was nevertheless true, for at the very least it must have been easier for him to obtain a place at University as a mature student in 1919 than it would have been in, say, 1914.

Fox's other achievement during this time was to get married. After breaking off his engagement to Maisie Barnes he had had a succession of casual girl friends but no firm relationships. His sister Mary (Babs) vividly recalled the role that she had played in marrying off both of her brothers, the first inadvertent but the second for her favourite brother quite intentional. Her own education and life had been very restricted. Charles Fox had a rooted objection to spending money on a daughter's education and appointed a series of suitable ladies as Governess for both his daughters. Maisie's younger sister Laura was one of those who fulfilled this role for Babs but after a few months, to the concern of the family, she suddenly gave notice and left to marry Norman. Their father never approved of this match, nor of any of his children's marriages though he came to accept them in the end. In 1913, at the age of 21, Babs was finally allowed her freedom and sent to London with a small allowance to study the violin at the Royal Academy of Music. She was very talented and able to pursue a professional career eventually becoming First Violin and Leader of the Oxford Chamber Orchestra. During her time at the Academy Babs shared a study with an advanced student Mary Congreve-Pridgeon, a most accomplished pianist and singer. She was the elder daughter of a well-to-do family who lived at Steyning in Sussex. Her grandfather, George Congreve, had made his fortune manufacturing Congreve's cough mixture, and provided very generously for his daughter and subsequently his grandchildren. In 1882 his daughter Jesse had married Arthur Pridgeon, a penniless cleric of Irish antecedents who had a Cambridge degree. Arthur was a man of outstanding charm and lover of the sporting life with a distinctly eighteenth century flavour. A favourite dog often followed him to church services, lying in reverence and repose under the pulpit throughout the proceedings. George Congreve had purchased the living at Steyning to enable them both to live in circumstances appropriate to his daughter's upbringing. In acknowledgement of this generosity Arthur changed his name to Congreve-Pridgeon. The Vicarage was a large comfortable house with spacious grounds, a small farm and woodlands with shooting rights, which enabled Arthur to live a life he could never have imagined. The parish was a wealthy one and with his wife's private income there were few restrictions on their lifestyle. The children were encouraged to invite their friends, and Babs spent several happy weekends with this slightly eccentric but happy and popular family.

During the late spring of 1914 Babs had received a letter from her brother to say that he had a fortnight's holiday in the summer and had no ideas as to what he was going to do. For the previous five years he had attended the Imperial Yeomanry camps but now that his service was complete he was at a loose end; did she have any suggestions? She mentioned her brother's letter to Mary, and the result was an invitation to Steyning. When I talked to my aunt Babs, then aged 95 and in a Nursing Home in Malvern, she clearly had a vivid recollection of writing to her brother with this invitation and telling him that the parson was an interesting man with whom she was sure Cyril would get on. What she could not remember was whether she had

Figure 13: Cyril and Olive, Steyning 16 May 1916

advised him that there were two very attractive unmarried daughters to keep him company! As the photographs of Fox at this time bear out, he was a very handsome man and very much one for the girls, so she thought it unlikely that he went there totally unprepared! However he was certainly unprepared for the sight of Olive whom he first saw coming down the stairs of the Vicarage 'looking', as he afterwards recalled to his daughters, 'just like an angel.' For them both, Babs recalled, it was love at first sight, but courtship in those days took time; with the war having just started and Fox's commitments at the Laboratory and in the Army, it took even longer. Having overcome her parent's concerns at the twelve years between them Cyril and Olive were married at Steyning Church on 16 May 1916 (Fig. 13). It was to be another three years before they were able to set up home and live together as man and wife, for after a brief honeymoon Fox returned to Cambridge and his wife to Steyning.

War duties, even for those on Home Service, would have meant an extremely lonely existence in Cambridge so Olive, like so many other war-widows, lived at home waiting for the day when the war would be over and married life could begin. She joined her husband for the occasional weekend or days at Cambridge and he travelled down to Steyning for leave; brief interludes of snatched happiness from his extremely busy wartime duties. Marriage and war clearly went together for the Fox family. Dorothy, the elder sister married Major Colson of the Machine Gun Corps who was later promoted Lieutenant Colonel but badly gassed in 1917. He remained an invalid for the rest of his life. Babs eloped and found lifelong happiness with a then penniless artist, Bernard Gotch, who was later to become well known for his watercolours and etchings of the Oxford Colleges.

Shortly before the end of the war Fox returned to full-time duties at the Laboratory and Olive set up home in rented accommodation in Cambridge. Since he was a University employee he had to be fully reinstated and his salary restored from 1 October 1918 to its pre-war level of £200 a year. This was clearly insufficient to support a man in his position and with his new responsibilities, so in early 1919, following his discharge from the Army, he successfully applied for a considerable rise. At the same time the Agriculture Board decided that the Superintendent should be provided with official accommodation as close to the laboratories as possible. Coincidentally an adjacent property, Red Gables, came on to the market and was purchased by the Board for £1000. The Field Laboratories Committee minutes in March 1919 show a deduction of £50 for rent from his new salary of £400. As soon as Red Gables was ready, Olive moved in. Her financial independence enabled her to employ a cook-housekeeper and the garden was tended by the laboratory groundstaff. She had been relieved to be able to leave Steyning, for a few months earlier her father had died of cancer and her mother had to pack up the Vicarage and move to a smaller house in the village. Her happiness at being united with her husband was completed when she became pregnant and on 3 April 1920 the first of their two children, Felicity, was born at her mother's new house in Steyning.

* * *

That Fox had intermittently continued his archaeological studies of the Cambridge area throughout the war is evident from the only work he is known to have published prior to his 1921 paper on Anglo-Saxon monumental sculpture. This was an article entitled Ancient military earthwork in the Cambridge district printed in *Buzz* in June 1918. Written as a military exercise in observation and reasoning, it is a microcosm of his regional research covering the gamut of historical remains, from Iron Age dyke to Cromwellian castle, all amply illustrated with sketches and distribution maps (Fig. 14). The exercise provided for a Cadet to travel on the road from Chesterford to Newmarket and described the military fortifications from different historical periods that he would encounter: '…roads carry traffic; traffic means wealth; wealth, or the want of it, breeds war and in consequence successive tribes, races and nations, prehistoric and historic, have constructed here these banks, ditches and fortresses of earth and stone which are so numerous and which are the silent but certain witnesses of forgotten wars.' Each period, from Stone Age to the Normans, was examined with particular attention given to its military purpose to the importance of southern Cambridgeshire regionally and nationally. He established that 'certain natural features of a district are so important in war that certain sites are bound to be prominent vital key positions century after century.' In conclusion he states of an Iron Age hilltop fortification just outside Cambridge: 'if East Anglia should ever again lie under the curse of war, Cambridge – and the dominating ridge on which Vandlebury [sic] stands – will loom as large in future military history as it has done in the past.'

This article was a foretaste of what was in his mind. The illustrations were his own work, for he had become a highly proficient draughtsman, his maps, sections and line drawings showing the same clarity of purpose and illustration of intent as his prose. He was also a most competent artist of architectural studies though few of his

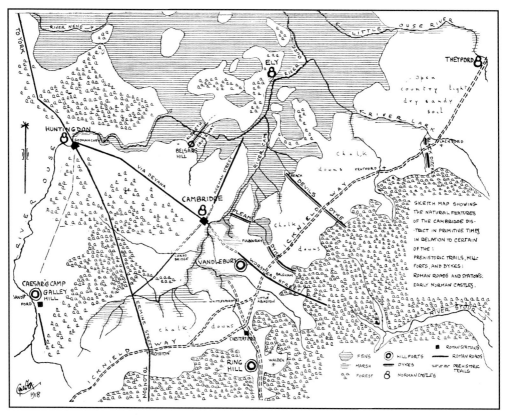

Figure 14: His first 'Distribution Map' published in 'Buzz' June 1918

drawings have survived beyond the illustrations reproduced in his articles and books. One survival is a drawing of Low Farm at Elsworth dated 29 July 1917 (Fig. 15) and is typical of his style. It was a particular favourite of his that hung on his study wall wherever he lived. The origins of this facet of his scholarship cannot be established. In my discussions with his sister Babs it was clear that her brother had always been able to draw but that he had had no formal instruction to her knowledge. It may have been encouragement of his talent by a gifted schoolmaster or more likely by his father's boyhood friend and protégé, Joseph Benwell Clark. JBC, as he was known, was a talented painter, etcher and illustrator who taught at the Slade and in 1894 with William Calderon founded the School of Animal Painting. Many of his pictures, which covered most of the walls in the family home, included buildings and architectural features that would have provided the young Cyril Fox with fine examples of perspective and artistic technique.[2] JBC was Godfather to his elder sister Dorothy and a regular visitor so there would have been ample opportunity for Cyril to discuss his work and technique with him at home.

THE LOW FARM
ELSWORTH.
29 -vii - 1917

Figure 15: Low Farm, Elsworth, Cambridgeshire by Cyril Fox 1917

Within a month of moving into Red Gables, Fox was informed that the future of the Field Laboratories and with it the post of Superintendent was not likely to survive for more than two to three years. He also realised that, in the longer term, he needed a better income to support his family. Furthermore the war had crystallised his ambitions and he was anxious to concentrate on archaeology and to obtain a degree with a view to achieving a University Lectureship or similar appointment. Fox later wrote, 'Professor G. H. Nuttall, the Chairman of the Agricultural Board, suggested that I should try Cambridge and offered to enter me at his own College Magdalene. He added that my absences from the station would not be noted "so long as the organisation functions properly." I expressed my gratitude and being interested in the early history and pre-history of Eastern Britain was recommended to approach Professor Chadwick' who agreed to take him on. As Professor Stuart Piggott was to write nearly fifty years later 'never has the axe of officialdom descended with such beneficial effects for archaeology.'[3] In October 1919 he entered Magdalene College Cambridge as a Fellow Commoner and started his studies of early history and archaeology. The formative years were complete. At the age of 37 he was to embark on a new life that would bring – along with fame but no fortune – personal satisfaction and that inner fulfilment that he had sought for the past twenty years.

Notes

[1] *The Society of Antiquaries of Scotland* XXXVIII 1904
[2] *Dorset Natural History and Archaeological Society* – Dorset Worthies No. 20
[3] *Br.Acad.* LIII p. 400

III

Archaeology of the Cambridge Region 1919–1922
Magdalene and the Cambridge Dykes

Life at Cambridge in the immediate post-war period was relaxed and enjoyable. The undergraduates were a mixture of young men straight from public school, who had missed the war themselves but had seen their families decimated by the carnage of the Western Front and a large number of survivors of the war with vivid and personal memories of their involvement, for whom the war had delayed or interrupted their university ambitions. There were also a few mature students, who had belatedly decided upon a university education and were taking advantage of the practice of most Universities to keep a few places for older men. Everyone had high hopes for the peace but by the winter of 1919–1920 cracks were appearing in society's class-ridden structure. Unemployment was rising and Lloyd-George's Coalition Government faced problems of revolt at home, in Ireland and abroad. But these national trends scarcely impinged upon life in the universities, which maintained their ordered routine virtually oblivious to the changes in the world outside their cloistered walls.

Magdalene, which was to become Fox's *Alma Mater,* was one of Cambridge's smaller and least wealthy colleges. Before the war there had been as few as 60 students; following the appointment of Arthur Christopher Benson (1862–1925) as Master in 1915, major changes took place. Graham Chainer in his *Literary History of Cambridge* wrote that Benson 'expended a fortune on improvements to what had been a run-down and impoverished college, money raised by the extraordinary popularity enjoyed by the stream of mellifluous, spinsterish books that flowed from his pen.' In 1919 over 200 students were entered at Magdalene. Although most of them were British, there were men from all over the world and of all races and creeds. According to college records in some twenty or so survived in 1985, including a Burmese, a French nobleman, a South African and two Indians. For those I was able to trace most had memories as fresh as when they went down giving a vivid insight into life at Cambridge at that time.[1] Unfortunately, for the present study, only one could actually remember Fox from those days for 'undergraduates hardly breathed the same rarefied air as Fellow Commoners', who were treated like Dons. Furthermore although Fox 'lived in' during his first year, 'his rooms were in the New Master's Lodge for Professor

Benson had established himself in the Lodge down by the Street where he lived a rather secluded life.'

Magdalene, as those survivors of the 1919 intake remembered, was a very small college (Fig. 16), none of the development of the Courts on the other side of Magdalene Street had yet begun and Cambridge was a much quieter place. Cattle fed peacefully on the Backs and were often driven from Jesus Green to a byre in active use underneath one of the uninterrupted line of old houses opposite the college. The motor vehicle was a comparative rarity on the streets, a happy contrast to its dominating role to day. Undergraduates arrived, like public schoolboys, with a cabin trunk and tuck-box of books and belongings. For the eighty or so allocated rooms in college, luggage was delivered by the railway company to the Porter's Lodge where it was piled high until the porters took it up to the rooms; for the rest it was delivered to their lodgings, which were scattered all over Cambridge. Rooms in the Courts were completely bare; the first thing to be done was to go out and buy second-hand furniture, cooking pots and china at 'well known shops for that purpose.' Dinner was the only meal included in college fees, so food had to be purchased either from the college kitchens or in the town. 'We learned from the bedder [a college servant who looked after the rooms and also served in Hall], that Cambridge Market sold butter in inches, so we ordered loaves of bread, a ration of two inches of butter a day and daily milk. The milk mostly went off and the butter rancid because there was only one small closet on each floor to act as larder. Magdalene First Court had ivy all over the walls and beautiful window boxes of bright red geraniums. These were watered by the gardeners but the addition of tea leaves, sour milk and rancid butter made them grow immensely.' There were then of course no lavatories or basins on the staircases; slop pails of water were provided and taken away by the bedders. WCs and bathrooms were in a corner on the ground floor, beyond the Pepys and Bright's buildings, so every morning a procession of undergraduates in dressing gowns made their way across the courts carrying towels and sponge bags to the baths. Rooms were heated by open fires, which were cleaned out and laid by the bedders and left with a bucket of coal together with a kettle full of water for making tea on the gas rings.

Traditions at Magdalene die hard; the standard of food in Hall was adequate, though somewhat sparse in those post-war years, and the candle-lit atmosphere made dining a warm and friendly an occasion. This is as true to day as it was in 1919. Women were not allowed in college without a chaperone – in any case there were few girls about at the time. Professor Benson was a bachelor who did not encourage the presence of the fair sex and the number of undergraduates at Girton and Newnham was small. As one 1919 freshman wrote to me; 'I don't think we thought about it, there was so much to do and girls were something nice in the vacation' but it cannot be certain that he spoke for them all!

May Balls were not the annual feature they have become in modern times; there was only one Magdalene Ball during Fox's time as an undergraduate, an occasion he

Figure 16: Magdalene College, Front Court and Dining Hall with (inset) Fox as an Undergraduate 1920

remembered for the rest of his life. The marquee was erected in the Second Court, a dance floor laid beneath glittering fairy lights, and an orchestra played the popular tunes of the day. The Hall, cleared of refectory tables and long benches, was set out with dozens of small candle-lit tables so they could dine in style. The men were all in evening dress, the ladies in flamboyant ball gowns, the champagne flowed as they danced until dawn when breakfast was served.

Apart from the Master, the two men, who presided over the college and its activities, were A. S. Ramsey, the President and Senior Tutor, and Thomas Peel, the Bursar. Ramsey, whose son Michael was to become Archbishop of Canterbury, effectively ran the college during the prolonged absence of the Master for most of the period 1919–1921. Professor Benson, despite his temporary withdrawal from day-to-day management, still kept in close touch with all that was going on. To undergraduates, whom he used to invite for coffee in his rooms, he seemed a genial but rather formidable character. 'It was a surprise to find out how much he knew about us' one wrote 'sport, work whatever you like.' It was this ability to understand his undergraduates and to recognise and encourage their talents that has made him remembered with affection by all who passed through Magdalene's doors during his Mastership, however brief their stay. To Fox he became a friend, confidant and professional adviser, whose wise counsel was sought and prevailed, especially in 1924, when difficult decisions were required on his future career. Ramsey, a highly talented mathematician, was an equally awesome person, who seems to be universally remembered for his wife's 'jolly tea parties', commonly known as 'doing a Ram!'

Peel, also a lecturer at the Engineering Laboratory, had served under Sir Charles Parsons, the inventor of the steam turbine. In addition to his college and university duties, he ran the local power station for the Cambridge Electric Light Company, the Parsons family firm. The building housing the steam turbines and generators – which were very advanced for their day – was on the opposite side of the Cam to the college and had an unmistakable hum which was apparently comforting to the engineering students but a minor irritant to those of other persuasions. Another colourful character was the Dean, Stephen Gazelle. He was later to achieve eminence in the Foreign Service and be knighted. In 1919 he was known as a delightfully entertaining and flamboyant man with a ready greeting for one and all and usually dressed in a bright leather waistcoat and Churchill type hat.

For students, gowns were required to be worn on most occasions – lectures, tutorials, Hall and, most irksome of all, on the streets of Cambridge after dark. The University Proctor and his Bulldogs, responsible for discipline throughout the university and known as 'Prog and Bullers', were on patrol to ensure adherence to this rule with the penalty of a stiff fine if an undergraduate was caught not wearing his academic dress. However there were apparently two or three time- honoured sanctuaries from proctorial discipline, one of which was the cobbled area on King's Parade in front of the entrance gates to King's though how one escaped from this sanctuary none of the 1919 undergraduates could recall.

The academic routine was not demanding with rarely more than two or three lectures and one tutorial a week for most students – the engineers and scientists had laboratory work to do in addition – so there was always ample time for sport and extra-curricular activities. Magdalene, being such a small college, provided a better opportunity than most to get one's "colours" or "oars" by representing the college on the sports field or the river. For the non-sporting men there was always the Junior Common Room Debating Society and if really talented the Union or, for those who preferred the boards, the Cambridge University Dramatic Society. Above all this was a chance to combine academic study with social activities and, for most under-graduates, another two or three years of freedom before earning their living.

This did not all apply to Fox, with a young wife to support and a job to hold down, but nevertheless he and his fellow undergraduates certainly enjoyed his time at University. As one of the ex-service undergraduates wrote to me ' it was a really marvellous experience to be at Cambridge just after that horrific First World War. Strangely perhaps we, who had been abroad in the Forces, hardly ever discussed or even mentioned our experiences. What a relief it was to be once more in civilian clothes – those in the Forces were obliged to wear uniform even on leave in those days – and to enjoy the free and easy life of the University.' Cambridge was well endowed with eminent men such as Quiller-Couch, Rutherford, and Thompson, a veritable posse of Knights of the Realm, as well as an abundance of undergraduates also destined to achieve their place in history – Kingsley-Martin, P. M. S. Blackett and Lord Louis Mountbatten amongst them. For them all, known or unknown, dons or undergraduates, perhaps the most endearing factor that runs through their reminiscences, be they formal biographies or informal letters, is the deep affection they have for their college or the University and the happiness with which they recall their Cambridge days. Without doubt this was true of Fox, for whom the mere mention of Magdalene would bring a gentle smile to his face and usually an anecdote of its personalities in his time.

*   *   *

Between leaving the Army in January 1919 and entering Magdalene in October, Fox had spent every moment that he could spare from his duties with the Laboratory continuing his researches on the Cambridge region and finalising his theories on the relationship between soil and settlement. By now determined to publish his ideas he had produced an outline for a book on the history of the region, which he discussed with Cobbett and other members of the Cambridge Antiquarian Society. He had been a member of this Society for many years and had on many occasions listened to papers presented by members on archaeological and historical subjects but had never produced one himself. Through the winter of 1919–1920 he had researched monumental sculptures of the Anglo-Saxon period but, like other first-year students, he was at the same time grappling with his academic studies of archaeology and history in preparation for Mays (the end of year examinations) and had no time to spare. During the summer and autumn he was less pressed; having decided that he would not be including this subject in his planned book he clearly believed it would be a suitable topic with which to open his account with the Society. This first paper, read in February 1921, is particularly interesting since it illustrates Fox's approach to evidence and his determination to provide a logical and understandable historically and geographically related chronology from the material available to him.[2] Before commenting on this paper and the Cambridgeshire Dykes papers that followed, which were partially incorporated into *Archaeology of the Cambridge Region*, it is important to set the archaeological scene in the early 1920s.

Archaeology, particularly British archaeology, as it was taught in the universities and as it was generally practised by the well-to-do antiquarians, who formed the majority of the people able to indulge themselves in this subject, had advanced little from the Victorian era. In broad terms it consisted of observation, excavation and reporting the site and/or the finds with little or no attempt to relate the discovery to its geographical position or to give reasoned arguments concerning its relationship to similar sites and artefacts. There were of course some archaeologists, like Pitt-Rivers and Williams-Freeman, who did not subscribe to this general philosophy, but most excavations were assessed individually. Some produced identical or very similar objects or methods of construction and could not be ignored; these, few and far between, were insufficient to alter the normal course of archaeological practice.

Writing to Professor Glyn Daniel in 1960 Fox summed up the position: 'British Archaeology when I began was ignorant of or indifferent to fundamentals. The background of collected knowledge (attained incidentally by individual studies of periods and type objects) on the important theme of the varied environment, with the island open to early settlers, and their choice, had never to my knowledge been considered as of importance itself, nor had distribution patterns been analysed to determine how and why they differed.' Like all generalisations there were exceptions. O. G. S. Crawford and Mortimer Wheeler were notably eminent examples of the new professional, but their ideas and practices were only just being formulated in the early twenties and were far from filtering through to university teaching, nor had any major publication indicated the possible direction that archaeological analysis should take. In the late Victorian period, General Pitt-Rivers had established and put into practice his ideas for improved excavation technique. Expensive in time and manpower they were almost totally ignored so that pre-historic or historical sites were still, in the somewhat exaggerated words of Wheeler, 'being dug up like potatoes.' As Professor Stuart Piggott aptly wrote 'the atmosphere [at excavation sites] was at its best that of amiable amateurism, at worst of destructive ignorance.' In such a world Wheeler and Fox were, independently each in their own fields, 'looking for a professional job where the profession had yet to be created.'[3] Anglo-Saxon monumental sculpture in the Cambridge district, read in this context can be seen to be a pointer towards the establishment of those fundamentals that Crawford, Wheeler and Fox found lacking, which in the following decades these three would lead a newly professional archaeology to achieve. The paper sets out in traditional fashion the accumulated finds and knowledge of pre-Conquest crosses and gravestones from this region to find, through commonality of design, their artistic origins and date. Having established in this way that there was a distinct Cambridge school, the paper goes on to investigate the derivation of its art forms and, what was new to British archaeology, the geographical and historical reasons for the distribution pattern.

All the work that Fox had undertaken thus far was restricted to an examination of the writings and finds of others and his own visual assessment of the wide variety of pre-historic and historic sites in the area. Whether he attended or assisted in any excavations before 1921 cannot be determined; there is no acknowledgement of his service or mention of it in any biographical notes that survive. In February 1921 an opportunity arose to carry out an excavation on a section of Worstead Street on behalf of the Cambridge Antiquarian Society[4] to determine if the Roman road was of original construction or built on a pre-Roman causeway. This was a very simple excavation; after two sections had been cut (Fig. 17) the answer was readily found to be the former. Its importance was not in itself but that it immediately established Fox

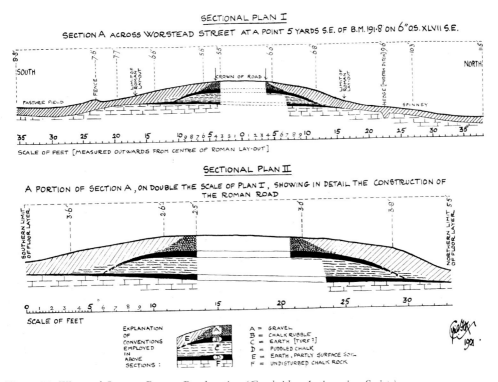

Figure 17: Worstead Street – Roman Road section (Cambridge Antiquarian Society)

not just as a willing and extremely competent excavator but as a man who published his results very quickly.

The subsequent excavations that Fox undertook on behalf of the Cambridge Antiquarian Society involved the Cambridge dykes. Dykes are linear earthworks providing a low level defence or boundary. Their construction involved excavation of a ditch or 'fosse' with the spoil forming a bank or 'vallum' that was usually on the defended or internal side. The vallum can be up to 20 feet (6m) high, with a ten foot deep (3m) ditch, or a barely discernible rise and fall in the landscape where ploughing and natural erosion has virtually brought the dyke back to ground level. In the normal course of building surface material from the fosse will form the base of the vallum, just above natural ground level, with sub-soil on the top. Careful examination of strata in the vallum can reveal a wealth of information as to the construction and purpose of the dyke and occasionally firm pointers to its date. The most renowned of these earthworks is Offa's Dyke, which runs through the Welsh Marches from the Dee to the Severn, but there is a group of eight dykes and ditches to the south and north-east of Cambridge – the largest being Devil's Dyke – whose purpose and date had never been positively established. Although there was some antiquarian interest in excavating dykes they did not provide the 'rewards' that were frequently obtained from barrows, so few had been scientifically examined.

Fox's work on the Cambridgeshire dykes was initially undertaken with Dr W. M. Palmer and later with T. C. (Tom) Lethbridge.[5] The Fleam Dyke excavations were undertaken in 1921 and 1922 with the primary objective of determining its age. Seven sections were cut across the fosse, with 'nothing whatever being found that threw any direct light on the date of the earthwork or its builders.' However a strange feature of these sections was the appearance of a constant 'shelf' on the vallum side of the fosse (Fig. 18). Various hypotheses as to its purpose were raised on the site at the time (and repeated for posterity in the paper) resulting in the assessment that it was necessary to undertake a complete cross-section of the whole dyke. Analysis of the soil strata suggested that the dyke had twice been raised from a small ditch and bank that, at its original level, could have done little more than mark a boundary; the 'shelf' was the remains of the ditch from the first stage of construction. Further consideration of the evidence from the 1922 excavations brought forward the theory that construction had been interrupted. It was thought that the differences between successive earth deposits to build up the dyke were mainly due to varying methods of construction rather than purposeful enlargement. Since evidence of Romano-British 'rubbish', all of it heavily abraded, was found on the original natural ground *below* the first stage of the vallum a date no earlier than the middle to late Roman period was proposed. Study of the historical evidence made it likely that a date as late as the 7th Century AD could not be discounted. Fox surmised that Fleam Dyke, together with the Bran Ditch and Devil's Dyke, formed defensive boundaries from forest to fen across the only access to East Anglia from the south-west.

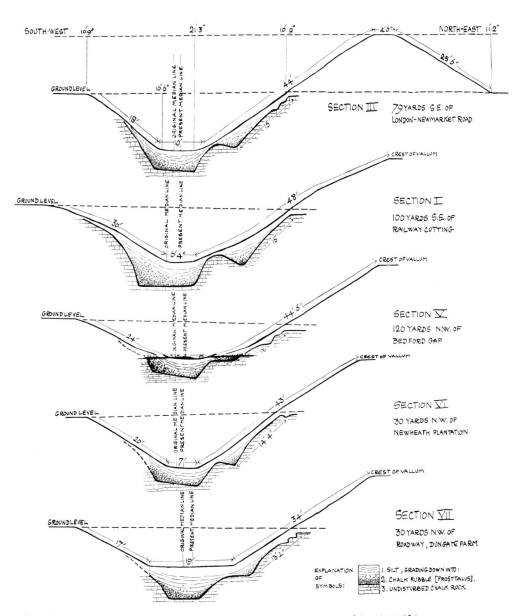

SOUTH-WEST 16'9"   21'3"   10'9"   4'6"   NORTH-EAST 11'2"

GROUND LEVEL   10'6"

ORIGINAL MEDIAN LINE
PRESENT MEDIAN LINE

18'   25'6"
44'
15'   SECTION III   79 YARDS S.E. OF
10'   LONDON-NEWMARKET ROAD

CREST OF VALLUM

GROUND LEVEL   4'8'
30'   SECTION I
6'4"   15'   100 YARDS S.E. OF
RAILWAY CUTTING

CREST OF VALLUM

GROUND LEVEL   44'6"
24'   SECTION V
120 YARDS N.W. OF
BEDFORD GAP

CREST OF VALLUM

GROUND LEVEL   43'
20'   SECTION VI
14'4"   30 YARDS N.W. OF
7'   NEWHEATH PLANTATION

CREST OF VALLUM

GROUND LEVEL   34'
17'   SECTION VII
19'   13'2"   30 YARDS N.W. OF
ROADWAY, DUNGATE FARM

EXPLANATION
OF
SYMBOLS:
1. SILT; GRADING-DOWN INTO:
2. CHALK RUBBLE [FROST TALUS].
3. UNDISTURBED CHALK ROCK.

PLANS OF FIVE SECTIONS CUT ACROSS THE FOSSE, FLEAM DYKE, MAY 1921

Figure 18: Sections through the Fleam Dyke (Cambridge Antiquarian Society)

Figure 19: Excavation of Devil's Dyke 1924 (Cambridge Antiquarian Society)

Figure 20: Work on the Dyke with Lethbridge and Palmer 1924

Clearly Fox was still not wholly satisfied with his answers, pursuing his investigations with a series of excavations of Bran Ditch and of Devil's Dyke in 1923 and 1924 (Figs 19 and 20). Devil's Dyke, much longer than Fleam Dyke, appeared to have been constructed in one continuous operation. The evidence of abraded artefacts on natural ground beneath the vallum once again suggested a later date than local historians had supposed. His examination of these remains was exceptionally detailed (Fig. 21). 'Ordinary investigation of the soil under the vallum,' he wrote, 'would certainly not reveal, except by fortunate accident, the minute and abraded sherds and other relics on which my conclusions are based. It took three of us four weeks to examine 300 square feet of the ancient surface in the three sections exposed; the soil was compressed by the weight of the bank and each lump had to be broken up by the fingers.'

This examination of these minute pieces of pottery revealed that all were abraded; some could be dated not earlier than the 2nd Century AD. 'Now the vessels from which these minute and worn fragments came were, we may suppose, for a time used, then broken, then carted away as manure, then by agricultural operations reduced to their present dimensions. These processes take time – a long time. All the Roman or Romano-British pottery is however in precisely the same condition as the Early Iron Age ware. It is therefore likely that the vallum was not thrown up until some time after the supply of Roman pottery had ceased; that is until some time after the latest fragments to be cast onto the fields had had time to be reduced to

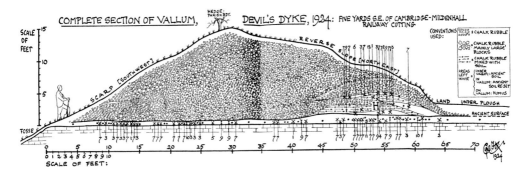

Figure 21: The main section through Devil's Dyke (Cambridge Antiquarian Society)

the same abraded condition as the earlier wares.' Thus the evidence from both dykes was the same. The conclusion was inevitable that the same people constructed them and at roughly similar times; the better construction of Devil's Dyke probably indicated that it was the second to be built.

Fox then related the construction to historical need. They had to be younger than the 2nd century AD for pottery of that age was beneath the vallum. They had to be older than the 9th century AD when written records report their existence. In what century in between must they have been made? No requirement could be found for the protection of Norfolk in Roman times, and the only period that would fit all the facts was the 7th century, when the 'East Angles were exposed to attack by, and finally succumbed to, Penda and his Mercians.'

This first series of excavations illustrates Fox's determination to get as near the truth as the evidence that survived and the elapse of time allowed. If the evidence was not initially or entirely clear it would be pursued unremittingly; if a better hypothesis emerged Fox was not concerned to openly admit that his initial judgement was wrong. McKenny Hughes had cut a section in the Devil's Dyke in the late 19th century. Finding 'a few objects of Roman date in the surface of the bank….. [whereas] under the bank there was no trace of anything of the kind' McKenny Hughes came to the conclusion that the dyke was pre-Roman – the accepted belief in 1920. It had to be of that era since there was nothing Roman under it. Having come to his own, very different, conclusion for the date of the dyke, Fox was not content to dismiss McKenny Hughes as mistaken or incompetent. He needed to discover *what* had prompted McKenny Hughes to come to that conclusion. Firstly he rightly believed, in accordance with archaeological practice of the day, there was inadequate supervision, which meant that minute pieces of heavily abraded pottery under the vallum were likely to have been missed or dismissed. This contrasts with the painstaking sifting of evidence undertaken in his own 1921–24 series of excavations. Secondly, and more important, was the detailed analysis of the soil that composed the vallum. This showed that the area of bank in which these sherds were discovered was the original topsoil from the first cutting of the fosse, which had been deposited on the far side of the vallum to mark, for its builders, its extent. That was why inside this portion of the far side of the vallum were pieces of Romano-British rubbish that had littered the surface of the field. The nearer the dyke was to former Roman settlements the greater their profusion, the further away the more rarely they were found. It was McKenny Hughes' misfortune that there were few noticeable remains in his section, and all of these found in and not *under* the bank.

Recalling this excavation and the many senior archaeologists who initially doubted his findings, preferring McKenny Hughes' thesis to his own, Fox wrote, 'I told Sir William Ridgeway of the Samian sherds we had found under the vallum which showed the Devils Dyke to be *not* pre-Roman; Ridgeway you remember had committed himself to an Icenian origin. He stepped out (onto the dyke) and said 'Fox knows as well as I do that Samian (or rather Arretine) were imported into Cambridgeshire long before the Claudian conquest!' But he winked at me and did not oppose the publication of the papers in the CAS proceedings.'

The reports of these excavations aroused considerable interest amongst archaeologists and historians but no one was really in a position to challenge this seemingly irrefutable evidence for the late construction of the Cambridgeshire dykes.[5] Bushe-Fox, writing to Fox after publication of his paper in 1925, said; 'The Devil's Dyke was a jolly good bit of work but I cannot help feeling that on archaeological evidence alone it might have been formed in the 4th Century. As you rightly say it is difficult to see what purpose it would have served at that period and I expect you are right about its date. However there may have been all sorts of queer goings-on on the East Coast towards the close of the Roman occupation.'

Looking back Professor Glyn Daniel has stated that 'the excavation of Devil's Dyke was a pioneer work of very great significance in the history and development of archaeological technique, as was the Beacon Hill barrow dig' and perhaps that is its greatest achievement. By the time the final excavation report was published in 1925, it had been read to the Cambridge Antiquarian Society in May 1924, Fox had long since completed his Cambridge degree and presented his thesis to an astonished University and the archaeological world.

*   *   *

The academic route that Fox had taken to achieve his degree was to say the least unusual – almost as strange as his preparation for university life – and involved the invocation of an obscure University rule known as Regulation One. Professor Glyn Daniel, who came up to Cambridge as an undergraduate in 1932 and studied under Professor Chadwick, remembered hearing of the celebrated use of this regulation from Fox's great friend Tom Lethbridge, as well as from J. M. de Navarro and

Chadwick himself:[6] 'Fox, through the Cambridge Antiquarian Society and the good offices of such people as Cobbett, Lethbridge and Professor Nuttall, had come to the attention of Professor Hector Munro Chadwick as a potential mature student. Chadwick, who was then Professor of Anglo-Saxon, had created in 1918 a new subject for the English and History Tripos – Anglo-Saxon and kindred studies – and thought that with some modifications this would be an ideal degree for Fox to undertake. Chadwick's modification was to substitute a dissertation on archaeology in the Cambridge region for the language paper, which involved very complicated linguistic achievements, Anglo-Saxon, Norse, etc, and this was not a forte of Cyril.'

Having obtained a first in the 1920 Mays[7] and presented Chadwick with his work on his dissertation, which had grown far beyond the original concept, 'Chadwick said to him 'Oh! this is much bigger than a paper for tripos, my dear boy, it ought to be a Ph.D.'. This came as a great surprise to Cyril, and a great surprise to everyone else, because in 1920, the Ph.D. was not well established and hardly anyone, except Hector Munro Chadwick, knew about Regulation One. This precept stated that people, who had not taken any other degree, could under special circumstances take a Ph.D. To the best of my knowledge,' Professor Daniel continued, 'Cyril was the first person in the University, certainly in the archaeological world, to take a Ph.D. never having taken a degree before. This was entirely due to Chadwick's appreciation of the rules and his being in a position to approve the application when submitted.' Professor Daniel was able to put this knowledge of Regulation One to good effect when many years later he was able to approve the second application by an archaeological student, Brian Hope-Taylor, to proceed direct to his doctorate without taking a preliminary degree. By a striking coincidence, Hope-Taylor's Ph.D. topic, the great early mediaeval site of Yeavering in Northumberland, was of much the same period as Fox's date for the Cambridge dykes; by another Hope-Taylor's last excavation was of the Devil's Dyke when the Newmarket by-pass cut through it and again its date and purpose were examined.

Time for Fox was no longer pressing since the routine submission of essays and tutorials, a necessary part of the BA degree course, were no longer required and he had two full years to present his expanded paper on archaeology in the Cambridge region. Research primarily in the surrounding countryside and the Cambridge Museum of Archaeology and Ethnology, as well as other local museums and private collections, and an intensive programme of recording, writing and editing followed. Only the previously described fieldwork and his continuing duties at the Field Laboratory interrupted his studies. The thesis was given the title *Archaeology of the Cambridge Region* and completed in July 1922; it was accepted by the University at the end of September, and published by the Cambridge University Press a year later.[8] As is stated in the Prefatory Note 'the high cost of production, in particular of the series of coloured maps which are essential to my scheme, made it necessary for me to find the sum of One Hundred Pounds additional to that which the Press was prepared to expend.'

Amongst the list of contributors who ensured that this thesis was published complete were Professors Chadwick and Nuttall and the Master of Magdalene as well as his father and sister Babs and his 'dear friend Cobbett.'

Commenting on this major work Professor Stuart Piggott was later to write 'publication of his thesis placed the almost unknown Cyril Fox, almost overnight, in the front rank of archaeological scholarship. The thesis must surely rank as one of the most remarkable ever submitted in the archaeological school of any University.'

In later life Fox was often asked how this book came to be written in middle age by a man with no previous track record or apparent archaeological expertise. His answer to the first part of the question was that 'until I was middle aged I had no opportunity for work outside the hard necessity of earning a living.' To the second part the 20 years between leaving school at 16 and entering University were his archaeological apprenticeship where he fashioned his own expertise. Whilst earning a living he completed his studies far more thoroughly than any undergraduate and evolved his theories on the relationship between geography, geology and history by practical examination of the evidence around him and the archaeological material that had been preserved. As he states in the introduction 'the work was undertaken in order to provide a basis – which does not exist at present – for the future detailed study, period by period, of the archaeological remains of the district.' In a comparatively small area, 44 square miles with Cambridge at its centre, he was able to undertake the research work and the visual fieldwork himself although he would have been the first to admit this had taken a great deal longer to accomplish than a normal degree course permits.

The theme of the book to which it returns time and time again is the relationship between developing man and his environment as expressed in his various activities by studying the distribution of his artefacts and settlement sites (Fig. 22). The maps that form the majority of the appendices establish quite clearly that this distribution is closely related to the terrain and the natural vegetation regarded as prevalent at the time and which, in turn, is dependent on the nature of the soil and sub-soil. It is the author's contention, amply supported by the distribution patterns from Neolithic times to the Anglo-Saxon period, that early settlement and soil are bound inextricably together. Although provenance of many of the early finds cannot be attributed more closely than to a parish, it must be accepted that settlement started on the dry, well drained and open country and moved, as civilisation progressed, onto the boulder clay areas that were originally forest covered. 'That Neolithic man hunted in the woodlands may be taken as certain; that outcasts took refuge there is highly probable; and that stone implements will, from time to time, here and there, be found in such areas is to be anticipated. But it is clear from the rarity of such finds as hitherto recorded, that settlements of this Age in the forests were very infrequent.'

The affronted claylands were the last to be occupied. As they were often potentially the best soil for arable crops their clearance was a significant element in the progression of civilised life in the ages that followed. In his sequence of ages a

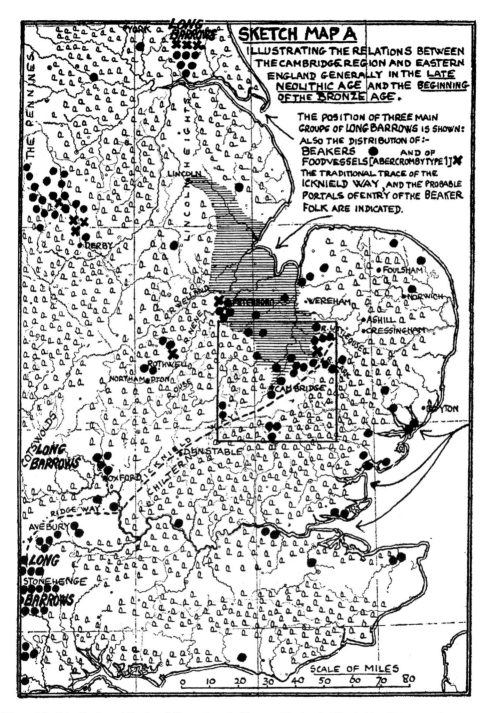

Figure 22: Distribution of Beaker folk artefacts in Eastern England (Cambridge University Press)

combination of his own theories and the necessity to rationalise man's progress inevitably forced Fox into conflict with existing archaeological dogma and generally accepted assumptions. In discussing the advance of agricultural activity into the clayland forests during the Roman occupation Fox came into direct conflict with Haverfield, the then acknowledged expert on Roman Britain. Fox contended that 'there is nothing to suggest a wholesale and general destruction which should have transformed the forest uplands of the Cambridge region into the prosperous corn growing districts such as for the most part they are to-day.' Haverfield's evidence of earlier clearance was based on the existence of Roman houses in this area. Fox countered this theory by saying that the fact that 'the majority of which are on chalk slopes or gravel terraced bordering streams is such that their presence cannot afford proof that the hundred square miles and more of dense woodland in this area had been cleared.' In his opinion much of the forest remained untouched from Neolithic times through to the Anglo-Saxon period and later. That re-afforestation occurred during the Dark Ages must be taken as inevitable, and it was probably the end of the Danish occupation before stability and the return of civilisation allowed re-occupation of the claylands and further inroads could be made into the virgin woodlands.

Fox was always a very gentle man whose inclination was to persuade rather than openly to confront. Though expressed in the gentlest of terms he nonetheless forced home his arguments in such precise terms that the reader was under no misapprehension as to the logic of his deductions and the fallibility of previous hypotheses. This compassionate treatment of his archaeological elders, however misguided he may have considered them to be, invariably won him their friendship and meant that he had few if any virulent critics.

Inevitably there were anomalies and errors in his thesis. Only theories could be offered for the unexplained break in the progressive cultivation of the southern fens during the Early Iron Age, despite rich reminders of man's presence in the Bronze Age. In this march land between hostile confederations, perhaps with different stages of culture, Fox suggested that the most likely cause for the absence of finds was that warfare on this interface made it untenable. His chapter on the dykes, which was written in 1922, perforce had to accept the McKenny Hughes pre-Roman dating; it was rendered obsolete within twelve months by his own researches. Nevertheless this thesis, which is a broad ranging historical survey, invites additional research and challenges to accepted doctrine; it fully accepts that further research may well make some of his conclusions obsolete. Hidden in the second and third chapters are reclassifications of the Bronze and Iron Ages, treatise subjects in themselves and which have to a great extent stood the test of time; other parts have been overtaken by events.

Twenty-five years later in a remarkable tribute to the timeless nature of this work, the book was republished by the Cambridge University Press.[9] Included in this 1948 edition is an additional appendix 'Reflections on the Archaeology of the Cambridge Region' that had been written for the *Cambridge Historical Journal* in 1947. This personal analysis of the book and the very frank acknowledgement of its shortcomings in certain areas is essential reading, if only to understand the state of archaeological art in 1920 was such that these errors were inevitable. Grahame Clarke and C. W. Phillips, who had developed the Fenland Research Committee in 1932, were able to establish that the occupation of the fens was more extensive than was apparent from the Cambridge Region study. Similarly Fox's belief that the permeable soil areas, the first to be occupied, were clear of forestation had been established to be inaccurate by 1947. 'We now know that such soils became open in the consequence of settlement … Clearance as at first practised was a temporary affair, Neolithic agriculture was extensive and many of these plots re-established themselves as forest as the farmers and their stock moved on. The forest was cleared by fire, the axe and the secular activity of grazing animals; and the temporary cultivation gradually became permanent. Towards the end of the pre-historic period in the Cambridge Region then the equation 'permeable soil = open country' was doubtless sound.' Fox therefore concluded that in his own opinion the basic hypothesis was still sound but that some of the definitions required changing. Later still Professor Christopher Hawkes wrote 'this topographical approach, which must for the most part be attributed to the influence of his friend Dr Cobbett, was not elaborated in a way that would make it dated. Hence despite the further march of progress (since 1947) it has not become obsolete or even obsolescent and is still in current use to day.'

A wide press followed the 1923 publication expressing general recognition that this book was breaking new ground in archaeological science. In *The Field* (17 Jan 24) under the heading 'Three Thousand Years of Cambridge,' the reviewer wrote; 'This noble volume is for the serious archaeologist; it is within its prescribed limits complete and any other books which deal with the same or cognate subjects will have to be additions or state their conclusions with reference to it.' W. G. Clarke's article in the *Eastern Press* headed Dr Cyril Fox's Brilliant Study (20 Dec 23), reprinted in the *Proceedings of the Prehistoric Society of East Anglia*, suggested 'it should provide considerable encouragement to the ordinary field worker. It is often impossible for him to perceive the value of his more or less isolated finds or of his accurate records of archaeological material, which he cannot assign with any certainty to any particular period. …these bare records and the specimens themselves provide the raw material for an archaeological Darwin…' *The Times Literary Supplement* (7 Feb 24) suggested that 'the publication ….marks a very distinct step forward in the historical interpretation of archaeological evidence,' and H. J. E. Peake in the *Museums Journal* (Mar 24) exhorted Curators considering publication of monographs on the archaeology of their region to consult this volume in the first place as being the best and most thorough archaeological monograph which has yet appeared.

Additionally Fox's treatment of his subject brought a wider audience than would normally be accorded to an archaeological or historical treatise provoking reviews in the geographical and geological publications. O. G. S. Crawford, Archaeology Officer to the Ordnance Survey, writing in the *Geographical Journal* (Apr 24) said, 'the book [whose] treatment is chronological and geographical will be a landmark in the history of archaeology.' In the *Geological Magazine* (Jun 24) he added that although 'the book is almost outside the scope of geology …nevertheless the writer shows that he is fully alive to the significance of geological structure and the distribution of the superficial deposits as controlling factors in human settlement…and [his book] cannot fail to appeal to a wide circle of readers beyond the bounds of archaeologists.'

In addition to these published critiques there were a flood of mostly congratulatory private letters. Foremost amongst these must have been the letter from his father, who had been so supportive of him throughout his apprenticeship and whose own literary skills had been sought for the final stages of publication. 'My dearest CFF,' he wrote, 'Many thanks for your very handsome gift of your first work – I am proud of my boy and doubly so to see his name affixed as author to so excellently printed a tome. The whole format… is perfect and the delight with which I shall read through the work again, with my mind and eyes freed from looking for possible printer's errors as when proof reading, will know no bounds. …it would appear to me that it should be one of reference and a text book for all time. That you will find more scope for your energies and archaeological learnings I know – but if you do nothing else your name will be quoted long after your old Dad has mouldered into dust.' Charles Fox died 30 years later in September 1953 aged 94 with his faculties intact to the end, able to appreciate that his proud words were fully justified.

Amongst letters from his 'archaeological peers' is one that was probably treasured most of all since it was to O. G. S. Crawford that he owed so much for helping him with his distribution maps and for support throughout the long years of genesis of his thesis. 'Dear Fox, Your book is an eye-opener. My word you will make some people sit up. It is absolutely unique. There is nothing like it in existence, others have produced excellent regional monographs, but there are none, which have the wide range, equal balance (between such diversities as e.g. The Roman and Neolithic) and truly scientific method. The topographical outwork is of course its chief feature but the accurate "attention to detail" is a far harder achievement and one rarely found in Geographers.' This was high praise indeed from the 'Master'.

There were of course some that found fault, usually those with their own hobbyhorses to ride. One such kept presumably as an amusing reminder of the archetypal antiquarian of the day reads 'Dear Sir, I have just had a look at your fine book …I shall never have time to read it…. My object in looking into your book was to find out whether it lent any support to my theories about the 'Tribal Hidage,' but your only reference to this interesting document (page 239) is to Mr Corbett's [sic] essay on it… It seems to me to be obviously erroneous from beginning to end…. Yours very truly J. I. Brownbill.'

A letter kept for very different reasons came from Olive at Steyning. His wife had gone home for the birth of their second daughter, Penelope born on 26th November

1923. 'Darling, I was so glad to get your dear letter this afternoon at tea time and to know that 'Boy's Book' had really arrived. I am disappointed that I was not there to share the pleasure of first opening it with you. I hear a pawsel [sic] has come for Grannie which no doubt contains her copy which I long to have up and open. … Mousie is going to start reading the parts she has not already read first. I was only wishing the other day I had some intelligent reading here …and am so proud of "Boy's Book," all my love Maimie.' This extract from Olive's letter, one of only seven that have been found to survive her death, indicates a considerable community of academic interest between them although, according to Babs, she was certainly not an intellectual. However as a wife, mother and companion she provided her husband with everything that he required and their relationship, from the letters between them and the memories of their two children, was deep, affectionate and fruitful.

This letter also points up the use of nicknames, which are a recurrent feature in Fox's life. They were much in vogue in the late Victorian and Edwardian periods and the habit, which originated in his childhood, remained with him for the whole of his life. They were not used all of the time, it clearly depended on the mood of the moment. Within his own family he was called 'Peter' his brother Norman was 'Chuff' and Mary 'Babs'. Dorothy insisted on her own name although occasionally answering to the common abbreviation 'Dot'. Ernest Gaye knew the brothers as 'Pouter' and 'Chuffy'. His first love, Maisie Barnes, called him by his second name 'Fred' whereas to Olive – Mousie or Maimie as she called herself – he was 'Bird' or 'Boy' but signed himself 'Burd'. The children were called 'Sissa' and 'Tiny' and they called their father 'Mallard' and 'Mannikin' whilst their mother was alive but this ceased with her death. The practice continued with his second family but the nicknames did not continue beyond our childhood.

Notes

[1] The description of Magdalene and University life at this time is taken from 1985 interviews and letters to the author from the survivors of the 1919 intake.
[2] Anglo-Saxon Monumental Sculpture in the Cambridge District *Camb.Ant.* XIII
[3] Biographical memoirs of the Fellows of the Royal Society December 1977
[4] Excavations in the Cambridge Dykes I – Worstead Street *Camb.Ant.* XXIV
[5] Excavations in the Cambridge Dykes II, III and IV – Fleam Dyke (with W. M. Palmer), Devil's Dyke and Foxton *Camb.Ant.* XXIV, XXV, XXVI
[6] Interview with the author in 1985
[7] For this Fox was awarded the College Prize, a sum of £2 12s 6d, sent to him by the Bursar on 21 June 1920 with this caution 'the understanding has always been that this should be spent upon books which should be stamped with the College Shield and Crest.' The prize, *Saxon Obsequies discovered by the Hon. R. C. Neville*, published by John Murray in 1852, was presented in 1998 by the family to Magdalene College Library together with the formal notification of marks and the award from the President A. S. Ramsey, and a letter written by the author.
[8] *Archaeology of the Cambridge Region* Cambridge University Press 1923
[9] Reprint of *Archaeology of the Cambridge Region* with Appendix from the *Cambridge Historical Journal* CUP 1948

IV

Further Excavations in the Cambridge Region 1922–1924 The Search for Pastures New

His thesis, *Archaeology of the Cambridge Region*, not only gave Fox his doctorate and his Fellowship of the Society of Antiquaries but also opened the door to a lifetime of work in his chosen field. Throughout his three years at Magdalene he had retained his post as Superintendent of the University Field Laboratory and his full salary. As there is no mention in the committee minutes of the 'leave of absence' granted by the Chairman, must be assumed that this was an internal arrangement agreed to privately by the committee unlike his officially authorised war duties. However as a Fellow Commoner for the first year and then a Research Student, he clearly had more time to undertake his laboratory duties than was possible during the war. It therefore seems unlikely that there was any pressure for a report on his activities from the Agricultural Board such as there had been in 1915.

Towards the end of 1922, when his thesis was virtually complete and his researches far less time consuming, Dr Louis Clarke, Curator of the Cambridge Museum of Archaeology and Ethnology, approached him for help in reorganising the Museum's archaeological collection. The Board of Archaeological and Anthropological Studies had appointed Clarke as Curator on 12 May 1922 to succeed Baron Von Hugel, the Museum's founder, who had resigned due to ill health. The Museum's minutes record that Clarke was invited 'to take up his appointment as soon as possible' and that his 'salary was to be £600 per annum.' Louis Clarke, so called because he was the fourteenth child, came from a wealthy Lancashire family that had made its fortune in coal. Of independent means, the salary was of little concern, he can be considered typical of the gifted amateur antiquarians, who filled the majority of the few archaeological positions of the day. Professor Christopher Hawkes remembered him well 'in pince-nez and flowing white dustcoat with all the buttons undone rushing around the Museum checking on everyone's activities. At eleven o'clock precisely he would stand in the middle of the ground floor display shouting "*tea*" at the top of his high noted voice. Everyone had to stop whatever they were doing and assemble in the staff room [now the student's common room] so that "*everyone will get to know each other otherwise they will hate each other*".' As a visitor to the Museum over 60 years later it was rather amusing to find that the tea ceremony at eleven o'clock was still observed by the staff as a lasting memorial to this generous and talented man. I was also informed that this is common museum practice to give an opportunity for staff to cross-examine visitors! To-day we call this bonding but the idea has obviously been around for a lot longer than the protagonists of this modern practice realise.

Once settled into his new appointment, Clarke realised that he needed additional professional staff if the archaeological and historical artefacts were to be properly catalogued and displayed. His approaches to the Board for the necessary funds were unsuccessful; nevertheless, Fox clearly states in his memoirs and it is a matter of public record that he became Assistant Curator at some time in the Autumn of 1922 presumably shortly after being granted his doctorate. The minutes of 2nd May 1923 record that 'Dr Fox[1] began early in December the rearrangement of early antiquities in order to facilitate the study of British Archaeology by students taking Section B of the English Tripos.' No official record exists in the Museum minutes or in the University archives of the appointment; the well accepted rumour in archaeological circles that Clarke told the Board 'that if they wouldn't pay the salary of his assistant then he would' must be assumed to be true. If Clarke did pay Fox's salary the sum in question was perhaps £100 a year[2] and it seems likely that Clarke transferred part of his own salary to ensure that this philanthropic act remained anonymous. This supposition is given additional weight by Fox's own recollection that he was 'paid' though it is clear that he never had any knowledge of the source of this funding.

As an additional task, which continues to this day, the Curator and his Assistant(s) gave lectures to University students. This duty gave them the status of Lecturers in Western European Archaeology. The University clearly acknowledged Fox's position, despite the lack of any official appointment by the Council, which stood him in good stead when seeking a more responsible appointment in 1924. At the time Professor Chadwick, as Disney Professor, was the only archaeologist on the faculty. His expertise was Anglo-Saxon, so the introduction of a man whose knowledge ranged from Neolithic times to the Dark Ages was clearly of great value to the University, especially if his services were effectively free.

Fourteen months later Fox received the first of many honours that were to come his way when the Master of Magdalene wrote to him on 16 February 1924. 'My dear Fox, It is a very great pleasure for me to write to you to say that at the College meeting you were elected a Kingsley Bye-Fellow for the ensuing year. It is only a one-year appointment. The minimum value is £25 but the College have voted that it should be £50 in your case. It is not therefore I fear, a very valuable endowment, but it practically gives you for a year the status of Fellow and the prestige of this for the future. This is partly in order that the College may mark their appreciation of your valuable and distinguished contribution to archaeological studies and partly as an expression of the high personal regard in which you are held here. I hope anyhow that I shall have the pleasure of hearing that you will accept it. Ever yours A. C. Benson.'

Fox much appreciated the offer and their concern for his financial situation; he accepted by return. Eight days later he was admitted and the traditional admission for the new Fellow was read. '*Auctoritate mihi commissa, ego, Arthurus Christophorus Benson, Praefectus hujus collegii, admitto te Cyril Fred Fox, Philosophiae Doctorem, in sodalitatem hujus collegii. pro domino Kingsley, in nomine Patris et Filii et Spiritus Sancti.*' On the same day, 26 February 1924, Professor (later Sir) Ellis H Minns wrote, 'My dear Fox, I only saw by a report that I happened to read yesterday that Magdalene had made you a Bye-Fellow. I hope that the Bye means as little as possible and the Fellow as much. It is most satisfactory to learn of the appointment not only on personal grounds (of which one needs say nothing) but also I think it is the first time that a College has recognised local archaeology in any way.' This letter is of particular importance since it clearly indicates the place that archaeology held in the University in the 1920s and the pleasure felt by the few professionals of the day that a man of talent had joined their ranks and been given public recognition for his work.

*   *   *

Throughout his time at Magdalene as undergraduate and Fellow, Fox was an extremely active field archaeologist presenting his results on a variety of subjects in a succession of papers to the Cambridge Antiquarian Society and the Prehistoric Society of East Anglia. These included four excavation reports in addition to the Fleam and Devil's Dyke papers previously described. In December 1922 he gave the results of his excavation of Anglo-Saxon inhumations at Foxton, which he found to be on the edge of an Early Iron Age village. In January 1923, with his friend Louis Cobbett, he presented their findings on the Saxon Church at Great Paxton[3] and in November of that year with Earl Cawdor described the excavation methods and results obtained from their dig at Beacon Hill Barrow at Barton Mills in Suffolk.[4] In March 1924, with Tom Lethbridge, he added to the knowledge of Cambridge dykes when he reported on their excavations of the front line of Iceni defensive ditches[5] and in December he produced an analysis of the excavation undertaken with Louis Clarke at Bulstrode Camp.[6]

Once he had obtained his doctorate he was also supplementing his income by writing articles for the *Cambridge Chronicle* and undertaking book reviews for the monthly anthropological magazine *Man*. To give himself a wider audience he provided articles and papers on a variety of topics and artefacts for the Society of Antiquaries and adjacent County Archaeological Societies. All of these activities ensured that by 1925, when he was actively seeking a permanent and more prestigious appointment, he was a well-known and highly respected professional archaeologist.

His scientific approach to archaeological research is well illustrated in his comments in November 1924 on the Pigott collection from the Early Iron Age Settlement at Abington Pigotts in Cambridgeshire.[7] This paper had to be based on artefacts alone;

the site had been completely dug over during coprolite (phosphate) extraction at the end of the 19th century. The introduction sets out his objectives with absolute clarity. 'It is remarkable that so few attempts have been made to illustrate continuity of settlement on a given site through successive culture phases in East Anglia. No more valuable study could be undertaken by any field archaeologist than the careful examination of successive deposits on such a site. Especially useful would be the analysis of the transitional phases, showing the extent to which the art and craft workers of one period influenced the technique and style of their successors and descendants. Such a study should also throw light on the material, social and economic effects on the peasantry of the district of invasion and conquest, an evil from which East Anglia seems to have suffered every 500 years or so from about 1000 BC onwards. I cannot offer you first hand such a study but it may be worth while as an approach to the ideal to illustrate a collection of objects from a settlement which seems to have been occupied during the three (or four) culture phases for a total of some 2000 years.'

Destruction of this site prevented positive identification of use later than the end of the Roman occupation, although sufficient evidence existed to presume that there were limited numbers of very poor inhabitants under mediaeval times. However throughout the Iron Age, a relatively prosperous community continuously occupied the site at Bellus Hill; their pottery wares in particular provided a graphic demonstration of improving skills during settled times and the influence of invasion and conquest. How much more he could have wrung from an untouched site can only be guessed at. Judging from the wealth of information obtained from the artefacts alone it could have been considerable.

A typical untouched site, though unfortunately proving to be short of artefacts, was Beacon Hill, which for many archaeologists is still considered to set the standard by which an excavation should be judged.[4] As already mentioned, these ancient burial mounds were routinely examined by antiquarians in the hope of finding some exciting remains. They vary in shape and size. The earliest are rectangular from the Neolithic era of Britain's first farmers around 3500 BC. There are a few very large barrows from the Roman period, 55 BC to 440 AD, but most are circular and belong to the Bronze Age 'Beaker Period', 2300 to 1500 BC. This classic prehistoric barrow is a round mound, perhaps 30 feet (9 m) across with an encircling ditch. It may stand perhaps 10 feet (3 m) high; though farming, natural erosion and rabbits can reduce this to a barely visible rise in the landscape. What all Bronze Age barrows hold in common is some kind of circular plan and a primary purpose of holding a burial. Usually these burials had grave goods; objects that we presume were indicative of the rank of the deceased, primarily male, and equipment that he might usefully take with him into the next world (Fig. 23). In the 'Beaker' burials there is a skeleton and usually the beaker itself, a handsome pot invariably decorated with geometric patterns, (Fig. 24) though rarely found intact. The beaker was probably filled with water and used in the course of burial ritual. The remains were then entombed in stone or wood to form a cairn and covered

Figure 24: Handled Beakers from Grantham and Whitby (Cambrian Archaeological Association)

Figure 23: Interment grave goods from Beacon Hill Barrow (Cambridge Antiquarian Society)

with the mound of soil. Later Bronze and Iron Age burials, many found as secondary interments in shallow pits dug into the side of an earlier Bronze Age barrow, were often cremations instead of inhumations. Here the Excavator would often find a special urn, decorated like a beaker but less well made, usually upside-down and fragmented, containing white cremated bones. If he was lucky there would again be grave goods such as bronze daggers and even objects of gold.

It was this that attracted the Victorian and Edwardian antiquarians. A narrow shaft at the very centre would hopefully bring the excavator's labourers to the central primary burial with its beaker, grave goods or cremation urn. William Cunnington's men, who in this style worked through many of the Wiltshire barrows in the early 19th century, would expect to dispose of a barrow in less than a day. By Fox's day, then, the obvious spoils of the barrows were known about and in many cases already quarried out. Some finds were retained by the excavator or found their way into museum collections, others were lost; few were recorded and none were analysed or systematically examined. The work on Beacon Hill was carried out in 1923 with Lord Cawdor. They revived the technique of total excavation (Fig. 25) advocated so forcefully by General Pitt-Rivers, whose great studies in his Dorset estate of Cranborne Chase set, in the late 19th century, the standard for large-scale archaeological fieldwork. What was new was the degree of expert supervision and precise recording that even that old war-horse would have admired. In his treatise, *Archaeology of the Cambridge Region,* Fox had stressed the vital need for provenance and accurate positional records of artefacts in relation to each other if full value was to be obtained from their discovery. At Beacon Hill he put this theory into practice, determined that nothing would now escape the archaeologist's inspection. 'It has been abundantly shown in past excavations,' he wrote, 'that if the contents of a barrow are to be fully revealed, it is necessary that it should be turned over from end to end, and the floor

Figure 25: Beacon Hill Barrow excavation with Earl Cawdor 1923 (Cambridge Antiquarian Society)

examined for the presence of a grave or graves. We were more conscious of our responsibility for making a complete and accurate record of the character and contents of Beacon Hill, and for preserving it as a landmark, because so many barrows in this district have been wantonly destroyed (little or no record of their contents being preserved) and so few apparently untouched examples are now available for investigation. The work was continuously supervised by one or other of us, and… that risk of overlooking a small deposit might be reduced as far as possible practically the whole of the work with the pick on the face (of the advancing section) was done by ourselves, the labourers being employed in shovelling away the loosened earth. No work of any importance was done in our absence. Two parallel rows of numbered pegs were driven in one foot apart on either side of the barrow at right angles to the face … and on the discovery of a deposit its position was fixed (Fig. 26). Finally when the barrow had been turned over from end to end in this manner, it was rebuilt and the turves which covered it replaced as far as possible.' The final sentence adds an amusing postscript for the ordnance survey purists. 'It should be noted however that it is now sited some 5 yards to the NW of its original position!'

The barrow had no primary central grave; its original purpose remained uncertain. Construction took place during the Early Bronze Age, then dated circa. 1700–1400 BC, using local sand. By careful examination of the soil, they were able to prove it had had time to compact and suffer wind erosion before the barrow was enlarged by being covered with boulder clay. Secondary interments included inhumation and post cremation burial of three different types dating from the Early to Middle Bronze Age but not into the Early Iron Age. The tribe using this barrow was in all probability exceedingly poor, at least in material possessions: only one personal object was found, a necklace, and that was made of bone. This detailed lesson in barrow excavation did have its problems, as the Reverend G. Engleheart pointed out in his letter of 10 January 1929. 'I am glad that there are some who will turn the whole thing over. But it would cost an awful sum to treat some of our big Wiltshire barrows so.'

Recalling this excavation, during the course of an address to the Cambridge Antiquarian Society in 1952, Fox said: 'Beacon Hill Barrow, where Lord Cawdor and I put into practice Van Giffen's idea of complete excavation, commanded a marvellous view of the Fen borders and their villages and to our astonishment the whole countryside came to see us at work on August Bank Holiday. Cawdor had to appoint voluntary wardens to keep the crowds back. Mansfield Forbes of Clare, a dear friend of all of us, was one of our diggers – this day he was on barrow work. One of the wardens, chosen by chance, was a stocky middle aged chap in a black Sunday suit and bowler hat. He was staring at Manny's efforts with the barrow, on and off the plank, with growing impatience till he could stand it no longer. Taking off his coat, waistcoat and bowler 'Here' he said to Manny, 'look after these, I can't look at you any longer' and he barrowed for us for the rest of the day.'

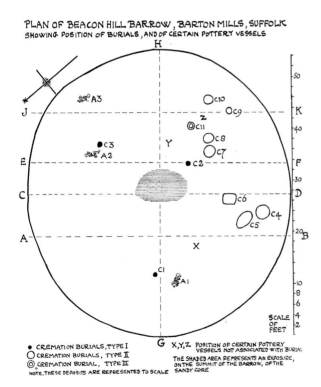

Figure 26: Plan of Beacon Hill Barrow excavation (Cambridge Antiquarian Society)

Today this excavation is acknowledged as being the practical foundation of modern techniques. Paul Ashbee in his book, *The Bronze Age Round Barrow in Britain*, wrote; 'The modern period of barrow study began in the third decade of this century when both field study and excavation began to be seriously and systematically used as avenues of research. The pioneer work in the new field study was an article on barrows by the founder of *Antiquity*, O. G. S. Crawford, which appeared in the first volume of that journal... In the realm of excavation, the fact that a barrow is a complex structure, explainable in terms of human activity, was emphasised and demonstrated by Sir Cyril Fox when he dug barrows at Barton Mills [Beacon Hill] in Cambridgeshire and Ysceifiog in

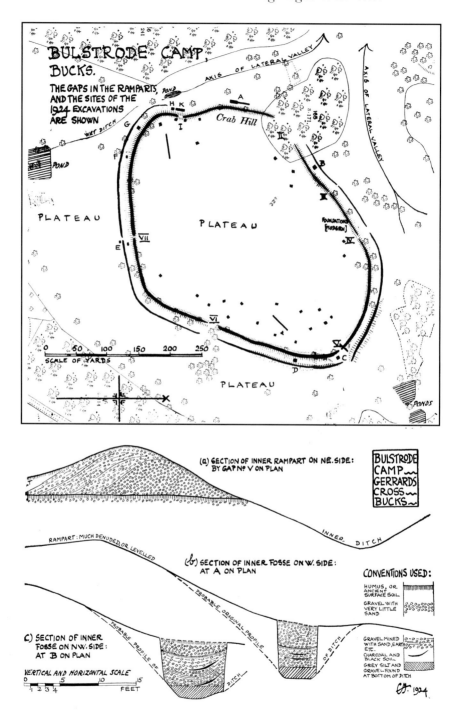

Figure 27: Excavations in Bulstrode Camp (Buckinghamshire Archaeological Society)

Flintshire – indeed he almost resuscitated the living ritual and procedures of burial.' Beginning with these excavations he continued 'total excavation of round barrows has become the accepted standard.' Van Giffen, to whom Fox referred, was a Dutch archaeologist, who had developed the same idea of complete excavation to recover the complex sequences within barrows in the Netherlands.

The last of the 1924 excavations was undertaken in June, in association with his Curator Louis Clarke, at Bulstrode Camp in Buckinghamshire.[6] This was on the estate of Sir John Ramsden, who authorised and paid for the work. It was not a particularly noteworthy or interesting site. The weather, being unseasonably wet, prevented them from excavating all that they wished – provoking the phrase 'there was too much water in the ditch to encourage us to apply the test of the spade.' However the drawings at the back of the paper do provide two of the clearest and most attractive examples of Fox's early work as a draughtsman (Fig. 27). As with his use of the English language so with the pen he always set out to present his findings in a manner that ensured understanding and was at the same time pleasing to the eye. His instantly recognisable printing was invariably done by hand in a bold yet fluent style, which was to be the hallmark of his work throughout his life. Whilst many might argue there have been greater archaeological authors than Fox, it is certainly the case that few have had the ability to present their written findings with illustrations and diagrams of such clarity and artistic understanding.

* * *

Although the total salary that Fox received from his three appointments was probably sufficient for his needs there was no prospect of promotion and the future of the Field Laboratories was uncertain. Furthermore he was anxious to obtain a more responsible post where he could devote all his time and effort to archaeological activities. In June 1924 the position of Keeper of Antiquities at the National Museum in Dublin was advertised and Fox applied for it immediately. In a letter dated 1 July 1924 H. J. Lawlor, Secretary to the Council of the Royal Irish Academy, wrote to inform him that the Council 'have selected two persons, of whom you are one, from the candidates for the Keepership of Antiquities. I am directed to ask you to be good enough to attend at the Academy House on Tuesday July 15th at 11 o'clock for a personal interview with representatives of the Council. One of the selected candidates will be nominated on the same day on behalf of the Council to the Minister of Education: and the Council will do their best to secure that the formal appointment will be made with as little delay as possible.' This routine letter sets the scene for an extraordinary sequence of events lasting nearly four months. It involved Mortimer Wheeler, the newly appointed Director of the National Museum of Wales, Professor Benson, the Master of Magdalene, and Lawlor at the Irish Academy; it ended in January 1925 with Fox in Cardiff instead of Dublin.

Wheeler used to tell a polished story of how in the summer of 1924 he met Fox for the first time at the Society of Antiquaries. After being introduced and learning of Fox's interest in the Keepership in Dublin, Wheeler magnanimously offered him the Keepership of Archaeology at the National Museum of Wales. The surviving correspondence tells a different tale. Fox certainly went to Dublin for his interview on 15 July. He was verbally informed that he had been selected and two days later received a confirmatory letter from Lawlor that had been signed the same day. 'I have the pleasure of informing you that you have been nominated to the Government for the post of Keeper of Antiquities in the National Museum. 'When we receive a reply to our recommendation we shall at once communicate it to you.'

Fox had returned immediately to Cambridge, but before leaving Ireland on the Boat either rang and a left a message, or more likely sent a telegram to his friend and mentor Professor Benson at Magdalene. This was to inform him of the result and to say that he would in due course be resigning from the Kingsley-Bye Fellowship. Benson replied that night addressing his letter to Red Gables in Cambridge. 'I read your message with mixed feelings. I am personally *very* sorry that you should leave Cambridge – you are and have been a delightful colleague and we *all* feel that. And I am vexed with Cambridge for being stupid enough to let a first rate man go when he is at the top of his game. On the other hand I am glad that you should have an unquestioned position and an opportunity of congenial work and, I suppose, an adequate stipend. Well you shall do your work triumphantly in Ireland and return to Cambridge later on.'

On arriving home Fox made provisional arrangements for his move to Ireland. He obtained a quotation from a Removal Company, which he wrote on the back of the envelope containing Professor Benson's letter. 'Door to door (2 vans) about £40 per van including Customs offices and packing and accepting all risks.' He also wrote to Mortimer Wheeler, concerning a mutual colleague's failure to obtain a particular appointment; in this he mentioned his own success in Dublin. This evoked the following reply dated 19 July 1924. 'My dear Fox', which even allowing for Wheeler's ebullient character was hardly the form of address to be used in the 1920s to a man he had never met, 'Your omen was propitious and poor Wace is once more turned down… About yourself. My very heartiest congratulations, but I must confess to v. considerable disappointment also. I had hoped against hope that you might have been willing to undertake a joint post here as Keeper of Archaeology in the Museum and Lecturer in Archaeology at the University College. The minimum salary is £400 plus £200 (I happened to be getting £500 plus £200 and it is just possible that we might arrange this after a short time). Expenses for field work are of course paid and the duplicate post is really a v. free one. Ample scope for good work, plenty of excavation and so on… This letter is quite unofficial and does not commit the Museum or the College but,' Wheeler typically adds, 'between ourselves, it comes to much the same thing. If you care to consider this alternative proposition write to me at once at Herne Hill, London.'

Perhaps the seeds of doubt were beginning to be sown. Fox had clearly expected to receive confirmation of his Irish appointment by this time (21 July) and presumably wrote a holding reply. Indeed he may have decided to go to London after all to discuss the Welsh Keepership with Wheeler – that would of course form the basis for the apocryphal story of the meeting at Burlington House. Certainly he discussed the whole affair with Benson, whose diary records 'Fox to see me – difficulties arise about permanence of his Irish appointment but he has the offer of a Welsh Professorship [sic – perhaps Benson considered the combined post to be equivalent] which he would like better.'

On 2 August Lawlor wrote to say that despite urging the Government to ratify the appointment, the Academy had now received a letter from the Civil Service Commissioners 'which will at least cause delay if not uncertainty of appointment.' This uncertainty, he explained was being caused by new regulations which no longer gave the Academy the absolute right of nomination. This was again discussed with Benson, 'Fox to see me – the Irish Academy throws him over.' It was presumably on Benson's advice that Fox then wrote in mid August to Wheeler, who was excavating the Roman Fort at Brecon, to accept his offer. 'My dear Fox' he replied 'needless to say I am delighted. But you must not expect *immediate* developments here – everyone is away and it will not be possible to do much before the middle of September.' Three weeks later Wheeler wrote again to advise that progress was being made but with Museum and University College having separate organisations it would take time. 'Your case will be considered (and I doubt not approved) by a joint committee of the two institutions.' At the same time Fox received a letter from Dr E. J. Gwynne of the Irish Academy explaining the situation there to which he replied with a certain degree of anger. 'I quite understand that the Academy is not responsible for the failure to appoint its nominee and I appreciate your expressions of regret at the inconvenience caused to me. If I understand your letter aright the right of presentation to the Keepership, which the Academy possesses, is void. My selection for the post by the Academy goes for nothing, and the matter will be dealt with afresh by a selection board appointed by the Irish Civil Service Commissioners on which the Academy is in a minority. The situation, which has its humorous side, is sufficiently clear and I cannot suppose that you are serious in suggesting that I should renew my application for the Keepership when the Board is so constituted. I have no intention of doing so and here the matter rests as far as I am concerned. I have gained a little knowledge of human nature, a set of maps of Dublin and District, which I purchased in a short-lived mood of optimism, and the recollection of a very pleasant visit to a fair city.'

In a later letter Lawlor was to add the final touch to this Irish situation comedy. 'It appears that in 1924 an Act was passed making all appointments subject to Civil Service Commissioners. But of this Act the Academy had no knowledge … it was not even reported in the newspapers. I think it unusual to make an Act of Parliament apply to action taken and almost completed, before it came into existence.' Fox always believed he was turned down because he was an Englishman; certainly they appointed a German, Walter Bremer, in his place. At any rate by then it seemed that the better Welsh appointment was virtually secured as the Museum Council had recommended Fox to the Joint Committee on 19 September.

There was to be one final twist to the tale that perhaps accounts for Wheeler's brief mention of this appointment in his own autobiography *Still Digging*: 'On my promotion to the Directorship (Sir) Cyril Fox had been persuaded to come from Cambridge.' Benson had been exceedingly upset that Fox should have even thought of leaving Cambridge in the first place. His diary entry on 15 July reads 'vexed that between them the Agricultural and Archaeological Boards have not found him a post here. He has just published the best archaeological volume of the last six years and "therefore I die in exile" as Jerome said.' Presumably Benson sounded others for their support but nothing happened until October when Fox received a letter on which he sought Benson's advice. 'Fox to consult me – Now when he has accepted a Welsh Curatorship the General Board [the body within the University of Cambridge which controls appointments to the University's academic staff] offers him £300 a year here. But I tell him he can't throw Cardiff over and the Cambridge offer is a precarious one.' A few days later 'Fox came for further counsel. The Cardiff people set him free – but it would be highly impolitic to change now.'

After this temporary setback Fox attended an interview at the University College on 26 October and was accepted. The Joint Committee made the formal appointment on 14 November with effect 1 January 1925. To add gilt to the gingerbread there was an article in the *Western Mail* headed 'National Museum of Wales – Appointment of Dr Fox of Cambridge.' This gave details of his career and achievements and reported: 'the Board of Celtic Studies have voted a special grant to enable Dr Fox to bring his special experience to bear upon the great dykes of the Welsh borders, which have never been thoroughly mapped or explored and are at present only dated by tradition.' This work and the extension of the hypothesis behind *Archaeology of the Cambridge Region* into the national scene in the celebrated book *The Personality of Britain* were to be the major achievements of the next decade but all this was in the future. Now it was a question of packing up and moving to Cardiff.

Earlier in the year he had bought plot No. 10 in Millington Road, on the western side of Cambridge, from King's College for £300. He had not started to build his house there so it was fairly easy to dispose of. More difficult perhaps was his letter of resignation as Superintendent written to Professor Nuttall on 27 October 1924. 'It is with very mixed feelings that I write … asking you to accept my resignation to take effect upon December 31 1924. I say mixed feelings; I feel very deep regret at severing a connexion [sic], which has lasted twelve years with a body, which under your chairmanship has always treated me with kindness and consideration. But now that owing to lack of funds it has been decided to reorganise the administration and do away with my office I feel that the sooner change takes place the better for everyone concerned in the matter... I suggest that I should hand over my books, papers and money to a person or persons nominated by the Committee at the end of term.'

A second letter, written on the same day, addressed the question of expenses incurred at his residence Red Gables. 'Last Autumn I had a good deal of papering and distempering etc ... at a cost of £17 6s 11d. This was done in reasonable expectation of indefinite occupation and in view of the changed circumstances which have made it necessary for me to seek employment elsewhere I venture to suggest that this expenditure might be charged to the Field Laboratories a/c. During my tenancy I erected a garden house (£20) and a garage (£25). Other fixtures, which I shall leave behind, are sunblinds (£5 10s). I make no *claim* for any allowance in respect to these items but they add to the amenities of the dwelling and if the Committee see fit to make me an allowance of, let us say one third cost price (£17), I shall be obliged.' On this slightly mercenary note Fox departed from Cambridge in his Morris Tourer for the two-day cross-country journey to Wales with Felicity on a dicky seat behind the gearbox and Penelope in a shawl in her mother's arms.

A quarter of a century later, reminiscing on his Cambridge days, he said, 'Cambridge was my kindly nurse, my spiritual home, and I have more archaeological memories of her folk than I have time to recall.' He had been happy there, he had married, he had had two children (Fig. 28), he had achieved all that he could have expected of himself but new challenges beckoned and a new country was there waiting to be explored. Most satisfying of all it was made abundantly clear that it was him and no one else that these Welsh institutions wanted to undertake this work. The Secretary of the Cambrian Archaeological Association, with which Society Fox was to have such a long and fruitful relationship, summed up these feelings when he wrote in November. 'At a meeting of the Committee of my Association, held at Shrewsbury, I was directed to convey to you an expression of the gratification felt on your appointment as Keeper of the Department of Archaeology at the National Museum and to offer you a hearty welcome to Wales. The Principality is fortunate in securing the services of so eminent an archaeologist.'

Figure 28: Fox with his daughters Felicity and Penelope in the garden at Red Gables 1924

Notes

[1] Until he was knighted in 1935 he was always known as Dr Fox and in parts of Wales that practice continued for at least another ten years to my personal knowledge.

[2] This salary is based on the knowledge that Fox's total remuneration *increased* following his appointment to the National Museum of Wales where he was initially paid £600 of which £200 came from the University. Since his salary as Superintendent of the Field Laboratory was £400, including £50 rent allowance, and the Kingsley Bye-Fellowship awarded in 1924 paid him £50 a year, it is reasonable to suppose that he would not have accepted less than £100 for this part time appointment

[3] Saxon Church, Great Paxton, Huntingdonshire (with Dr Louis Cobbett) *Camb.Ant.* XXV

[4] Beacon Hill Barrow, Barton Mills, Suffolk (with Lord Cawdor) *Camb.Ant.* XXVI

[5] Excavations in the Cambridgeshire Dykes IV & V (with W. M. Palmer) *Camb.Ant.* XXVI

[6] Excavations in Bulstrode Camp (with Dr L. C. G Clarke) *Records of Bucks* IX

[7] Objects from the Settlement at Abington Pigotts, Cambridgeshire *Proc.Pre.E.Anglia* IV Part II

V

Foundations for a Welsh Progress 1925
Introduction to Wales and Offa's Dyke

The most striking contrast in the geography of the mainland of the British Isles is between the geologically old mountain areas of the north and west and the younger and lower escarpments and vales that make up the rest of the country. For a man brought up in the Isle of Wight and Hampshire, who had spent most of his working life in East Anglia, the contrast provided by a move from Cambridge to Cardiff was a dramatic one. Fox's youngest sister Babs could not recall her brother ever going north of York or west of his birthplace Chippenham; she was certain that his interview at the National Museum of Wales and the University College in October 1924 was the first time he had set foot in the Principality. Now he was about to embark on a lifetime in this country; its geography was to become as familiar to him and as much loved as the Cambridgeshire he had just left.

The Celtic inhabitants of Wales, like Scotland, had strongly resisted all attempts to colonise their nation; the rugged terrain had made their defensive task all the easier. The Roman occupation scarcely affected Wales except for the border strongholds of Chester and Caerleon that controlled coastal access to the north and south. Isolated garrison forts, such as Segontium near Caernarfon and Y Gaer, Brecon, which Wheeler was excavating, had been established much further west. In the early mediaeval period the territorial ambitions of the Welsh Princes provided constant problems for English border Kings which gave rise to the construction of one of Europe's largest man-made barriers – Offa's Dyke. Like the Cambridgeshire dykes that Fox had explored so well, Offa's Dyke is a great boundary earthwork, the history and precise purpose of which was virtually unknown at that time. Very much larger than any of the Cambridgeshire dykes it runs north-south through what later became the border counties of England and Wales and Wheeler was determined that Fox's experience and knowledge of the Cambridgeshire dykes should be brought to bear upon this monument. 'Plenty of excavation with all expenses for fieldwork' he had written in his initial offer and he was to make good this promise in full measure. Never one to let grass grow under his feet, Wheeler initiated applications through the Museum Council and University College for the necessary grants as soon as he received Fox's formal acceptance of the post. The University's Board of Celtic Studies response was the special grant that had been reported by the *Western Mail* when greeting Fox's arrival in Cardiff at the start of 1925.

The National Museum of Wales, which had been granted its Royal Charter in 1907,[1] was the youngest of the national museums in Britain and still at an early stage of development. There had been intense rivalry between Cardiff, Swansea and Caernarfon over the site for this new prestigious institution, finally resolved when a special committee of the Privy Council selected Cardiff as the largest centre of population. From its inception the Museum had been intended to be different from other national museums in that it was regarded as essential and fundamental to be national in fact as well as name. Not a general museum of interest only to the immediate locality it was to be 'entirely devoted to a really national object, the scientific representation, namely of the geology, mineralogy, zoology, botany, ethnography, archaeology, art, history and the special industries of Wales.' (Appendix III provides a more detailed summary of the history and pre-1925 achievements of the Museum and its staff)

Dr William Evans Hoyle, the Director of the Manchester Museum, had been appointed its first Director in November 1908. He was an eminent zoologist and a recognised specialist in museum organisation and procedure as well as in the planning of museum buildings. Evan Hoyle's influence over the design for the National Museum of Wales, won in an open competition by the London based partnership of Dunbar Smith and Brewer, is quite clear. Externally the building was required to be in harmony with the City Hall and Law Courts and be capable of being built in stages: Internally Evans Hoyle dictated a departmental layout that maximised space for display and study, and provided ample facilities for storage and administration. Funding was never likely to be available for the whole of the four-acre site; the design needed to allow for various funding options. In the event Treasury approval was given for the estimated sum of £230,000 to build and equip the first portion – amounting to approximately one third of the complete building. Treasury practice seems to change little with the passing years, they agreed to contribute half this amount providing the other half was raised independently. The Foundation Stone was laid in 1912 by His Majesty King George V and the builders began work on the southern block, that included the main entrance, and part of the west wing. The war interrupted construction and fund raising to the extent that it was 1922 before any part of the building could be opened to the public. It took another three years and an extraordinarily generous gift by Sir William Reardon Smith Bart. before the cost of the initial stage of construction was cleared. Even at that time it was an impressive building (Figs 29 and 30) with a grand flight of steps leading into a spectacular galleried entrance hall dominated by the central dome (see illustration to Appendix III) with an innovative pattern of departmental galleries, offices and basements for storage areas and workshops. Being incomplete, departments competed for space and the central hall was somewhat crowded and confusing (Fig. 31).

Figure 29: National Museum of Wales from the south-east 1921 (work was being completed on the main entrance steps) (National Museum of Wales)

Figure 30: National Museum of Wales from the south-west 1925 (National Museum of Wales)

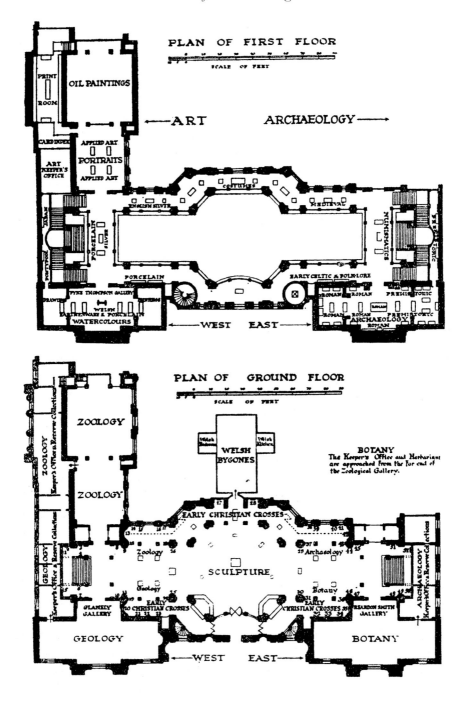

Figure 31: National Museum Galleries 1925 with Welsh Bygones Gallery added in 1926 (National Museum of Wales)

Appointments to the Museum staff had been equally slow. Although the staff of the Municipal Museum had been taken over in 1912 it was 1914 before the first departmental posts were established – Keepers of Art and Archaeology and Assistant Keepers of Botany and Geology. In 1919 these four departments were given equal status and a fifth, Zoology, was created. This then was the situation when Fox arrived at the beginning of 1925. His senior curatorial colleagues (Keepers) were Isaac J. Williams, previously Curator of the Castle Museum in Merthyr Tydfil as Keeper of Art, London University geology graduate Dr Frederick J. North, Aberdeen Natural History graduate Dr James J. Simpson and Downing College Cambridge botany graduate Harold A. Hyde. Captain Archibald H. (Archie) Lee, initially appointed in 1909 as Secretary to the Director, had by this time become the Museum Secretary and was the Museum's senior administrative officer. All were generally acknowledged to be 'good museum men.' Wheeler had held the Keepership of Archaeology since 1920 and with it the lectureship in Archaeology at the University College of South Wales and Monmouthshire. In 1924, following the resignation through ill health of Evans Hoyle, he had been made Director.

Wheeler's arrival in Cardiff had been fortuitous to say the least. Having had an exciting war he had returned to the Royal Commission on Historical Monuments and was employed as a recorder of pre-1714 buildings and their artefacts. He found this work extremely tedious and had applied for the Keepership in a fit of pique 'rather as a means of letting off steam than with any expectation or indeed hope of success. I had never heard of the National Museum of Wales, did not know where Cardiff was on the map, and had a growing dislike of museums. Why I was appointed to the Cardiff posts is still hidden from me ... I had no sort of qualification. I came away from the interview with a heart of lead not because I had failed but because I had succeeded. Apart from a handsome civic centre, the streets of Cardiff seemed unbearably mean and dingy, the people in them unbelievably foreign and barbaric... Having said that I must hasten to add that my following six years (1920–1926) in Cardiff were both busy and happy ones and the kindliness with which Wales received a stranger in its midst is unforgettable.'[2] If Wheeler's arrival in Wales had been a surprise there could, in the words of Jacquetta Hawkes, 'have been little doubt in anyone's mind, including his own, that he would be given the Directorship.' Furthermore 'he had also seen to it that he would have a first rate lieutenant for he had persuaded Cyril Fox to leave Cambridge to take his vacated place as Keeper of Archaeology.'

The situation that Wheeler had inherited in 1924 was, in his opinion, highly unsatisfactory. 'In 1920 the building was a façade backed by concrete and scaffolding. Most of the collections were still housed or stored in a murky suite in the City Library. Work on the new structure had ceased and the building fund was £22,000 in debt. Everything had come to a standstill. After a profitable war Cardiff was suffering a financial setback which augured ill ... in 1924, stagnation had set in with an air of permanency.' When submitting his application for the Directorship Wheeler had indicated his determination, should the Council appoint him, to restore momentum to the construction work and to clear the outstanding debt. He was not afraid to voice his opinions or to sing his own praises. Jacquetta Hawkes continues 'In his handsomely printed application … Wheeler set out his proposed policies with an authority and confidence that would have been considered presumptuous in an ordinary young Keeper seeking promotion. Nor was he afraid to offer thinly veiled criticisms of the existing regime,' stating that, 'it is essential that even in the remotest parts of the Principality the existence of the National Museum should be known and its influence felt. The present position in this respect leaves much to be desired!' That these words were a synthesis of the views of the founding fathers in 1903 is not in itself surprising. The fact that it was necessary to spell them out a mere 12 years after the foundation stone had been laid is indicative of the torpor created by the war; more importantly it drew attention to the desperate shortage of funds to complete even the first stage of the project.

Wheeler must also have impressed the Council with his achievements during the four years he had held the Keepership. 'He had more than a score of substantial learned articles to his credit, including a few on pre-historic subjects, he was on the councils and committees of half a dozen national societies, including the Board of Celtic Studies, and had been elected a Fellow of the Society of Antiquaries. These things all in addition to his excavations and administrative and missionary work for the National Museum, and his considerable success as a University and public lecturer.'[3] He was also about to publish *Prehistoric and Roman Wales,* which set out to provide a series of studies of prehistory and archaeology in Wales for the general reader. Even allowing for Wheeler's egotistical view of his role at Cardiff, it is clear he was even then a man of considerable stature. The mantle that Fox was about to inherit was not going to be an easy one to assume especially as the former Keeper turned Director was mounting guard from his office in the dome.

The archaeological collection at Cardiff, for which Fox was now responsible, had its origins, like the rest of the museum's artefacts and specimens, in the former Municipal Museum[4] established in 1868. When Cardiff submitted its application to the Privy Council the whole of this collection had been offered as a core contribution for a National Museum. Although the archaeological collection had not been particularly noteworthy before 1890, pride of place being given to geology, botany and art, there had been a remarkable expansion in this department during the late 1890s and the early part of the twentieth century. This was primarily due to the activities of its formidable and cantankerous curator John Ward. As Douglas Bassett reported in his history of the National Museum 'the prehistoric collection was largely Welsh – its most notable feature a series of Iron Age bronzes, mostly related to horse trappings and many enamelled, found at Seven Sisters near Neath in 1875. In 1911 it was enriched by the purchase of the large and important collection of stone implements made by the late Mr H. Stopes – the father of the redoubtable Marie Stopes. One of the last acts of the Municipal Museum Committee (before transfer to the National Museum in 1912) had been to form a collection to illustrate old-fashioned Welsh life – the obsolete and obsolescent objects, conveniently called "Bygones". Inevitably the inception of the National Museum gave a great stimulus to the acquisition of first class specimens from all parts of Wales. Among them were the remarkable shale bowl inlaid with gold of about 1000 BC from Caergwrle (donated in 1912), the mediaeval silver chalice and paten from near Dolgellau deposited by HM King George V and the Kenfig Mace.'

After the foundation stone had been laid in 1912, a series of temporary exhibitions, was organised in a building erected for this purpose in the City Hall quadrangle. The selection of Welsh antiquities, exhibited from June to October 1913, included items from the Cardiff collection and a number of objects illustrating old manners and customs. 'The organisers had some difficulty in deciding whether to call these objects "antiquities" – that might imply a greater age than they possess – or "bygones" – which although convenient is hardly a recognisable English word as yet – or "old fashioned things".'[5] Whatever the title it is evident that this folk material formed part of the Archaeological Department almost from its inception. It was to become ever more important until, like a cuckoo in the nest, it was to virtually demand and obtain independence, as a department in 1936 and as a satellite museum at St Fagans in 1947.

* * *

Having spent Christmas 1924 at Steyning the family moved from Cambridge to Cardiff for the start of the New Year. They rented a large comfortable semi-detached Edwardian house, Ash Cottage, in Heath Park Avenue, and settled down to the routine life of a professional family in the mid 1920s. Fox was quickly immersed in the problems of his department, working his way through the storerooms beneath the City Library where most of the accumulated artefacts from the Municipal Museum had been deposited in 1919–1921. Evenings at home were dominated by the need to read up on Welsh history and archaeology and to prepare for his university lectures and tutorials. His sister Babs believed that this determination to grapple with his new responsibilities meant that unfortunately he had little time for Olive and their two children. Their upbringing was a matter he left almost entirely to his wife and to 'Nanny'.

There was also a backlog of Cambridge matters to complete: Some reviews and comments on artefacts, on which his opinion had been sought, and two excavation reports.[6] The first, Bran or Heydon Ditch had been excavated with W. M. Palmer in the summer of 1923 and read to the Cambridge Antiquarian Society in March 1924. Uncharacteristically, there had been insufficient time to prepare the paper for publication. This was probably due to the lack of evidence obtained and hence, once it had been read, there was no urgency to publish the results.

The second, a joint excavation of the La Tène and Romano-British cemetery at Guilden Morden in Cambridgeshire with Tom Lethbridge undertaken in September 1924, was rather more important. It had long been known that the knoll near Ashwell Street overlooking the Cam valley contained an early cemetry since 'it includes the parish chalk pit wherein from time to time Roman pottery, burials by cremation and skeletons have been found by quarrymen.' A plethora of interments and cremation burials, with no sense of order and often one on top of the other, indicated that this ground was in use from 1 AD until the end of the Roman period, though not for Christian burial. The three weeks available for this excavation did not allow for examination of more than a portion of the site; dating was clearly established and

Figure 32: On site at Guilden Morden 1924

further light thrown on the change from inhumation to cremation during the period of Roman occupation. As the authors wrote in their summary 'early La Tène burials in the Cambridge region are by inhumation but during the first century BC the intrusive cremation culture reached the Cam valley ... in this period fall the earliest burials at Guilden Morden. Cremation was the normal rite in Britain during the first two hundred years of Roman occupation but a considerable body of evidence from Cambridge and its neighbourhood has shown that inhumation was not infrequent during the earlier part of the period' (Fig. 32). This site was of especial interest to the historian for it provided examples of both cultures throughout the early part of the Roman occupation. It also confirmed Fox's previous suspicions, expressed in *Archaeology of the Cambridge Region*, that inhumation as practised by the La Tène Celts survived in places throughout the first and second centuries AD until becoming general practice again with the arrival of Christian traditions.

Olive settled in happily in Ash Cottage. She accepted her husband's preoccupation with his work in the Museum as inevitable and encouraged him in his endeavours. She quickly established herself at St Dyfrig, her local church and through the parish priest with the Christian Mission in dockland. She joined the Cardiff Art and Choral Societies integrating easily with all whom she met – rich and poor, professional and trade. This was the way she had been brought up and neither the move nor her newly acquired young family gave her cause to change. She was a very spiritual person and took great personal pleasure in her 'good works' in the docks. At the same time she was well aware that she was both beautiful and exceedingly well dressed. As is often the case at this period of time it seemed to make no difference to the poor and homeless; on the contrary, it appeared that they themselves took pride in the appearance of their benefactress. Though Olive's financial independence ensured that she need not be concerned with the drudgery of housework or of looking after her young family, she was a warm hearted and caring mother who had a very close and loving relationship with her children. Felicity, however, proved to be rather a handful: 'ungovernable' was the word Cyril used to describe his precocious five-year-old. In September 1925 she was sent to a boarding school at Mumbles on the Gower peninsula. She subsequently continued her education at Cardiff High School.

In the course of his examination of the mass of accumulated archaeological material in the City Library storerooms, Fox's attention was drawn to two recently acquired Bronze Age funerary beakers. He had a considerable knowledge of the subject as pertaining to eastern and southern England and decided to investigate the Welsh connection. The results were published in *Archaeologia Cambrensis*, the proceedings of the Cambrian Archaeological Association that would report so much of Fox's important work over the next twenty-five years.[7] Beaker design and patterns provides information on cultural influences and tribal movement. Fox used this opportunity to cover not just the Carmarthenshire and Brecknockshire beakers (Fig. 33) but many of the Museum's earlier acquisitions from all over Wales. The whole was then related, with the aid of the now familiar distribution map, to finds in the rest of the United Kingdom to provide a progression of 'beaker-folk culture' and movement of people in the period 2000–1500 BC. As with his Cambridge thesis, Fox was able to relate soil to settlement. He indicated likely migration routes from the well-established centres of beaker folk in eastern and central England to the western seaboard and into Wales. The presence of the Midlands 'barren triangle', supposedly heavily forested and then devoid of any traces of beaker burials and the absence of any trace of beaker folk in the Cotswold areas, seemed to preclude these as routes to the south Glamorgan plain

Figure 33: Cwm Du Beaker (Cambrian Archaeological Association)

and thence to Carmarthenshire. More likely was a sea crossing from Exmoor. This accorded with the beaker types and in particular with the bar-chevron decoration, which had been found on both sides of the Bristol Channel.

The Brecon handled beaker offered far more of a problem. A beaker of this type was extremely rare. Apart from two finds in Cornwall and Dorset, it appeared to be made only by tribes in northern or eastern England. Fox did not attempt to find or to offer a final solution. Citing known sixth century AD Anglo-Saxon movements towards the Welsh border, he suggested the Warwickshire Avon as a possible route through the barren lands. Due acknowledgement was given to Abercromby and Crawford but, with a gentle dig at his Director, Fox wrote:. 'The discovery of the beaker (Cwm Du) … is noted by R. E. M. Wheeler in the Bulletin of Celtic Studies but its importance for the history of beaker-folk in Britain warrants more extended treatment.' Either Wheeler failed to read this sentence or he totally agreed with it for he was effusive in his comments. 'This really is an epoch-making paper in the full sense of the term. It will form the basis of all future research in Brit. beakers. I am filled with enthusiastic admiration. It will do both the Museum and *Arch.Camb.* a lot of good incidentally.'

These researches enabled Fox to write up other burial furniture, four sepulchral vessels of the Bronze Age from North Wales, a late 'Celtic' bronze mirror and platter from Merioneth and the superb Abercromby A 'Shefford' beaker.[8] This was just the start of a wealth of archaeological papers, mostly for the Cambrians but also for the Antiquaries, *Antiquity* and other appropriate Society journals. These papers and many others that followed were in due course to form the background to two major undertakings, published long after retirement, *Pattern and Purpose,* a study of Celtic Art and *Life and Death in the Bronze Age,* but the present gave no indication of those tasks. Rather it was as though his mind, frustrated by his long years of apprenticeship, had to give vent to an insatiable need to study and to write. Both of these needs were of course admirably satisfied by Wheeler's 'suggestion' of an initial task – Offa's Dyke.

* * *

The results of the survey of Offa's Dyke and the associated Wat's Dyke were initially published between 1926 and 1934 in *Archaeologia Cambrensis.* Nearly thirty years later the British Academy decided to publish the complete and where necessary updated text in one volume. There in his Author's Preface, Fox provides his own introduction to the task that Wheeler had set him and explains how, over the years, he achieved it. The Preface provides an uniquely personal view of this major undertaking and of his method of working; as such it is worthy of inclusion at length.

'This detailed record of archaeological fieldwork on the western frontier of Mercia – Offa's Dyke, the 'Short Dykes' and Wat's Dyke – was a piece of work which, though carried out with care and alertness of mind, has recognisable defects because it was a pioneer effort in which a suitable technique of survey and record had to be evolved. I learnt however from experience and the narrative gains breadth and significance as it proceeds. It is in brief a detailed account of a series of journeys, with notebook and camera, level and staff, along the borderlands of north and central Wales, across Herefordshire and down the Wye valley following the line of Offa's Dyke; and of a return to the north when this was done to follow the line of its precursor, Wat's Dyke. A significant counter-attraction was provided by 'Short Dykes' – little barriers across ridges or valleys – met with here and there in the central zone in the course of the survey…

The Council of the Museum had approved sufficient annual leave of absence for the fieldwork involved in the research. Nothing could have been better devised; it provided the finest introduction to Wales and the Welsh and largely accounts for the affection I have for both. Many a good friend, many a remembered acquaintance, did I make in manor houses and farms, in the fields and on the moors – for the follower of the line of any ancient 'running earthwork' must be trespassing all the time – and when the day's work was done, in inns and country hotels, I, a lowlander born and bred, learnt in this undertaking the profound physical and cultural significance of a border where highland and lowland meet, visually, and by talking to men and women who had always lived in the 'debatable land'.…. The record of the survey represents the gradual growth of comprehension of the range of information – technical, military, political and economic – which can be obtained from the study of a running earthwork, and increasing understanding of the best way to set it out. It is the history of a pilgrimage, mental as well as physical, and that is I hope part of its interest. It shows how the author, grappling with unexpected and baffling problems in the first year thereafter improved his methods and increased his understanding of the way the Dykes were laid out and constructed, the part likely to have been played by the Mercian State organisation and so forth. Thus the reader interested in field research can learn something more than facts gathered and marshalled; why the dykes were aligned thus and not otherwise, why they are large here and small there; and can share, I hope, the excitement of discovery of the mind behind the work and the varying quality of human material through which shape was given to the concept.

The survey was started at the north end of Offa's Dyke in Flintshire because the barrier was being studied from the Welsh side and *in preparing a map ribbon one should work from left to right.* This immediately involved me in difficulties. I could not find the course of the dyke – or approve the line of my predecessor in research – from its apparent fade out near Newmarket, Flintshire to the sea 3 miles away; and as Bishop Asser, writing in the ninth century, affirmed that King Offa built it *mari usque ad mare,* this represented a real frustration at the outset. On the other hand, looking at the matter in the perspective of the years, I think that had I started at the south end, I should have failed to provide the solutions for the problems there met with, that came easily to mind fortified by five years' experience of the methods employed by the Offan engineers. I now consider it likely that the work was begun in the centre, completed in the south and in the north left incomplete' (Fig. 34).

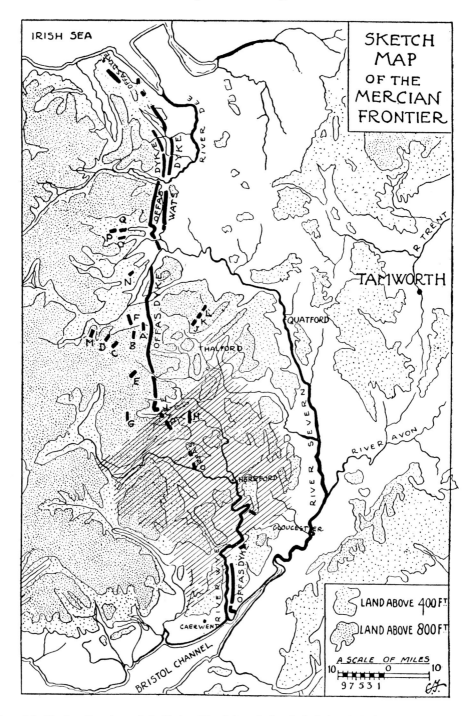

Figure 34: Mercian Frontier and the Dykes (Cambrian Archaeological Association)

Figure 35: Fox and Phillips (at foot of the Dyke) on Offa's Dyke, Denbighshire 1927 (Cambrian Archaeological Association)

Throughout the survey Fox was accompanied by D. W. Phillips (Fig. 35), who starting as one of his university students subsequently became a 'partner' in the enterprise, though all reports and drawings were undertaken by Fox himself. Phillips was a 'good companion, his fiddle always accompanied him on these expeditions and his talk, interlarded with appropriate music (either invented or drawn from memory) will be remembered, I am sure, in many an inn parlour on the Welsh border till our generation passes away.' At the suggestion of the Rev. Ellis Davies, Joint-Editor of *Archaeologia Cambrensis*, the 'Cambrians agreed to publish the results following each season's work.[9] After the survey had been completed, the Chief Inspector of Ancient Monuments asked for the map record to be forwarded to the Ministry of Works for scheduling the dykes as 'Ancient Monuments'. This it was hoped would perhaps prevent or reduce further destruction of the ancient banks and ditches.

The gradual deterioration of the dykes over the years meant parts of them, reported in 1858 as being 'manifest to all observers', were no longer obviously there. Historical investigations apart, there was an urgent need to survey the remaining identifiable portions of the dyke for posterity; and to indicate the probable course where it no longer exists. The historical requirement was to determine its date, whether conceived by one mind or several, to observe its relationship to other monuments and to attempt to determine its purpose. Excavation is a time-consuming and expensive task that can be left for succeeding generations unless modern building or road works dictate; the majority of sections were above ground and excavation was reserved for sites of very special interest.

One such was the Ysceifiog circle and barrow. Fox summarised his interest in this monument stating 'like travelling earthworks in general, well-defined changes in direction of the dyke coincide with hill crests or spurs. The use of barrows for the same purpose is a feature of this [Flintshire] section.' The relationship of the barrow and circle to the dyke and the fact that the dyke stopped short at the ditch on either side of the circle seemed to him to justify the expense and time of complete excavation. 'One must conclude that at the date when the Dyke was built, the enclosure defined by bank and ditch was recognised by the folk who built the Dyke as the sacred precinct of a tomb within it, and it seemed to me likely that monument and Dyke might have been nearly contemporaneous. My anticipations were not realised and the barrow proved to be much older than the earliest date to which the Dyke might be assigned.'

This typical passage, setting out his thoughts at the time in precise terms and with total candour, introduces the second major barrow excavation of his career. His method was the same as he had used at Barton Mills; he even used the same introductory phrases as in his Cambridge paper to explain his reasons for turning the barrow over and his method of recording the findings. Initially the barrow yielded very little save a single very deep grave pit filled with vegetation on which a man had been laid and then covered with a cairn (Fig. 36). Overall a mound had been erected, and into this mound three secondary cremation burials had been put at least 800 years

Figure 36: Ysceifiog – Barrow excavation at the half way point 1925 (Cambrian Archaeological Association)

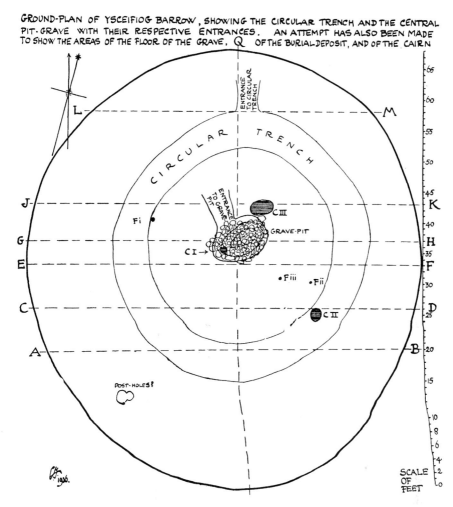

GROUND-PLAN OF YSCEIFIOG BARROW, SHOWING THE CIRCULAR TRENCH AND THE CENTRAL PIT-GRAVE WITH THEIR RESPECTIVE ENTRANCES. AN ATTEMPT HAS ALSO BEEN MADE TO SHOW THE AREAS OF THE FLOOR OF THE GRAVE, Q OF THE BURIAL-DEPOSIT, AND OF THE CAIRN

Figure 37: Ysceifiog – Plan showing entrances to Trench and Pit (Cambrian Archaeological Association)

later. There were three items of particular interest that led Fox to postulate on ritual associated with Bronze Age burials. Firstly the barrow was to the south of the centre of the Circle. Secondly, inside the edge of the mound was a circular trench with an entrance to the north. Inside the area contained by the trench was the grave pit – again with an entrance to the north. Trenches had been found before, but not specifically inside the mound or with special entrances both to the trench and grave pit (Fig. 37). Fox suggested in his paper that the absence of an exit from the trench into the inner area meant that this was a 'Holy Place' reserved for the priests or elders whose duty it was to bury the Chieftain or High Priest whose body was found in the pit. From this hypothesis, with the caveat that 'so long as the imaginative picture is dissociated from the exact record' he built up an account of this burial 4000 years ago.

'On a certain day, probably nearly four thousand years ago, five old men stood silent ands motionless on a level sward facing a circular trench; behind them was an empty grave pit. They were looking to the north. The country on which their eyes rested was parkland – pasture, heath, patches of elder, hazel and alder scrub, with birch, thorn and willow and groves of oak. No mines scarred the landscape and evidences of agriculture were very scanty, but familiar trees and the unchanged contours of the hills closely link their day to ours. Between this group and the curving bank of a newly erected earthwork (the Circle) two lines of men faced inwards on a broad passageway leading from the entrance to the Circle to the entrance to the Trench which fronted the waiting elders. Outside the Circle a numerous folk was gathered, men, women and children. Moving down the slope of the hill on the north side of the Circle a body of men is visible, four of whom bear a burden. These step slowly into the sacred area; passing along the processional way between the two lines of privileged spectators they reach the Trench. Entering the Trench the bearers turn to the right and immediately hand over their burden to the waiting group within, then with their fellows they take station outside the Trench. The Elders descend in turn to the grave-pit. A long time elapses. They are almost invisible but the spectators know that they have placed the Chieftain on his bed of white sand and are performing the traditional and essential rites of which they alone know the secret. Emerging, ceremonial lustration is performed in sight of all; orders are given for the filling in of the grave and the trench, for the erection of cairn and barrow, and the sacredness of the site in perpetuity is affirmed. The funeral feast, proclaimed on behalf of the dead man's successor, is then held. The people disperse.'[10]

This extraordinary but imaginative reconstruction of life and death in prehistoric Wales was new to archaeology. Previously historical or pre-historical speculation had been the province of writers of fiction. Yet here was an eminent professional archaeologist entering this field and asking his readers, on the basis of physical excavation of an early Bronze Age barrow, to accept his chronicle of events of 2000 BC as a likely tale. His justification for this venture into neo-fiction was that 'the large and growing public interest in the early history of the Principality makes one demand on the archaeologist. It is that after measuring, weighing, and restoring the dry bones, he shall endeavour to breathe into them the breath of life. It is a demand entirely justifiable. Our ultimate aim must be the reconstruction of the life of man in Wales in pre-historic times.'

The secondary cremation interments in the Ysceifiog barrow were not particularly noteworthy except that analysis of the charcoal twigs and branches, which indicated a mixture of Birch, Willow, Elder, Hazel, Hawthorn, Alder and Oak. This provoked another admission. 'This wide variety of species shows that any convenient firewood was used for pyres and disposes of the suggestion made by me in connexion [sic] with Bronze Age cremation burials in Suffolk that the use of oak for the pyres in this case may have had some ritual significance.' After all was completed the barrow was rebuilt in its old position. It was re-sown with grass to present, as nearly as possible, its original appearance. From it much had been learnt about Wales in the Bronze Age, but nothing relating to Offa's Dyke. In fact it was to be the following year before any form of dating was possible for the Dyke. The north Flintshire element was never very substantial; the cross-sections produced no artefacts from which dating might have been deduced. Being an earthen dyke, mostly of clay construction, as the topsoil of the vallum eroded it tended to meld with the soil in the base of the ditch, making precise dimensions of the Dyke difficult if not impossible to estimate.

In 1926 the south Flintshire and Denbigh sections were examined. Here the Dyke changed from a boundary bank with ditches on each side to a considerable work ditched on the Welsh side. At Ffrith it passed through a known Roman settlement. Although existing OS maps failed to show its course through the village, Fox and Phillips established its route, and sectioned it. The evidence was conclusive – sherds of Roman pottery and other artefacts, the majority well abraded, were found in the material of the bank and on the original soil beneath. This proved that here, as in Cambridgeshire, it was of late Roman occupation or Anglo-Saxon construction; noting the extent of sherd abrasion most likely to be the latter. Nothing found so far conflicted with the traditional ascription to Offa (ca 785 AD), the supposition which gave the Dyke its name. Other evidence of interest was that it was clearly established as having been adopted in later years as a route for north-south communications; this was in a part of the country where all natural lines of traffic were east-west. There was also an initial impression gained that it had been constructed 'under the direction of men trained in a military tradition and that to the builders Wales was an enemy country.'

That its purpose was not military but rather a political boundary was indicated during the 1928 survey in Montgomeryshire. Here the alignment in this mountainous region gave no military advantage. In one case it swung eastward towards country controlled by Mercia, reinforcing a view expressed in the 1927 report. 'The alignment of the Dyke may not represent … the free choice of a conquering race but a boundary defined by treaty or agreement between men of the hills and men of the lowlands. The latter, although the dominant partners in the arrangement, did not have matters all their own way.'

At this stage Fox was also prepared to give his views on the construction of the Dyke. He set out three basic forms of alignment: straight; sinuous along a straight line; sinuous or contour following. He then related them to the ability of the engineer visually to sight the line of posts from one high point to the next used as the guideline for the builders. Wheeler, writing to Fox very many years later, recalled a particularly vivid moment 'of you sitting on a hilltop, probably in Montgomeryshire, and looking along the wriggly course of the Dyke when you suddenly had the inspiration about the Dyke's relationship to former forest. If I remember rightly, the Dyke was straight on the south or cultivated side of the hill, and curly on the northern or bleak and forested side.' This theory was translated to a map of its course through Montgomery-shire showing suggested distribution of arable and low-level woodland in the seventh century. Once again Fox was entering the realm of conjecture rather than established archaeological fact.

In 1929 Fox and Phillips covered the 'mountain zone' of Shropshire, Radnorshire and northern Herefordshire. Here the Dyke is virtually complete and has a range of nearly a thousand feet climbing to a peak of 1408 feet on Llanvair Hill. For much of its length there is an eastern (Mercian) ditch instead of the more usual western one. On the higher ground this often presents little more than a boundary bank. In 1926 Fox had suggested that one mastermind was responsible for the overall plan of the Dyke, its dimensions and character. Individual sections were then allocated to local landowners or Chieftains, in proportion to the size of their holdings or fiefdoms. This view 'serves to explain not only the differences in method of construction but also the differences in scale.' The skill of the engineer was clearly apparent in this mountain section. 'Western facing slopes were skilfully selected and utilised; wide views to the west are normal, to the east rare although the tilt of the country is largely to the east.'

However problems clearly arose when local diversions from the master plan took place. This was either to satisfy an agreement to incorporate a particular summit or where two construction gangs had differing views on the route to their boundary. At Rushock, and less dramatically at Cwmsanaham, the Dyke diverges from its course to take in a high point but quickly returns to the natural route. At Hergan there is an angled junction which has no basis in the lie of the land. Fox's theory of two gangs at work seems to be supported with one, which finished first, working northwards and the other working south from Middle Knuck. 'The builder of the northern portion was forced to diverge from what he naturally regarded as the ideal line in order to link up.'

After five years of surveying, Fox now felt confident to give a reasoned explanation for the Short Dykes. One of these had been surveyed in 1928 and the remainder in 1929.[11] He found that they bore the same hallmarks as the main dyke but that their positioning on either side in defensive sites indicated a different purpose from Offa's boundary. Whilst they could hardly be termed barricades, they would present an obstacle to raiding parties, attempting to capture and drive back livestock. Their positioning to the east and west of Offa's Dyke could have been due to the ebb and flow of territorial gains; the Dyke being the eventual median line boundary. His further interpretation was that these short dykes were forerunners of the main dyke and that the engineer(s) applied the lessons learnt to the later and larger dyke.

One year later in 1930 his survey of Offa's Dyke was completed. The final section down the Wye valley to the Severn was more notable for its absence than presence; only 13 miles of this 60-mile stretch were previously marked on the OS map. As the survey increased this by only a matter of yards the problem was to account for the apparent decision not to build the Dyke in this section. For his solution Fox pointed to the geology of the region as, in his opinion, 'we have the whole construction in this area as Offa made it.' The parts that are missing are all to be found on the outcrop of Old Red Sandstone; now rich agricultural land, but in the Dark Ages and as late as Mediaeval times, very densely forested. He believed that the only reason for any Dyke construction in this area was for boundary definition and defence in those parts of the river valleys that had been cultivated by the Saxons.

The final problem associated with this area was to give a credible explanation for the positioning of the Dyke on the eastern side of the Wye when the river provided a natural 'political' boundary. Place names pointed the way to his interpretation and contention that the Wye was, by treaty up to the highest watermark, a Welsh trading route and that both banks were open for use. From this it followed that the agreed boundary for the line of the Dyke, between the high watermark of the Wye and the banks of the Severn, would have to be some distance back from the river on the eastern side. Work on Wat's Dyke was still outstanding but the field survey of Offa's Dyke was now at an end. The initial task 'set' by Wheeler in 1925 was complete.

*   *   *

The news in 1925 that the new Keeper of Archaeology was going to undertake this mammoth task had been warmly welcomed by the Cambrian Archaeological Association, both officially and privately. Several of the more active members joined Fox and Phillips whenever they could spare the time. Among them were two with whom Fox was to establish life-long friendships. W. J. Hemp, who lived at Roehampton, but later moved to Criccieth, was affectionately known to his friends as 'the Rabbit'. He was initially a Research Assistant and later Secretary of the Royal Commission on Ancient Monuments in Wales and Monmouthshire. He was also my Godfather, though why my parents chose a convinced atheist for this role defeats me. The other was Miss L. F. (Lal) Chitty, who came from Yockleton near Shrewsbury where her father was Rector. Both were to become working partners in several excavations and publications.

In 1970 at the first AGM of the Offa's Dyke Association Lal Chitty gave a talk entitled 'Days on the Dyke with recollections of Sir Cyril Fox'. Although some may say this was somewhat biased, she made no secret of her attraction to him, it nevertheless provides a picture of the survey by one who was there at the time. Fox was allowed three weeks each year and adopted a standard routine for these field surveys. The first week was spent walking the stretch of the Dyke determined for that season's study, noting points requiring special investigation and photographic record. The second, and part of the third week, was for surveying and any essential small excavations. The last few days were used to conclude any unfinished business.

Mr Fred Gay, the Archaeological Department's craftsman and photographer, and another Fox devotee, always spent the third week with them producing a photographic record for the reports. He told Lal Chitty that these were 'the best days of his year.' She also recalled that, 'sometimes Olive was able to leave their two young daughters in safe care and join Cyril for a short time (Fig. 38) … She [Olive] was an artist and gave him just the balance his intensely artistic nature needed, but she was also ambitious for him and keen that he should produce the finest work possible, which indeed he did assisted by his happy home background. The picnics, which Olive shared, were extra cheery occasions, a complete relaxation from the tense concentration on the survey before and after them.'

Her first introduction to the survey was in July 1927 when Charles Fox was spending a few days seeing his son at work. They were surveying at Craig Forda, a couple of miles west of Oswestry; one of the most impressive stretches where the Dyke dominates the crest of a deep ravine that falls steeply to the Morda River. The picnic on this occasion was less rewarding, the lunch had been left behind in the hotel so Lal's sandwiches and one banana was shared between the four of them. 'By half past three we were nearly famished and rejoiced to draw up at the Royal Oak, Treflach, but the good lady shook her head. 'No we don't do lunches, specially at such a time of day…. but if you don't mind waiting a bit and just have boiled eggs and bread and butter I'll go and see what the hens have laid.' Fox and Phillips continued their survey on either side of the pub until we were all called in to enjoy a marvellous spread. A

Figure 38: Olive on Offa's Dyke in Montgomeryshire 1928 (Cambrian Archaeological Association)

dozen boiled eggs, bread and butter, jam, lots of tea and even a home made plum cake – what a feast for hungry folk – I remember eating two boiled eggs and somebody else had four.'

After tea there was one more task – the ascent of Llynclys Hill. 'We descended to the great gap in the limestone range at Porth-y-Waen …and then climbed up to follow it [the Dyke] along the contours of open limestone moorland of Llynclys Hill towards the Blodwel Rock outlier of Llanymynech hill-fort. The sun was declining as we re-traced our footsteps – the views over the Berwyn country were glorious. Cyril was striding ahead, his hands in his pockets, the light glowing though his ears, rapt in concentration. We followed in respectful silence. Then Mr Fox said, "He was always like that, even when he was a boy. He would either be clinging to your arm, just as if he couldn't let you go or he'd be striding ahead like he is now, with never a word, as if you simply didn't exist." It was a fitting close to a good day.'

There were other days, other picturesque memories, like Cyril and Dudley (Phillips) pushing their way through horrid undergrowth round re-entrant angles at the head of cwms, whilst Olive and Lal took the high road above them. They were used to thickets, but their determination to follow every inch of the dyke, despite the almost impenetrable undergrowth, clearly impressed the ladies. Her lecture concluded with another word picture that will readily conjure up the image of the man for those who knew him or saw him at work. 'Perhaps you may catch a glimpse of a slight virile figure striding ahead, his ears set like a dog's on the trail, the wind waving his hair as he follows the shade of Offa, King of Mercia, along the crest of his wonderful Dyke.'[12]

The survey has been dealt with at length for two reasons. Firstly, it occupied three of the 52 weeks of every year from 1925 to 1931 and was a major contribution to the extension of knowledge of the Dark Ages in Wales and the Marches. Secondly, it demonstrates Fox's increasing interest in the environmental background and cultural activities and development of the peoples whose monuments and relics he was investigating. Geology and geography had provided his entrée to the theme of soil and settlement that ran as a continuous thread through his University treatise. Now he had taken this a stage further by giving his views on the reasoning for the construction for this great dyke, not only, as one would have expected, when judged as a whole but also for each section individually. His characteristic style was to determine the nature of the landscape with its key aspects – its height, its position, its geology and the vegetation that its soil would have supported – and then to think through how people of that era would have reacted to it. Here, he surmised, they would leave it largely as virgin woodland, there they would have cleared it for ploughed fields or used it for timber and pasture land. Despite these forays into conjecture and, particularly in the Wye valley area, his rejection of earlier accounts of Offa's Dyke, there is no evidence of outright criticism of this work or for that matter excessive praise. A succession of letters from friends and acquaintances, among them R. G.

Collingwood, Crawford, Tom Kendrick and Wheeler, acknowledged this 'fine work' and 'valuable contribution' but it was clearly believed that this was of a standard they expected of him and it set out the facts as they too saw them. The limited distribution of *Archaeologia Cambrensis* and publication in annual instalments were also factors in this lack of national interest. Much later, after publication in book form, there were critics but not at the time. He had also brought in advisers from other fields, mostly National Museum staff but also well-known archaeologists in Wales, and this clearly added weight to his arguments for those in a position to read his reports.

[1] The summary of the history of the National Museum of Wales has been taken from *The making of a National Museum* by Douglas Bassett, a former Director. *Soc.Cym.* 1983–1986. In order to reflect the diversity of the institution its bilingual name was changed in 1995 to the National Museums and Galleries of Wales – Amgueddfeydd ac Orielau Cenedlaethol Cymru. The English title of the Welsh Folk Museum became the Museum of Welsh Life at the same time but the Welsh title – Amgueddfa Werin Cymru was retained. The original names are used throughout the text.
[2] R. E. M. Wheeler *Still Digging, Interleaves from an Antiquary's Notebook*
[3] J. Hawkes *Mortimer Wheeler, Adventurer in Archaeology* p. 93
[4] The proper title was Welsh Museum of Natural History, Arts and Antiquities
[5] D. Bassett, The Making of a National Museum Part I p. 30 and 34 *Soc.Cym.* 1983
[6] Excavations in the Cambridgeshire Dykes (with W. M. Palmer) and La Tène and Romano-British Cemetery, Guilden Morden (with T. C. Lethbridge) *Camb.Ant.* XXVII
[7] Two Beakers of the Early Bronze Age recently discovered in South Wales *Arch.Camb.* LXXX
[8] Four Sepulchral Vessels of the Bronze Age from North Wales *Arch.Camb.* LXXX: A Late Celtic Bronze Age Mirror from Wales *Ant.J.* V: The Shefford Beaker *Beds.Hist.* XI
[9] Offa's Dyke – A Field Survey I – N. Flintshire *Arch.Camb.* LXXI: II – S. Flintshire & Denbeigh *Arch.Camb.* LXXXII: III – Shropshire *Arch.Camb.* LXXXIII: IV – Montgomeryshire (with D. W. Phillips) *Arch.Camb.* LXXXIV: V – The Mountain Zone (with D. W. Phillips) *Arch.Camb.* LXXXV: VI – The Wye Valley (with D. W. Phillips) *Arch.Camb.* LXXXVI
[10] The Ysceifiog Circle and Barrow *Arch.Camb.* LXXXI
[11] Offa's Dyke – A Field Survey V – The Mountain Zone p. 60–67 *Arch.Camb.* LXXXIV
[12] Extracts taken from a copy of Lal Chitty's lecture notes supplied by a member of the Offa's Dyke Association

VI

The National Museum of Wales 1926–1930
Promotion and Challenge

Presenting the Offa's Dyke survey as a single piece of work in the last chapter has set aside the passage of years and the major events that took place in this critical period in the development of the Museum as a national institution. The financial position when Wheeler took over as Director in 1924 has already been referred to as precarious; it was a particular feature in his application for promotion. Douglas Bassett[1] states that the building fund was exhausted in 1921 with £5,000 owing to the contractors and 'that the situation became more serious, even though building had been suspended in 1922, the overdraft at the bank was £16,684. In 1923 it had increased to £19,000 and by November 1925 it was £21367.' It is clear that Evans Hoyle's illness prevented him from grappling with this seemingly insoluble situation; Wheeler's arrival in the Director's chair was fortuitous in both its timing and the nature of the man himself.

Wheeler was nothing if not full of enthusiasm and drive; he tackled the financial crisis head on. In contrast to the detailed account of his work as Keeper, Wheeler's autobiography gives scant attention to his considerable achievements as Director; other than elimination of the Museum's debt by Sir William Reardon Smith, Bart. and consequent resumption of the building programme. Sir William was a wealthy Cardiff ship owner, coal exporter and company director; he and his wife, Lady Ellen were to become the Museum's most generous benefactors. Wheeler's 'bald summary of several months of hectic and anxious work' that covers the first sixteen months of his appointment is dealt with in three sentences. 'On my appointment events happened in speedy succession. A private visit to the Treasury in Whitehall resulted in a substantial increase in the Government grant, and a subsequent open battle between myself and the Museum Treasurer … led to the resignation of the latter and the appointment of Reardon Smith, who marked his appointment by coming to my office and writing a cheque for £22,000. With our debt thus cleared, an appeal was launched [jointly by the Museum and the City of Cardiff] and in a few weeks the builders were once more at work.'[2] But Wheeler's heart was never truly in Wales; he was always on the lookout for a suitable appointment at the centre of things in London. Less than two months after the debt was cleared, such an opportunity was presented to him.

(Sir) Charles Peers wrote in early January 1926 offering him the position of Keeper at the London Museum. He accepted immediately but stipulated that he remain at the National Museum until 1 July to allow for the selection of his successor without undue haste.

*   *   *

Since completing his first season of work on Offa's Dyke, Fox had been kept busy with his University College work, writing up reports of his own excavations, and surprisingly perhaps of excavations that others had undertaken, as well as papers on various artefacts that interested him. During the summer of 1925 Mr Charles Thomas of Whitland examined and partially dug two local Bronze Age barrows. Messrs A. G. O. Mathias and J. D. Beddoe of Pembroke similarly opened up another Bronze Age barrow at Rhoscrowther, on Kilpaison Burrows in Pembrokeshire. In each case Fox visited the site and advised the local team. He was then asked if he would produce the report for publication based on their findings. It was probably a question of doing the job himself, or accepting the fact that important information obtained from these sites would never be published, so he accepted the inevitable. In his Kilpaison Burrows paper[3] he drew attention to the similarity of funerary urns found in West Wales to those from other parts of the British Isles. He noted that the influences that manifested themselves in the designs of these Welsh urns seemed to have come from the more distant north of England and Ireland rather than the closer southern parts of England. This led him to consider the likelihood of a cultural unity around this 'inland' (Irish) sea and to question the reasons for it. He drew a line from Torquay to the Tees, to form a boundary between the 'highland' and 'lowland' zones, where cultural development proceeded on different levels. In the eastern lowlands new cultures of Continental origin tended to be imposed, whereas in the highlands they were absorbed. Little attention was paid to this innovative theory at the time; in six years time it would be a different story.

In addition to these routine tasks, much of which he undertook at home in the evenings and at weekends, Fox carried out one piece of interesting research that provided the material for a paper read to the Society of Antiquaries in December. Three months earlier, Mr Thomas Jenkins, a carpenter from Llangorse, Brecon, recovered an oak dugout canoe from Llangorse Lake (Fig. 39). Although Mr Jenkins had known of the existence of this canoe for some years, the lake had not been low enough for him to recover it. It was purchased by Lord Glanusk and sent to the Museum for treatment. Fox took the opportunity of his detailed study of this canoe to investigate the distribution pattern in Britain of monoxylous craft – boats or canoes constructed from a single piece of timber: His classification was based on that provided by Wilde for Irish craft in the mid-nineteenth century. The resulting paper[4] was a classic in its time, although the author readily admitted that the list of 34 canoes, 31 of

Figure 39: Llangorse Canoe 1925 (Society of Antiquaries of London)

which he used as the basis for his classification, was known to be incomplete: his personal copy includes a 1926 typed amendment adding another 14 craft. Fox expanded the three Irish groups to five, with sub-groups for internal fittings such as stern-boards and thwarts. The paper was warmly welcomed; it continued to provoke correspondence for over twenty years from those who knew that he was or might still be interested. Louis Cobbett wrote at the time 'Splendid! Your super excellent paper on your dugout much appreciated. I expected just a detailed description of your old boat and lo a sumptuously illustrated monograph on dugouts in general and jolly well done too if I may say so.'

To help him with his departmental work Fox nominally had an Assistant Keeper, V. E. Nash-Williams, one of Wheeler's first students and a member of staff since obtaining his degree at Cardiff in 1922. He had been excavating at Caerwent and Caerleon for much of the time since Fox's appointment and was unable to ease the excessive workload that was increasing inexorably as Wheeler's efforts to publicise the Museum's national role bore fruit. Wheeler had described this crusade 'to secure some general acceptance in Wales at large of a "National" Museum situated in the cosmopolitan, un-Welsh and peripheral city of Cardiff' in typically direct fashion. 'Wales, save when united in opposition to England, was an aggregate of parish-pumps rather than a nation. The thirteen counties could not for a moment be expected to focus on Cardiff; the last thing the mountains were prepared to do was to come to Mahomet. And if for Mahomet we substitute a young and rather determined Englishman, that is what happened. My senior colleagues were sometimes disturbed at my frequent absences in the hills, but I knew that my policy was right. By lectures, excavations and other contacts, I took the Museum into the highways and byways of Wales and eventually, by offering practical assistance to the poor little local museums up and down the country, built up a Welsh federation of museums with the National Museum in the chair and periodical training schools at Cardiff.'[5]

In March 1926, at the same time as Wheeler's departure to London was made public, Fox submitted a Memorandum to the Museum Council on the work of the Archaeology Department and the need for an additional assistant. This provides a succinct summary of his work as Keeper and University College Lecturer and an insight into the pressure that he was under to hold down these two appointments whilst, at the same time, providing the flow of academic papers that were an essential corollary to his excavations and research. It goes without saying, although not mentioned in the report, that his own hours at least equalled and probably well exceeded those of his staff.

Although Wheeler had made a start on the organisation of the Department, his main focus had been in the field and little real progress had been made on cleaning, indexing and displaying the artefacts. Of the eight listed essential tasks Fox had only managed to tackle two, and new collections and individual artefacts were arriving all the time to add to the backlog. His staff consisted of Nash-Williams, who in addition to his own excavation work was also assisting the Director at Y Gaer, Mr Fred Gay the General Assistant, craftsman and photographer, Miss Cooke the typist and Mr D. Hall a young lad under training. As a Lecturer at the University College, which had claims upon one third of his time, he informed the Council. 'I have to give in term-time four lectures a week, I have College meetings to attend, examination papers to prepare and mark three times a year, students to interview, returns etc. I am also an external examiner in Archaeology to the University of Ireland, work that is linked with my teaching appointment. As a Museum official in the time thus limited I have routine work which, as all Keepers will agree, occupies a very considerable time – correspondence, reports, visitors. External lectures are of great value as extending the influence of the Museum, but they are a tax on time and energy. I had two in Holywell and one in Carmarthen last month and have one this week in Cardiff and two next week also in the City.

Visits to affiliated museums are an important part of the Keeper's duties; I have done my share of this work since I was appointed. Inspection of sites of archaeological importance where excavations are going on cannot be omitted. I have spent much time visiting Whitland and Crosshands, Carmarthenshire and Rhoscrowther, Pembrokeshire, the results of which journeyings are in the museum galleries and in the pages of Archaeologia Cambrensis. As a member of the Royal Commission on Ancient Monuments in Wales and Monmouthshire much work has begun to fall upon me. Such work (all honorary) is an essential part of the duties of the Keeper under present conditions. Almost more than anything else it tends to raise the status of the Keepership and has on this ground rightly been encouraged by the Committee and Council. Fieldwork – survey and excavation at Offa's Dyke – occupied one month of the past summer … and frequent visits to the excavations at Caerleon are necessary. Thus the normal routine of a Keeper under the existing conditions … will under no circumstances permit of prolonged and continuous curatorial work. When to these duties is added the task that should properly fall on the assistant to the Keeper the situation becomes, and is, impossible. I have for months been unable to give more than an hour or so at a time to any job however important.'

Fox went on to deplore the lack of any executive presence in the Department, for days or weeks at a time; and the undue burden placed on his General Assistant. Mr

Gay had been working overtime almost continuously, organising and arranging the Bygones Gallery and running the Department in the absence of the curatorial senior staff. Since it was vital that Nash-Williams be allowed to continue his fieldwork, he would not be available for routine curatorial duties. Fox therefore requested the Council to note the need for two extra Assistant Keepers, but only asked them to approve the appointment of one.

Although there is no supporting evidence it must be considered possible, indeed likely, that Wheeler was determined to expand the Archaeology Department; he may well have suggested to Fox that a memorandum on these lines would be strongly supported. The Art and Archaeology Committee met on 14 April 1926. They fully accepted the memorandum resolving 'that with a view to making possible for at least one official of the department to be continuously on duty in the Museum, this Committee recommends the Council to appoint an additional Assistant in the Department.' This was agreed at the next Council meeting and the post was advertised nationally. Nineteen applicants were shortlisted to G. H. S. Bushnell, Iorwerth C. Peate MA (Wales) and W. F. Grimes BA (Wales). Peate had already had experience in his research degree in geography, anthropology and archaeology – working under Professor H. J. Fleure at Aberystwyth – and was considered a competent archaeologist. Grimes, a student of Wheeler and Fox at Cardiff, had only just obtained his degree in Latin! Nevertheless, Grimes was selected and took up his post on 1 September. Peate was deeply disappointed; feeling with some justification that he was far better qualified for the post. He firmly believed that Fox had unduly influenced the selection committee (of which he was not a member) in favour of his pupil.

*   *   *

The Council meeting at which Mortimer Wheeler's resignation was received was held on 26 March. The Council congratulated him on his new appointment but regretted his leaving the National Museum. They placed on record their high appreciation of his services and the interest taken by his wife in Museum affairs. They then went on to consider the question of his successor. They resolved: Firstly, 'that the vacancy be not advertised'; Secondly, 'that a Committee consisting of the Officers of the Museum with Principal A. H. Trow [University College, Cardiff] and the retiring Director be desired to make enquiries regarding possible applicants, to draw up a short list and report generally to the Council in regard to the matter.' Discussing this procedure in 1986 with Dr David Dykes, the then Director, he could only comment 'it could never happen like that nowadays, but of course the Museum was then very much more its own master than today.' On both counts – not advertising the post, and including the then Director in a committee to recommend a successor – this resolution smacks of pre-selection; there was only one person who could be responsible for it.

Wheeler's autobiography, not surprisingly, gives no details of this 'coup' but does include one short phrase (my italics) that speaks for itself. 'Behind me I should leave a going concern; I could also leave a successor in whom had absolute faith for on my promotion to the Directorship (Sir) Cyril Fox had been persuaded to come from Cambridge to assume the Keepership of Archaeology *and he (I was determined) should now take charge.*' At a subsequent meeting of the Council, the Committee was strengthened to be more powerful and slightly more representative; to all intents and purposes this was a paper exercise. They produced their report in June with a short list of two candidates; Professor Fleure, Head of Geography and Anthropology at Aberystwyth and Dr Fox, Keeper of Archaeology at the National Museum of Wales. Their report, which is somewhat weighted in favour of Fox by including his administrative experience, is reproduced in full at Appendix II.

It was somewhat ironic that Fox's contender on the short list should be Fleure since he, from the evidence of the correspondence that survives, had been among the first to congratulate Fox on his appointment as Keeper. Herbert John Fleure had been a major figure since the end of the war as an influential geographer and anthropologist. He had been a Professor of Zoology before creating a combined Geography and Anthropology Department at the University College of Wales in Aberystwyth, the first of its kind in Britain; he had carried out important research in all these subjects. Being so well established it is surprising that he had allowed his name to be put forward for the appointment. Both nominees were well known to the Council; extraordinarily they were apparently not required to submit any form of application or to attend for an interview. As the enlarged Committee included the President, Lord Kenyon, and the Vice-President it may safely be assumed that they had made up their minds in committee – with suitable guidance from Wheeler? The full Council meeting on 25 June formally approved their choice. Suffice to say that the Council minutes merely record the resolution 'that Dr Cyril Fox FSA be appointed Director of the Museum and that he take up his duties on 1st July 1926.' From raw undergraduate at Cambridge, to one of the most senior professional academic appointments in the nation, had taken him six years and nine months – an astonishing progression by any standard.

The press reports of this appointment were most flattering. The *South Wales News* commented that 'In appointing Dr Cyril Fox to the directorship of the National Museum of Wales the Council of that institution has secured the services of a man with a European reputation.' The inference from the use of the word 'secure', when Fox was already a member of the museum staff, can only be that without this promotion, they considered that he would be following Wheeler to greater things elsewhere. The *Western Mail,* devoted a long article to 'Dr Fox's Important Work in Wales.' It reported on ' his eighteen months of sterling work, under the trying conditions that must obtain in an institution of the scope, outlook and magnitude of the National Museum of Wales, while still in the process of formation, and necessarily still in the childhood of its real archaeological work both in the institution and in the field... In succeeding Dr Wheeler [as Keeper] Dr Fox faced a task not one archaeologist in a hundred would have succeeded in carrying out. It meant that Dr Fox not only had to find his feet in the Museum itself but he had to take over a large part of the responsibility for the field work with the Roman antiquities ...and old Welsh hill camps that Dr Wheeler had planned to carry out and also to prepare for his own work on the dykes... In all of this work he has been especially successful. Just recently he has been engaged in arranging the new room that has been selected for the exhibition of "Welsh Bygones"... The general public will not of course realise the tremendous labour that has been entailed in the arrangement, selection and labelling of those relics of a Wales that for the most part died before history began to be recorded. But the experts will be able to judge not only the task, but also to a large extent the genius, with which it has been carried through and to appreciate from all his work, in Wales and at Cambridge, of the excellence of his selection for the greater post of Director of the Museum.' The 'new room', to which the *Western Mail* article refers, had been built behind the main Entrance Hall (see Fig. 31). Fox had managed to persuade the Council that this 'bygones' material needed to be separated from the rest of the archaeological collection and to build a small temporary gallery to house it.

This contemporary report is of especial interest on two counts. Firstly, it draws attention to the unfulfilled commitments that Wheeler left behind him after so short a tenure in the Director's office. Secondly, it highlights Fox's understanding of the importance of heritage and his 'genius' for displaying what were in those days called 'bygones': eventually under his guidance they were to become the genesis of the Welsh Folk Museum. Jacquetta Hawkes in her biography of Wheeler ably chronicles the endeavours of Nash-Williams, Nowell Myres and particularly his wife Tessa to honour these undertakings and does not attempt to hide the criticism that his early departure aroused. 'The move provoked unconcealed ill feeling in Wales among a few, who thought that Wheeler had used the National Museum of Wales as no more than a stepping stone in his career.'[6] Fox, who had established a very close and warm relationship with Wheeler, could not accept this; nevertheless now, as Director, he had the overall responsibility for these tasks – the major one, Caerleon would be with him for a decade.

*   *   *

During his last three months as Keeper of Archaeology Fox found time to research, classify and write up one more group of artefacts, in the same manner that he had so successfully applied to Beakers twelve months earlier. Again it was a 'local' find that sparked off his enthusiastic investigations. Mr and Mrs G. E. Blundell of Nottage Court, on the edge of Merthyr Mawr in the Vale of Glamorgan, who were to become very close family friends, had regularly found evidence of Bronze or Early Iron Age occupation on the warren and forwarded their finds to the Museum. In March Mr

Blundell, attending the Council meeting that was to receive Wheeler's resignation, showed Fox some crucible fragments he had picked up on the warren. Fox immediately recognised these as being similar to those found beside the Early Iron Age Glastonbury Lake dwellings. A favourable report from Taunton Museum encouraged him to pursue his enquiries; he visited the site at the end of May. Fortune smiled that day; whilst Fox was there Mr Blundell picked up from the surface of the sand a typical La Tène I type bronze brooch; a distinctive and diagnostic artefact of that period (Fig. 40). Together with the other evidence, this convinced Fox that here was a settlement of Early Iron Age people in the south Glamorgan plain that must merit further examination.

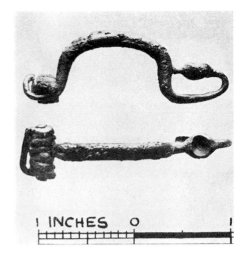

Figure 40: La Tene Brooch, Merthyr Mawr 1926 (Cambrian Archaeological Association)

Despite the pressure of work and lack of urgency to examine this site, the three of them carried out a four-day sectional excavation of the three most promising sites in June. This small dig showed that dunes had covered the site for at least 2500 years and that prehistoric settlements had existed there over a considerable period. The only datable object was the brooch, 400 to 300 BC. Discarded remains indicated that these La Tène folk were hunters and keepers of domestic animals but not agriculturists. It was therefore unlikely to have been in occupation after the early Roman period. Whether the settlement was seasonal, or driven away from time to time by sand movement, was unclear. What was evident was that with denudation the relics of successive settlements on these shifting sands could, and frequently did, end up in a single horizontal level. After major denudation this would usually be on the surface, even though at the time of occupation they may have been vertically quite widely separated.

The proven La Tène presence led Fox to examine the brooch in more detail, aiming to establish a classification and distribution pattern and to investigate how it might have arrived in South Wales. He identified three phases in their manufacture with finds ranging from Yorkshire and the East Coast to Cornwall and now Glamorgan. Since these people did not cultivate the land he needed to find a naturally clear route between the two coasts. He suggested that this was provided by the Jurassic Zone of comparatively open country, densely forested on either side, that linked north-east to south-west; here there could be unhindered movement for the Iron Age or even the Neolithic traveller[7] (Fig. 41). This original concept, that was to form a major part of his thesis published five years later as *The Personality of Britain,*

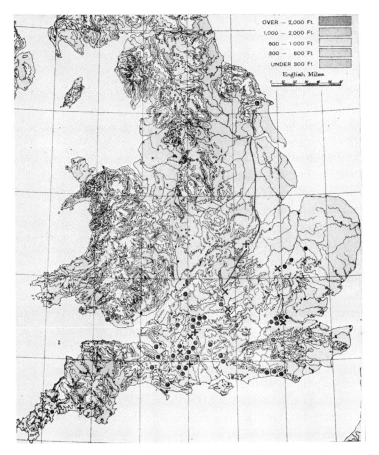

Figure 41: Distribution of La Tene (Type I) Brooches in Britain (Cambrian Archaeological Association)

once again illustrates Fox's ability to put himself in the position of the people whose remains he was examining. In so doing he sought the answers from to-day's questions from the land of yesteryear. The paper also provides more evidence of what was to become known as 'Fox's Law'; the separate but parallel development of the highland and lowland zones due to the absorption or imposition of foreign cultures after invasion. Originally raised in the Kilpaison Burrows paper, this too was to form part of the *Personality of Britain* thesis. With time, the latter theory has been recognised as an over simplification and in part erroneous, relying unduly on geographical determinism. It still retains a certain credence, but was certainly then seen as a most likely explanation of the different cultural groups found to the east and west of a Tees-Torquay axis.

Apart from his commitment to Offa's Dyke and to the Cambrian Archaeological Society's Annual General Meeting – a week of lectures and visits based on Hereford

– Fox found that as Director he had a comparatively clear diary. He tackled his new responsibilities with characteristic energy and enthusiasm. High on his priority list was completion of the second phase of the building programme and consequent reallocation of galleries to departments. This was to be followed by the official opening by Their Majesties King George V and Queen Mary, which his predecessor had set in train. Whereas for Wheeler it had just been an unconfirmed date in the diary, for Fox it became a reality when the President of the Council submitted a choice of days in late April 1927 for Royal approval. There was also the urgent question of his replacement as Keeper. As Nash-Williams was committed to Caerleon for the summer, Fox decided to retain an overseeing responsibility for the Department until his successor was appointed. To a degree he retained this oversight throughout his time in office: some would say with justification that he never left it.

Seven applications were received for the post of which two were short-listed for interview by the Council, V. Gordon Childe and V. E. Nash-Williams. On 18 October the latter was selected and took up his appointment immediately. Two months later Iorwerth Peate was chosen to take Nash-Williams' position as Assistant Keeper, thus completing the complement for which Fox had petitioned. Though each in his own way was to serve the Museum loyally for many years, relations within the Department and with their Director were not ideal. Peate's antipathy apart, this friction was to some degree of Fox's own making; despite his greater and broader responsibilities, he continued to take a deeper interest in the affairs of the Archaeology Department than was either necessary or appropriate. Nash-Williams, a true product of the Wheeler school, was essentially a 'Roman' and 'early Christian' having little concern for other periods and finding anything earlier rather boring. Although Grimes was made the prehistorian and Peate given general archaeological duties, which would appear to be a reasonable division of labour, Fox believed that the Keeper had to have much wider interests. He failed to realise that his own extraordinarily comprehensive studies were to say the least unusual, and should not be expected of everyone. Discussing this period with Grimes in 1986 he told me that Fox's continuing pre-occupation with his former Department was at first accepted by the Keepers as inevitable, but later it became a cause for an undercurrent of dissatisfaction.

*　　*　　*

Shortly before he was appointed Director, Fox was shown the remains of a Bronze Age 'encrusted urn' (Fig. 42) but there was insufficient time to examine the fragments or evaluate their significance until the winter of 1926–27.[8] The urn, brought to the museum by Mr G. E. Evans of Aberystwyth, had been found by gravediggers in a burial cist with no barrow to cover it in the cemetery of Penllwyn Calvinistic Chapel. Though complete at the time of its discovery, the urn had collapsed but was painstakingly reconstructed by Mr Gay. Encrusted urns were rare in Wales although, as the 1927

Figure 42: Penllwyn Encrusted Urn (Society of Antiquaries of London)

Antiquaries paper illustrates, more frequently found in Northern England, Scotland, Ireland and the Isle of Man; Fox's 'highland zone'. His analysis of the 43 known encrusted urns showed an artistic development commensurate with progressive movement of this culture from northern Britain to Ireland and Wales. Dating was difficult; none of the true encrusted urn burials, usually inverted over burnt bones in both flat cemeteries and barrows, contained artefacts. However a cemetery in Fife, which included an urn with a rudimentary form of encrustation, contained oval bronze blades (razors) dated by Montelius as around 1000 BC. From this Fox assessed the developed forms of the urn to be 900–600 BC. This seemed to accord with late Bronze Age burial practice but was admitted to be in conflict with Abercromby's belief of a much later date c.650–400 BC.[9] The importance of the Penllwyn urn is that, like the Merthyr Mawr brooch and the Cwm Du beaker, it helped Fox to build upon his ideas that subsequently would appear as *The Personality of Britain*. To the highland and lowland zones, and the Jurassic entrance to south-west Britain, was now added the concept of an Irish Sea Bronze Age cultural basin.

Fox's first submission to the Council as Director was his Memorandum on the allocation of gallery space to each department. This was initially when the eastern half of the south front was completed, the cue for the Royal opening, and later when the major part of the east wing was built. The Council had already decided in principle to allocate more space to Art and Archaeology, and to make tentative provision for an embryo Industry Department. Fox believed that the opportunity provided by the completion of a building, which was balanced on either side of the entrance hall, should be taken for a comprehensive review. 'I think' he wrote, 'the time has come when the Council should carefully reconsider the whole problem of accommodation in order to see whether a logical scheme cannot be prepared which may continue until the building is completed.'

The scheme that he proposed, accepted by the Council, was simple and has been retained to the present day in the major part of the building. The architectural grandeur of the building deeply impressed him and he was determined that nothing within the building should be allowed to detract from its nobility. His first and pre-eminent recommendation was that the Entrance Hall should be extra-departmental and under the personal control of the Director. 'This area constitutes an architectural area of special character and dignity differing from any other portion of the building constructed or in contemplation. It demands and should receive special consideration. It is moreover too extensive and its value, as an index of outlook and standards of those responsible for the policy of the Institution too great for it to be in the hand of any one Department... Directorial control would permit flexibility of treatment; the character of the exhibits could be modified – always with an eye to the architectural requirements – as our collections increase and objects of a suitable character come into the hands of the different Departments.' His proposal for the Director's guidelines were to 'emphasise the dignity and architectural effect of the Entrance Hall, the specifically Welsh character of the Museum and the wide scope of the Museum's activities.'

His second recommendation, from which the main reorganisation flowed, was that 'space be allocated on a scientific basis, making a clear distinction between "nature" and "man" (Fig. 43). The student or visitor... should visit Geology first to see what is known of the structure of Welsh hills and valleys; the flora and fauna of Wales should then be studied successively in the Departments of Botany and Zoology. Passing thence to Archaeology the evidence of life of early man in Wales would be examined and the tour ... completed by an examination of man's higher achievements in technical skills linked with imagination in the Art Galleries.' Grimes, in his obituary of Fox, wrote of this milestone in the history of the Museum. 'His period of office as Director was one of great development, with the completion of the Entrance Hall in 1927 and the later extension of the east wing, including the Reardon Smith Lecture Theatre in 1932. He thus had overall responsibility for the organisation of the galleries during a time when the museum more than doubled its effective exhibition space. It would be fair to say that not all of Fox's colleagues shared his view of the building, impressive as it was and is, as the nearly perfect setting for exhibits; at times the danger that the building might take precedence over the specimens seemed very real indeed.'[10] This is fair criticism, but cannot detract from the fact that those far-sighted and imaginative proposals have stood the test of time; they were left unchanged when the west wing galleries were opened in 1965.

Having completed his long-term plan for the reorganisation of the Museum and prepared all outstanding reports of excavations and research for publication, Fox with the help of his Secretary, A. H. Lee, turned his attention to the Royal Visit. Although the date had not yet been finally approved, this was not to be announced until March, it was privately known to be 21st April 1927. The Director, responsible to the Council for the arrangements, left all detailed planning to 'Archie'. Jacquetta Hawkes, in her biography of Wheeler, acknowledges the talents of this dedicated servant of the Museum and implies the debt that a succession of Directors owes to him. It is therefore a matter of regret that neither Wheeler in his autobiography, where he is not even mentioned, nor Bassett in his '*Making of a national museum*', gives the credit that is due to this extraordinary man. Jacquetta Hawkes wrote 'The Directorship brought with it a number

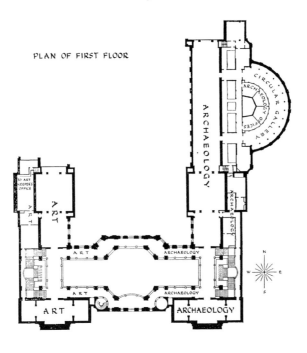

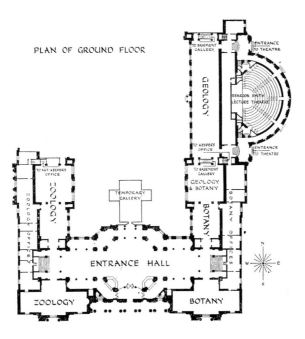

Figure 43: Re-organisation of National Museum Galleries as proposed by Fox in 1927 and implemented in 1932 on completion of East Wing and Reardon Smith Lecture Theatre (National Museum of Wales)

of personal advantages. One of them was in the shape of an agreeable, capable and ever willing Secretary. He was equal to all his new master [Wheeler]'s exacting demands and all possible burdens were put upon him. "Leave it to Archie" became a regular formula in the National Museum and remained so for long afterwards.'[11]

Discussing Lee's role with Peter Grimes in 1987 confirmed to me that all this was true; to these talents one should add his kindness, courtesy to the stranger and young visitors to the Museum (myself included), and loyalty. Above all he had an ability to run the establishment whenever his Director was away for extended periods on lecture tours, on excavations or, as was to happen to Fox on several occasions, through prolonged illness. As Grimes pointed out there was however another side to his character that did not always endear this former Adjutant to his senior or junior colleagues. He had a sharp tongue and a habit of basing his advice to his Director on information gleaned from junior members of staff, rather than that obtained from the Heads of Department. In my opinion, whatever his faults they were more than outweighed by his merits, he was certainly always kind to me. A secure base is an essential for the head of any organisation; Lee undoubtedly provided this for four Directors between 1922 and 1953 and this deserves greater recognition.

After such an introduction it goes without saying that the arrangements for Their Majesties' return to Cardiff to officially open the National Museum of Wales were planned with military precision and were impeccable – even the weather followed the plan. The *Daily Telegraph,* under the headline, 'King's praise for new Welsh Museum', reported that 'thousands of Welsh men and women joined in giving a great welcome to the King and Queen on their visit to Cardiff when, after a lapse of almost fifteen years since the inaugural ceremony which he performed, His Majesty declared open such sections of the National Museum of Wales as have been completed. In brilliant sunshine they drove in an open carriage through the city and were received at the foot of the steps by Lord Kenyon the President, who presented his predecessors as President [Lord Pontypridd, Lord Mostyn and Lord Treowen], the Officers of the Museum, Vice President Lord Aberdare and Treasurer Sir William Reardon Smith, the Director Dr Cyril Fox (Fig. 44) and Secretary and Marshall Captain A. H. Lee together with the architect Mr A. Dunbar Smith.' In his reply to the address of welcome the King reiterated the words used by the first President, Lord Pontypridd, in 1912 to describe the purpose of this new National Museum. This was 'to teach the world about Wales and the Welsh people about their own Fatherland.' He continued 'I am glad to know that its influence extends beyond the city in which it has found a home and that by means of affiliated museums, loan collections and in other ways, the whole Principality benefits from an institution the educational importance of which will be increasingly recognised by the people of Wales.' For the next 20 years the extension of this influence was to be the new Director's principal motivation and in its achievement his greatest reward.

*   *   *

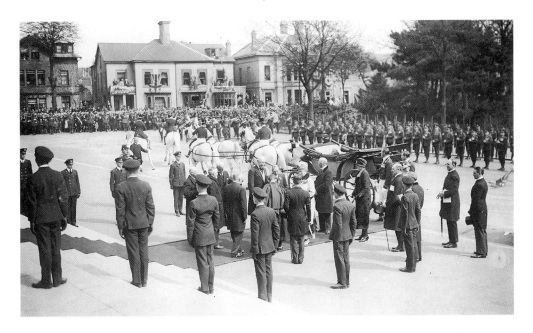

Top: Presentation of Dr Fox to His Majesty in front of the Museum

Left: The Royal party enter the Museum

Right: Departure of the Royal Carriage procession for civic reception

Figure 44: National Museum of Wales – Official opening ceremony by HM King George V – 21 April 1927

The ceremonial over, it was back to the administrative routine with occasional breaks for excavation and research. The years spent with the Royal Commission at Stansted and the Field Laboratory at Cambridge were now to bear fruit; that administrative experience, although on a much smaller scale, had covered a wide range of scientific disciplines as well as construction and finance. From the moment he arrived in the Director's office it was clear that Fox had the ability to take these diverse matters in his stride. Whether dealing with people, the routine of daily Museum life, or matters of great moment that affected them all, he moved from one to the other with ease. In particular, he quickly won the hearts of the junior members of staff in whose welfare he always took great interest. But, given the chance, even though it might mean a little more midnight oil or less time with his family, he would escape from his office to keep in touch with practical archaeology; excavations or research it mattered not. His problem, which he failed to solve for many years, was to achieve that balance between administrator and scholar that his constitution would allow.

One such escape was in the late summer of 1927. With his annual pilgrimage to Offa's Dyke long since over, he was glad of an excuse to head west to Pembrokeshire. Those two well known local antiquarians Mathias and Beddoe, with the help of a group of their friends, had opened the centre of a mound at Corston Beacon and invited him to attend the ceremonial removal of the capstone they had exposed. Hearing that Fox was driving to Pembroke, Grimes asked if he might come too; giving him an opportunity for an unexpected week-end in his home county with the chance of seeing his Director at work.[12] On arriving in Cardiff, Fox had exchanged his two-seater Morris Tourer for a larger black Morris Cowley. In those early days he could barely afford the running expenses, but the Museum's travel allowances were sufficiently generous to make it worthwhile and gave him the freedom he needed for his journeys around the Principality. Knowing the car fairly well, Grimes was a little surprised to see a bright green model in the Director's place in the park at the back of the Museum. In fact it turned out to be the same car, but after an accident during the Offa's Dyke survey that summer that had totally wrecked the offside wings, the whole car had been re-sprayed in a colour that seemed more appropriate to Olive's taste than his own. The drive to Pembroke was thankfully less eventful. Grimes took refuge in a local pub, whilst his Director availed himself of the hospitality of the local landowner, General Burleigh-Leach. Grimes recalled that, 'the following morning all were assembled, including the press, and together they stared at the large capstone. Thomas Meyrick, a local builder, suggested they needed a tripod [presumably with accompanying block and tackle] and vouchsafed the information that he had one in his yard, but didn't offer to produce it without some form of remuneration. In the end Mr Alan Colley, the tenant farmer, fetched his own and in due course the capstone was removed. There to the delight of all were the decayed remains of a skeleton and with it a bronze dagger knife.'

The *Western Mail* article was headlined 'From out of the Past! Remains of man 3500 years old.' and gave this rather romantic account of the discovery. 'The skeleton of a warrior chief, who was forgotten by his tribe two or three hundred years before Tut-ankh-Amen was laid in his tomb in Egypt, has been excavated at Corston Beacon… The large capstone, ten feet long and about four feet wide weighing about two tons … was raised exposing – what no man had seen for 3500 years – the bones of a man in a coffin formed of upright slabs of red sandstone. By his side was a beautiful riveted bronze dagger, seven inches in length, with a handle of horn. The dagger, which was covered with verdigris, was a conspicuous object in the grave. Such a blade belongs to the dawn of the metal age in Britain, about 1700 BC and in design and shape is derived from the eastern Mediterranean. The man who owned it probably controlled the peninsula south of Milford Haven and was buried in an eminence overlooking his domain.' Nearly sixty years later Grimes told me that the information given to the journalist suggested a person with a feeling for popular interpretation as well as detailed knowledge. At the time he was new to the scene and denied all responsibility for the article. He certainly convinced me that the source could only have been Fox himself. Grimes clearly believed that Fox was cleverly using the press to convey his message; archaeology and prehistory was not just dead old bones but alive and fun.

Mathias and Beddoe's enthusiasm for their successful excavation did not extend to recording and publishing their finds. Since they always presented everything to the National Museum, they suggested that the Archaeology Department might like to publish the results. So instead of just observing, Grimes found himself enlisted to do the work for them. He readily recalled for me the sequel to this occasion. The cist having been opened, the contents examined and photographed, the Director left him to get on with it. 'He gave me no instructions and casually assumed, as his former pupil, that I knew exactly what to do. In an absent-minded way, he had presumably forgotten that our degree course had not prepared us for this kind of practical work.' It was an exciting site, with an elaborate Early Bronze Age megalithic chamber that Grimes was later to study with such distinction; he found it a pleasure to draw. His recording was accepted without question, much to his surprise; 'Looking back' he commented 'I would certainly have checked up myself if I had been the Director.' The paper,[13] with Grimes' drawings and a Fox text, repeats the earlier established pattern. There was a distributional map and tabular list of all known flat-riveted knife-daggers, with an assessment of their historic development and likely route to western Wales. The map is of note as the work of Lal Chitty. It is the first of many, and the start of a long association of devoted (and unpaid) work, mapping and indexing Fox's researches.

* * *

Appointment as Director had brought a welcome increase in salary to £800 and within a few months, following the October 1926 general rise for senior museum staff, to over £900. For the first time since his childhood, money was no longer a major worry. Their rented property was convenient both for the Museum and for the city. For a while Olive was content to stay; her husband had no inclination to move. However this new found financial security, together with the pressing need to have more space with a larger garden for their growing family, meant that the restrictions of Heath Park Avenue drove them to look for a house in the country. Five miles north of the city a garden suburb called Rhiwbina was being developed by the Cardiff Workers' Co-operative Garden Village Society Limited on land leased from the Welsh Town Planning and Housing Trust. Started in 1912 with well-built community housing, there had been an eastern extension of small private dwellings immediately after the war. Now, in late 1927, planning authority was given for the western extension. Detailed plans were published in February 1928 showing much larger plots for substantial houses. This proved so attractive that they, and several other senior members of the Museum staff, were persuaded to obtain 999-year leases from the Trust.

Fox had a highly developed and acute appreciation of architecture. With his natural talent for draughtsmanship he might well have followed the architectural profession if archaeology had not claimed him. The Arts and Crafts movement embodied everything that most appealed to Fox, with its emphasis on hand finishing and freedom to express the characteristics of individual materials. The houses had to be designed by T. Alwyn Lloyd, architectural adviser to the Trust, but his ideas were very much in tune with their own and it proved a happy relationship.

The plot that they had chosen was No. 10 Heol Wen with an old tree-lined hedge for its northern and western boundaries. It was the last but one to be sold before the open fields that were, for as long as he lived there, to remain undeveloped. Alwyn Lloyd created a row of six properties of Georgian proportions (Fig. 45) fitted with modern conveniences, such as Crittall metal windows. Oak block floors ran throughout the ground floor and Fox insisted on a matching oak staircase with vase shaped finials to the banisters. The treads were left uncovered to reveal their polished beauty. We children of both families clattered about and frequently fell from top to bottom of the lower flight of this dreaded slippery staircase. Antique tin-glazed tiles in profusion lined the dining room fireplace; larger modern tiles of Persian inspiration were similarly set in the drawing room hearth. The garden vista closed with a very large rockery, a fashionable feature at the time.

With the passage of years, Fox found equal attraction to successive architectural styles; the Art Deco of the thirties and in his retirement the classical revival. He always retained a great affection for this typical twenties house; it had given him great pleasure, both in its creation and in the work that he had undertaken there. With four bedrooms, one of which became his study, ample reception rooms and a children's playroom downstairs, it was a comfortable family house. Originally designed and built with one adjoining garage, a second was soon added; Olive found it necessary to buy

Figure 45: Four Elms, Heol Wen, Rhiwbina Garden Village 1929

her own car to give her the freedom she needed to carry on with her activities in the city and the docks. The red and buff Triumph, known affectionately by the family as the Biscuit Tin, soon became a familiar sight in Tiger Bay (now Cardiff Bay), as well as Rhiwbina, and gave the Fox's certain kudos as a two-car family. The vast elms in the hedgerows that had given the house its name, Four Elms, have long since gone, as have the initials CF OF 1928 carved in a panel above the front door. To-day only the name remains and the memories of those of us who lived or stayed there.

Olive's artistic temperament made her an interesting and unconventional hostess. Meals appeared when she thought about such things, or when gently reminded by her husband that their visitors or family were expecting something to eat. The house was filled with her paintings. They all had titles giving the source of her inspiration. This could puzzle those unenlightened guests, who failed to appreciate the connection between a Welsh landscape and a Brahms opera! As one frequent visitor to the house remarked 'she was such a nice, kind and generous person one had to make allowances for these peculiarities, and just be thankful one's own wife had not got them!' Coming from such a happy home, both as a child and now as wife and mother, it was not surprising that Olive had a delightful and warm-hearted sense of humour. Her husband took his new position very seriously, he was very conscious of his status as Director; she was more inclined to frivolity, finding amusement in the most serious of public occasions, often to his unconcealed annoyance. She treated everyone on his or her merits, with little respect for his or her position. She would not hesitate to let others know, surreptitiously, that she had little or no time for some of the members of the Museum's Council, nor for some of its bumbling officials, whom her husband felt he, and she, ought to treat with the respect their position entitled.

As his name became known beyond the narrow confines of the archaeological and museum worlds, so the pressure upon his time increased. He had been appointed in December 1925 as a Member of the Royal Commission on Ancient Monuments in Wales and Monmouthshire (he was to be appointed a member of the English Commission some twenty years later) and was an external examiner for the University of Ireland. The Welsh Commission in 1925 had published a county report for Pembrokeshire, in the series of inventories, which were its main public activity. This Pembrokeshire report, memorably and publicly condemned for its incompetence in a review by Mortimer Wheeler, could not be repeated for its successor in Anglesey if the Commission was to flourish or even survive. Added to these statutory duties was an unending stream of invitations from all over the country to official functions, lectures and seminars, as well as excavations that other archaeologists considered might interest him or where his presence could be of advantage to them. He was often called upon to speak and was reluctant to refuse any opportunity to explain the unique role and responsibilities of the National Museum and its desperate need for funds. He was also very keen to promote his fervent belief in the role of archaeology in establishing a nation's heritage.

The time spent in travel and in preparation for these diverse engagements was considerable. It could only be taken from that previously set aside for academic research. A glance at the Bibliography will show how the spate of work between 1921 and 1928 was reduced to a trickle. Only Offa's Dyke remained inviolate: that three-week survey in the Marches was the only complete break that he allowed himself. When the family took their summer holiday beside the sea, or with Granny C at Steyning, he would drive them down, even join them for weekends, but spend the rest of the time working at home or in the Museum. In 1926 he had accepted a commission from Methuen to write a book on the archaeology of England and Wales in the Neolithic, Bronze and Early Iron Ages for which Lal Chitty would produce the distribution maps and index. What should have been his holiday, and most of his spare time, was devoted to this project. The details he had obtained for the Cambridge Region had been within the grasp of one man in his spare time. To undertake similar research for the whole country was a monumental task; after three years work, he was beginning to realise that it was almost beyond him whilst he remained at Cardiff.

Inevitably his health, never strong, began to give Olive and his doctor cause for concern. Though outwardly healthy, Fox's disposition was nervous and highly-strung; the legacy of his childhood and wartime illness was always present. He also had a tendency to hypochondria – a cold in the head would send him straight to bed, where he would remain until all symptoms had gone. He suffered periodical bouts of colitis for most of his life and the need to take regular doses of powerful laxatives aggravated his feelings of lassitude. On one occasion, en route to Edinburgh for a lecture, the strain of this hectic schedule proved too much, and he found he was unable to speak. A doctor was called and told him that he had to ease up and should never attempt to speak in public again. Rest, a lighter workload and 'Radio Malt' were prescribed. He took this advice for a short time, but feeling better he soon resumed his usual routine. As the twenties came to an end, it appeared that he had weathered the storm; he was now ready for greater things to come.

Notes

[1] D. Bassett *The making of a National Museum* Part II, p. 18, *Soc.Cym.* 1984

[2] R. E. M. Wheeler *Still Digging* p. 65

[3] A burial place of [Bronze Age[dwellers in the upper Taf valley, Carmarthenshire *Arch.Camb.* LXXX: A Bronze Age Barrow on Kilpaison Burrows, Rhoscrowther, Pembrokeshire *Arch.Camb.* LXXXI

[4] A Dug-out Canoe from [Llangorse], South Wales *Ant.J.* VI

[5] R. E. M. Wheeler *Still Digging* p. 65

[6] J. Hawkes *Mortimer Wheeler, Adventurer in Archaeology* p. 101

[7] A Settlement of the Early Iron Age on Merthyr Mawr Warren, Glamorgan; La Tène I Brooch from Wales *Arch.Camb.* LXXXII

[8] An encrusted Urn of the Bronze Age from [Penllwyn, Cardiganshire] Wales. *Ant.J.* VII

[9] As previously intimated, these dates are those discussed at the time. In the 1950s the new radio-carbon dating method and in the 1970s the 're-calibration' of that radio-carbon dating extended the prehistoric time-scale for Britain so that nearly all dates for Welsh and British prehistory in these discoveries of the 1920s through to the early 1950s are too young. The relative chronology – what is contemporary with what, and what succeeds what – for the most part stands.

[10] W. F. Grimes *Arch.Camb.* 1967 p. 208–10

[11] J. Hawkes *Mortimer Wheeler, Adventurer in Archaeology* p. 95

[12] Reminiscences with the author 1987

[13] Corston Beacon, an Early Bronze Age Cairn in South Pembrokeshire (with W. F. Grimes) *Arch.Camb.* LXXXIII

VII

Triumph and Tragedy 1930–1932
Personality of Britain and death at Llangennith

The beginning of the 1930s was dominated by Museum affairs with ill health, brought on once again by overwork, being a continuing cause for concern. The financial position was difficult; constant efforts were required from the Director and Council to raise the necessary funding for the construction and fitting out of the east wing extension and constituent Lecture Theatre. Building would not have been possible unless Sir William Reardon Smith, Lord Buckland and others, had expressed their willingness to donate the substantial sum necessary to supplement the Government grants. It had been approved by the Treasury in 1928 and was now just starting to be built. Since arriving in Cardiff Fox had been very active in the business of the Museums Association; he served on, and subsequently chaired, its Education Committee and took a deep interest in Sir Henry Miers' quest for a National Folk Museum.[1] As a countryman the preservation of national heritage, be it buildings, the environment or artefacts associated with traditional ways of life, each was to him a natural and abiding concern. This concern had first been given public expression in his Bygones Gallery opened in 1926. Now with his enhanced national reputation he was in a position to ensure that the National Museum of Wales could continue to provide a lead for the nation in this field. At the same time he was anxious that this developing interest in the collection and preservation of our heritage should not be at the expense of the environment. In 1928 he had helped to found the Council for the Preservation of Rural Wales (CPRW) and became a member of its executive. He used this platform for a broadcast in February 1930 on the 'Preservation of Ancient Wales' to plead for the protection of the natural environment that surrounds historic sites and ancient buildings so that in years to come visitors might continue to see their monuments in their native setting. 'How much of the beauty of Tintern, the joy and delight which its contemplation gives, depends on the unspoilt setting of meadow and woodland… The harm caused by ill-considered development, whether the loss be of old buildings, of historical associations or of man made or natural beauty or interest, is a harm done to a soul of a nation not measurable in terms of money.'

Although this broadcast, one of a series of three by CPRW officials, was directed

Figure 46: Left, Wheel Car from Radnorshire. Right, Truckle Cart – from drawing dated 1886 (Antiquity Publications)

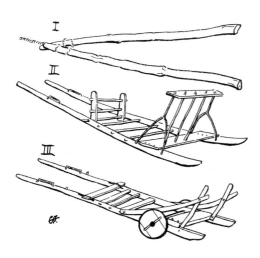

Figure 47: Evolution of the Truckle Cart (Antiquity Publications)

towards the more ancient relics of human occupation in Wales, he was equally vociferous in his campaign for the preservation of rural crafts and of the associated tools and workshops that were so rapidly disappearing as modern industrial techniques rendered them obsolete. In his opinion erosion of the environment in which these crafts had flourished was equally damaging to the nation and equally immeasurable in financial terms. His natural curiosity and fascination for such things led him to follow up a casual sighting of a Welsh handcart with an investigation into its origins. 'While engaged in field work near Llanbister in Radnorshire [Offa's Dyke survey August 1929] the writer saw by the roadside near a country wheelwright's shop, a remarkable vehicle the like of which he had never imagined. On being questioned the wheelwright said it was a "wheel-car" and was of a standard type used throughout the Radnor forest area. It had been made entirely by himself and his smith. He drew attention to a second example, half completed, in the shop. This was purchased for the Welsh Folk collection of the National Museum of Wales' (Fig. 46, left). His researches eventually encompassed all forms of rural transport in Britain, sleds, carts and wagons, and led to a comprehensive paper published by *Antiquity*[2] (Fig. 47).

This natural instinct to preserve for posterity anything that was in danger of disappearing had obviously been encouraged by his earlier research into the 'Bygones' material transferred from the Cardiff Museum. Mention has already been made of the public acclaim that followed the display of this material. As the *South Wales News* reported at the time 'A new department has been added in which appear all the characteristic features of the life of the people of Wales prior to the Industrial Revolution.' Actually the folk collection was not a separate department but still an integral part of the Archaeology Department. This new gallery in its prominent position opposite the main entrance to the museum, which included the re-creation of a typical Welsh bedroom and farmhouse kitchen, fired the imagination of visitors and was an instant success.

*   *   *

From its outset the Museum had had a tradition of encouraging its staff to undertake original fieldwork and other kinds of research, that would clearly be reflected in an enhanced reputation or add materially to its collection. Although satisfied that links, such as those provided by the Museums Association, would ensure that the Museum was taking advantage of the latest techniques to display its varied collections to their best advantage, Fox, like Evans Hoyle before him, was aware that foreign museums, particularly those in Scandinavia, had much to offer when considering the exhibition of 'folk' material. In March 1930 he informed the Council of his concern and it was agreed that he, with two of their members, should visit Norway, Sweden and Denmark, to assess the situation. Fox's companions T. W. Proger and Dr D. R. Paterson, were eminently suitable for this task. As senior members of the Council they had been well aware of Evans Hoyle and now Fox's interest in these Scandinavian museums. Proger, as an Hon.Curator of the Cardiff Museum, had helped to start the original 'Bygones' collection and Paterson, Chairman of the Art and Archaeology Committee, was an authority on Norse languages. The delegation left Cardiff on 23 May and returned on 9 June having spent four days in each capital and visited eighteen museums and galleries.

Their report noted that the display of material in traditional museums was of a similar standard to the United Kingdom; their ethnographic exhibits were certainly on a par with their own 'Bygones' Gallery. The Scandinavian field and folk museums had no such equivalent and made a great impression on all members of the team. 'Buildings (houses, bars, stables, churches, mills, workshops, etc),' Fox wrote, 'illustrating the mode of life and immediate environment of the people from the earliest times for which such constructions are available (XII and XIII centuries) down to the XIX century. These buildings are fittingly and spaciously set out in parkland – Field Museums – and ... in every case appropriately furnished with contemporary furnishings, often that which was made for the particular house. The intense interest aroused by an examination of these collections is heightened by the extraordinary effort made to create an air of reality. The storerooms of the farmhouses are in many cases *stacked* with dresses, furnishings, materials, etc, as they were when the buildings were inhabited. From the educational point of view the Field Museums are admirably arranged. The visitor goes to the oldest house first and the sequence of buildings visited illustrates the growth of civilisation, of comfort, of the desire for privacy. Attention is drawn to the evolution of the fireplace, of the retiring room, of the upper storey.'

For those that knew him it is easy to picture Fox's ebullient unbounded enthusiasm as he toured these living museums. They had been developed, not just to preserve old often decaying and unwanted buildings, but as a focus for folk activities, rural crafts, music and dancing. In this rejuvenated role they truly became alive rather than just a repository of times past. That this enthusiasm was transmitted to the Council is evident from their unanimous acceptance of the report and their resolution of 29th November. 'That the National Museum is incomplete without an adequate illustration of the life and work of people such as can only be offered by an open-air museum on the lines of that at Skansen, Stockholm.' At the same time it was decided that when the new galleries in the east wing became available, added emphasis should be given to the Museum's own collection. This should be done by adding a parlour and buttery to an enlarged and redesigned farmhouse kitchen, the reconstruction of four craft workshops, and by renaming the enlarged display 'The Welsh Folk Collection'

Although every department specialised in the Welsh aspects of their subject matter, be it geology, botany, art or archaeology, Fox recognised that a collection of material possessions, or the reconstruction of surroundings immediately recognisable by the older generation of Welsh people as typical of their childhood, could convey a national image more vividly than most other exhibits. He had therefore encouraged the newly appointed Assistant Keeper Iorwerth Peate, a Cyfeiling (Montgomeryshire) man, who already had a reputation as a writer and poet in Welsh and had a particular interest in all things 'Welsh', to specialise in this aspect of the department. Despite being appointed for 'general archaeological duties' Peate had made no secret of his lack of interest in prehistory and welcomed this suggestion to concentrate on the 'Bygones' collection. Six months later he was specifically appointed by the Council to 'curate and develop this collection.' The following year, under Fox's guidance, the Museum published Peate's detailed and richly illustrated '*Guide Catalogue to the collection of Welsh Bygones.*' This popular guide helped to initiate the systematic collection of folk material. Peate acknowledges that 'I had warm support from Cyril Fox in the work of cataloguing the collection and [it] was a discipline of the best kind. Every item went through my hands, to be measured … dated, and to identify its [geographical] source.'

Addition of the east wing almost doubled the Museum's exhibition space. All members of staff had a difficult time producing the many new exhibits, and reorganising the old, to fit into the new galleries. Fox had allocated a surprisingly large space to Folk Culture, even before the subject had been recognised or elevated to sub-department status; Peate and his trainee craftsman were particularly hard pressed. His autobiography continues: 'This involved a great deal of work – the planning, the choice of specimens and the placing of all these in new cases and designing labels for them.'[3] However Nash-Williams, the new Keeper of the Archaeology Department, took little interest in the subject; Fox perforce had to protect and nurture this potential sub-department to ensure its healthy survival.

Apart from his paternalistic role, overseeing the further development of the 'Bygones' collection, Fox maintained a close personal involvement in any written reports on items coming into the Museum, especially those resulting from his own endeavours. He also took great interest in the collection and display of specimens throughout the Museum, though it has to be said that he paid less attention to the exhibits and work of the three Natural History Departments than to Art and Archaeology. His extraordinarily comprehensive, almost panoramic, view of human development, enabled him to move freely in his analysis of the material possessions of peoples, from prehistoric times to twentieth century Wales, with the same unrestricted enthusiasm and, more importantly, acknowledged expertise. Writing in June 1931 to thank Fox for his copy of 'this fascinating paper on carts, carts and carts' Wheeler acknowledges this visionary breadth 'How I envy you the catholicity of your knowledge.' Peate was less complimentary in his autobiography. 'I remember [Fox] coming to my room one morning and seeing on my desk a number of photographic prints of drag cars and drag carts with wheels; photographs taken by my father… Without a word he took them and shortly I read in the journal *Antiquity*, his paper "Sleds, Carts and Waggons" the precise subject that I was working on at the time.' Perhaps, if he were alive, Fox would have a different account of this confrontation. As a brief aside it should be noted that all of Peate's photographs were given due accreditation.

∗   ∗   ∗

Although fieldwork in 1930 was restricted to the last of the Offa's Dyke surveys and a week in August at Kidwelly Castle, Fox was out of his office for much of the time. These outside activities involved committee work for the Archaeological Congress and the Antiquaries, visiting and reporting on Anglesey sites with W. J. Hemp for the Ancient Monuments Commission, touring with the Cambrians for their AGM at Menai Bridge and visiting 'affiliated museums' throughout the Principality. The latter was usually an unrewarding but important duty for the Director of a museum striving to improve its national image. In a paper read to the Museums Association during their Conference in Cardiff in June Fox described this pastoral role as a 'one-way street' that was intended to be of mutual benefit but in practice was somewhat one-sided.[4] Initiated by the Council in 1922 on Wheeler's recommendation, this 'affiliated' status enabled local museums to call on the expertise and assistance of National Museum staff, to improve their presentation and to give practical help in re-arranging their exhibits. Although there was no expectation of anything in return, it was hoped that these museums would better understand the aims and needs of a national museum; perhaps giving consideration to enhancing this Welsh national collection. The Museum also arranged an annual Summer School for their Honorary Curators for discussion and demonstration of matters of common interest. Fox also started a formal series of lectures throughout Wales by Museum staff, including himself, on topics pertinent to the collection in the museum in question.

As winter approached the symptoms of lassitude, and an inability to concentrate for any length of time that had given cause for concern in 1929, reappeared. A thorough examination initiated by the family doctor, Harold Couthard, produced a report in late October that Fox was suffering from hypertension and low blood pressure. His recommendations in 1929 were now instructions. 'You should take Saturdays and Sundays completely free from any administration or academic work and for three months at least remain in bed on Saturdays until lunch. You should have at least three weeks clear holiday every year, say a week at Easter and a fortnight during the summer. This is an absolute minimum for a man with your responsibilities if health breakdowns are to be avoided. I cannot regard archaeological research as a holiday.'

These somewhat old-fashioned remedies were observed for a while, Olive made certain of that, but even she found it hard to stop her husband from taking his 'rest' in his study and devoting his newly created 'free time' to the archaeological research so condemned by his doctor. In truth this was not wilful disobedience of Doctor's orders but boredom, for nothing else really interested him. He had no hobbies or interests other than his work; if that was denied, time hung round his neck like the proverbial millstone. That this total concentration on academic work, to the virtual exclusion of all else, was the principal cause for this temporary breakdown in his health, is almost certain. The inner compulsion to research and to inform the world of his findings, born in those long frustrating years before Magdalene College, had not yet abated; it took its toll. But there were other reasons. Although 'he was not given to laboured reworking of completed tasks'[5] he was a perfectionist. Prior to publication or oral delivery, he would write and rewrite his prose to ensure that, it not only conveyed his meaning but measured up to his highest standards of language.

He applied these same critical standards towards his work as an administrator, and looked for a similar approach to their duties from his senior colleagues and in particular his successor as Keeper, Nash-Williams. He was acutely conscious of his own dignity and status as Director; he had a hierarchical view of the responsibilities of others within the Museum. Credit for departmental achievements or research was automatically given to the Keeper, both in public and in private. This, as Grimes told me, was often to the acute disappointment of the originator, but in return it was required that the Keeper should be fully aware of all departmental activities and stamp his own authority upon their performance. Nash-Williams' pre-occupation with matters Roman, his absence on excavations and at the Caerleon Museum outstation for weeks at a time, meant that Grimes and Peate pursued their own paths. They dealt with interdepartmental and other enquiries or research as required, without reference to their Keeper. Fox was well aware of this unsatisfactory situation, but disliking any form of disciplinary action, shrank from confrontation, preferring to drop gentle hints in the hope that matters might improve. They never did. Nash-Williams continued on his Roman way and, perhaps by way of compensation, his Director maintained a more than usual interest in the Department's non-Roman affairs.

There was however one form of relaxation that Fox did permit himself, which gave him intense pleasure throughout his life, and that was walking. Although on occasions, especially in later life, he would walk alone, he much preferred congenial companionship and a setting, natural or man-made it mattered not, that provoked comment and discussion. Best of all was a round of contrasting countryside with perhaps an ancient site or mountaintop as an objective, a pub en-route for a pint, and a companion, who was new to the scene or at any rate appreciative of his views. Striding along, his arm frequently on his companion's shoulders, talking with unbounded enthusiasm, often quoting from favourite items of English poetry, he could change a mundane walk into an event that would never be forgotten. Stuart Piggott as a junior research assistant for the Royal Commission remembered his own first clear recollection of him 'striding across a Welsh moorland, hair blown by the wind, declaiming the "Hounds of Spring" chorus from Swinburne's Atlanta in Calydon.'[6] As reiterated to me 'What happy and treasured memory.'

* * *

Fox had first met Courtenay Ralegh Radford through their membership of the Archaeological Congress Excavation Committee, of which Radford was Secretary, and subsequently at the Antiquaries. Their acquaintanceship had become closer in 1929, when Radford was appointed Inspector of Ancient Monuments for Wales. Although based in London, this required frequent visits to the Principality. When business took him to Cardiff, he took advantage of the oft-repeated invitation to meet Olive and the children and to use Four Elms as a base. Their mutual interest in mediaeval history was combined when an opportunity arose for an excavation to investigate the origins of Kidwelly Castle in Carmarthenshire.

The Museum and the Society of Antiquaries were interested in polychrome pottery. Examples of this had been found at Kidwelly and presented to the Museum by the owner, Earl Cawdor. The Ministry of Works wanted to establish the constructional history of the castle before Radford wrote the guidebook. Much was known of the castle's history and it was easily dated. However the layout was a little strange; there was little distance between inner and outer curtains making the outer ward extremely cramped. It was known that a Norman castle had been built on or near the site but no trace of it had been found; the earliest surviving remains were thirteenth century. The excavation, sponsored by the Antiquaries with assistance provided by the Ministry of Works, was started by Fox in August 1930 and completed by Fox and Radford in

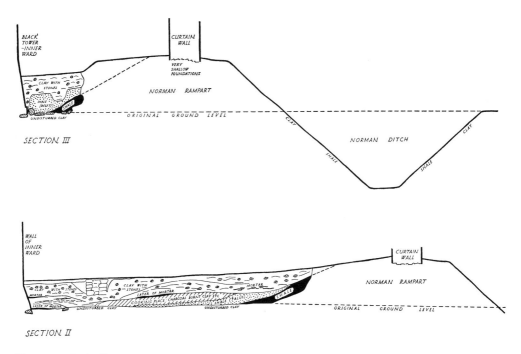

Figure 48: Kidwelly Castle – Sections establishing Norman origin (Society of Antiquaries of London)

March 1931. This established that the existing stone structures had been built on earlier foundations, replacing a Norman earth and wooden palisade fortress (Fig. 48). The inner curtain was the first to be rebuilt and needed to enclose as large an inner ward as possible – hence its earlier date and the restricted size of the outer ward. Some years later, when thought necessary or affordable, the physical characteristics of the site dictated that the outer curtain be raised on top of the then existing Norman ramparts. The six sections they had dug yielded fragments, mostly very small, of over a hundred vessels dated between 1100 and 1500 AD. However the most exciting find had taken place during repair work by the Ministry of Works, just prior to the start of excavations. A small midden in the outer ward was found to contain numerous potsherds. They were reconstructed by Gay, in the Archaeological Department workshop at the Museum, and found to represent no more than four almost complete vessels; three pitchers (Fig. 49), one of which was decorated in polychrome (see colour Plate 2), and a cooking pot. Although recognised as typical fourteenth century ware, the position of the midden at the foot of the inner curtain (ca.1320) provided firm evidence of a date of manufacture around the turn of the century.

The joint paper[7] presented to the Antiquaries in April 1932, suggested that this rare and valuable Mediterranean type ware was probably imported from southern France but, unusually for Fox, considered further research was needed before any final

Figure 49: Kidwelly Castle – Ewer illustrating the reconstruction work of Mr F. Gay in the Archaeological Department (National Museum of Wales)

conclusions could be drawn. It had been a highly satisfactory excavation for all parties and a useful opportunity for Fox and Radford to establish a most cordial working relationship; it was to stand them in good stead for a quarter of a century. Also present at Kidwelly, and to whom acknowledgement is made for his assistance, was the new Assistant Inspector Bryan O'Neil. He was to succeed Radford as Inspector in 1934 and became a particularly close colleague of Fox during the 1939–45 war.

The only other field activity in 1931 was the start of the Wat's Dyke survey. As Fox had commented in 1925 when beginning the Offa's Dyke survey, 'the investigation of that system of travelling earthworks cannot be considered complete until Wat's Dyke has in like manner been examined and the relation of one dyke to the other considered in all its aspects.' Although his assistant D. W. Phillips was away in Canada, he decided to press on by himself, with occasional assistance from friends such as W. J. Hemp when they could spare the time. The survey was scheduled to be completed in two seasons; unforeseeable circumstances would extend this to three. The combined results were published in one issue of *Archaelogia Cambrensis* in 1934.[8]

During this first year, Fox covered the northern section between the estuary of the Dee and Wrexham. There were many similarities to the northern part of Offa's Dyke, but although the line was clear there were long stretches where nothing could be found. The reasons for this might have been difficult to interpret were it not for his now considerable experience of the rationale behind Mercian dyke construction. There were no known sites of Roman or Dark Age occupation, and no objects of importance bearing on its age found on the bank or in the ditch, so Fox concluded that excavation would be a waste of time and money. Instead he concentrated on the more controversial parts of its alignment – many of the OS sheets were considered untrustworthy – and its design.

It was clear to him that the builders of this Dyke were sufficiently concerned about this northern flank, to plan for their barrier to be built right down to the Dee. However study of the missing sections led him to believe, on geographical and geological grounds, that this part of Flintshire included areas of dense woodland where no artificial barrier was needed. In the open country, where a barrier was required, it appeared to have been started at each end but never completed. This he explained by the sparse population in this largely uncultivated area and the consequent shortage of labour to undertake the task. He also considered that it was probably the last part to be built; it may well have been overtaken by events or by the decision to construct a new dyke a few miles to the west. Further south, except where the Dyke uses the River Alyn and some other smaller rivers and streams, it was virtually complete. This posed few problems, other than the physical effort involved in proving its non-existence in this densely wooded and steep terrain. At Wrexham, roughly half way, he called it a day and having finished his sections and, with Gay's support taken the necessary photographs, he returned to Cardiff.

*　*　*

Whilst working on Wat's Dyke Fox had had the opportunity to reflect on his writing commitments. Since 1926, when Methuen had asked him to write *Archaeology of Britain*, he had struggled with the necessary research and cataloguing of the mountain of material available, to extend his Cambridge regional thesis to the whole of England and Wales. He had been stimulated to accept the commission by O. G. S. Crawford, who had written towards the end of 1923. 'The next thing you must do is to bring out a textbook of British Archaeology. It is a crying need and will sell well.' Methuen had originally suggested a two-year contract, but this had been extended to 3–4 years. In 1929 when his health was threatened he had written to Methuen explaining the circumstances and asking them to find another author. But Methuen were adamant; not interested in anyone else, they intended 'to be more generous in the matter of time' and were 'confident that Fox would not fail them in the long run.' Having made his point as forcibly as he could Fox felt that he had little choice but to continue with the project; he promised nothing except to keep Methuen informed of progress. Lal Chitty had volunteered to produce the distribution maps and undertake the index. She produced the first batch of maps in the early summer of 1930. This stimulated Fox to start writing but he made little progress. It was this slow progress, when much of what he had to say could be produced quite quickly for a more limited publication, that that gave him cause for thought.

Coincidentally, shortly before leaving for the survey in North Wales, Fox had been asked by Sir Charles Peers, President of the Antiquaries, if he would be willing to give a key lecture on an archaeological subject to the forthcoming Prehistoric Congress. Peers had suggested the influence of Britain on its people. There seemed to be a connection between the two. This invitation had its origins at a meeting in 1929 in Berne. The Great War, as it was now being called, had brought to an end the old 'Congrès Internationale des Sciences Anthropologique et Archéologique'. Professor (later Sir) John L Myres and Professor Vere Gordon Childe, amongst others, believed that after a gap of twenty years it would be an appropriate time to revive this important international forum. Accordingly a committee meeting was held at which Myres and Childe represented Britain and Myres was elected Secretary. After considerable wrangling, statutes were drawn up for a new International Congress for Prehistoric and Protohistoric Sciences, and for the first Congress to be held in London. The invitations, being issued by Myres, were also subject to a certain degree of in-fighting amongst those anxious for the kudos of holding such a prestigious event, but equally concerned for the financial implications. Finally it was agreed that the Antiquaries would guarantee the event and that the Anthropological Institute would co-sponsor but take no financial risk.

In this circumstance it was understandable that the President of the Antiquaries should insist that he be nominated as President of the Congress and Chairman of the organising committee. Peers packed the committee with his own nominees and asked Fox to be the Welsh representative. Those attending the first committee meeting found that Peers had already decided on an outline programme under the broad title of 'Outstanding contributions of British Archaeology.' The Congress, scheduled for the first week of August 1932, would have a main lecture each morning and presentations of no more than 30 minutes in the afternoon. These would be to each of five groups, covering the spectrum from Human Palaeontology through Palaeolithic, Neolithic, Bronze and Early Iron Ages to the Transition from Prehistory to History. The Congress would open with a Presidential Address, outlining the history of prehistoric studies in Britain, and Peers intended that this would be followed by the keynote lecture on Britain's influence on its prehistoric inhabitants and invaders.

Fox had given considerable thought to this topic. His geographical approach to archaeology must have been the reason why Peers had nominated him. Therefore a title that reflected both the subject, and its geographical viewpoint, was essential. In the event he settled for 'The Personality of Britain'. He was also asked at this meeting to contribute to the delegates' handbook of prehistoric archaeology. Both were invitations he couldn't refuse, despite the considerable work they would entail and in any case it was work he would enjoy. The Methuen book was now definitely relegated to 1933.

*   *   *

Fox scarcely had time to settle down to the routine of the Museum after his 'three week holiday' in North Wales and to tackle the inevitable backlog of work when an urgent invitation arrived from McGill University, Montreal. The President of the Museum's Association, Sir Henry Miers, had recently visited McGill as part of a survey of Canadian museums, sponsored by the Carnegie Foundation. For some time McGill had felt the need for advice and recommendations for 'policy, future development and building programme for a modern University museum'[9] and sought his recommendation for this task. In proposing Fox, Sir Henry was recommending a Museums Association colleague and friend, whose administrative abilities were well established. Having studied the museum complex at McGill, Miers was also aware that it included an Ethnological Museum; expertise in the collection and display of 'folk' material was an essential qualification. In all respects Fox was admirably if not uniquely qualified.

Apart from the annual meeting of the Cambrian Archaeological Association, to which Fox was deeply committed, and another Prehistoric Congress committee meeting in mid-October, there were no outside commitments that could not be put off or cancelled. This was an excellent opportunity to spread the influence of the National Museum abroad and to mould the future of an entire Canadian museum complex. Sir Henry Miers request was considered by the Council on 25 September, in the knowledge that 'whilst no expense would fall on the National Museum of Wales, a month's special leave of absence of the Director would be necessary.' After discussion it was resolved 'that the Council has pleasure in authorising the Director to accept the invitation and to proceed to Canada after the meeting of the Court in October.' Accordingly he reserved a berth on the *SS Letitia,* of the Anchor-Donaldson Line, which was sailing from Liverpool on 24 October, returning by the same ship just under a month later.

In normal circumstances Fox had little interest in politics. He read the *Times* and *Western Mail* and the *Observer* on Sundays to keep himself informed on national and international affairs, but for political infighting he had little time; it rarely impinged on his museum or archaeological activities. However, the deteriorating economic situation that had plagued Ramsay MacDonalds' Government from the beginning, had led to the establishment by Parliament of the May Committee to enquire into the financial state of Britain and to propose economies. A run on sterling, that followed the May Committee's report, divisions in the Cabinet and warnings of swingeing cuts in public expenditure, made life for a museum administrator, so dependent on public funds, extremely worrying. At the end of September the rumours in the press that major economies would have to be made, proved to be only too true.

The *National Economy Act* imposed restrictions not only on expenditure but also on salaries. A Treasury Circular was received on 4 October; a special meeting of the Museum Finance Committee was held ten days later to decide on its implications. They reported that 'The Director, anticipating that the Council of the Museum would desire to meet the Treasury's request to curtail annual expenditure, having due regard to the efficient working of the Museum,' proposed savings of 5% for the rest of the financial year and a static budget for 1932–33. The circular had also informed all non-Government authorities that the cuts in Civil Service salaries that were being imposed ranged from 10% on salaries over £1000 to 3% for those earning less than £200. The Director proposed that Museum staff salaries be cut by similar amounts. A few days later Council endorsed these economies and Fox's salary was cut to £850. The Council added that they were particularly grateful to the staff for 'accepting these reductions' without complaint.

At the same time as these economic measures were being enforced the Bank of England raised the Bank Rate to 6%. Whilst private contributions in earlier years had, with Government grants, managed to sustain the building programme, there was an overdraft of some £6000 on the Building Account; interest charges would now be more than doubled. All in all it was a worrying time for to be leaving the country, albeit for only a month, but Archie Lee had shown himself to be more than capable of dealing with routine matters and in an emergency he could always be contacted by cable. Meanwhile the final stage of fitting out the east wing extension was progressing well; it was sufficiently advanced for Lee and the Keepers to plan their departmental moves into the new galleries. Council had just approved the appointment of an additional Uniformed Attendant, 'preferably with a knowledge of Welsh', and a cleaner to take up their duties before Christmas; there was also the question of an official opening to be considered. Tentative enquiries indicated that a member of the Royal Family would be prepared to attend but the new Lecture Theatre was some way off completion so all discussions on this could easily wait. Of more immediate importance was the fact that the country was facing its second General Election in two years and what the situation would be when that was all over. It looked as though Ramsay MacDonald's proposal for a National Government would receive electoral support but Fox would have to wait until he got back from Canada to learn the full details.

*   *   *

The *SS Letitia* was due to sail on an early tide; all passengers had been asked to board on the evening of Friday 23 October 1931. Fox travelled to Liverpool by train; a tedious journey that involved changing trains twice, but he was looking forward to a relaxing trip across the Atlantic and, being a poor sailor, hoping for fair weather. Arriving onboard he settled into his First Class cabin and changed for dinner where, together with David Allan, 'a dear old Scotsman', he sat at the Captain's table. Conversation at dinner that first night came round to the topic of the Sunday service; unless there was a minister onboard, this had to be taken by the Captain himself. Either the Captain was particularly persuasive or he had found a willing volunteer, for the following afternoon Fox wrote home to say, 'We reach Belfast at 8.0 PM and I hasten to send this note. You would think no haste was needed; but I have been asked to take the *Ship's Divine Service* tomorrow and I have to select hymns and psalms, reading and prepare a 10 minute sermon as the notices have to be out to-night. I shall be busy. I am going to take Isaiah 40.28 for my talk and read Isaiah 40 as the Lesson. … Service will be held in the 3rd Class Lounge so everybody will be present.'

This temporary priestly role was obviously convincing and successful 'The staff of the ship, I learn to my embarrassment, think that I am a Minister (in disguise???),' he wrote five days later, 'I am trying to live it down, of course not in ways a Mouse would disapprove of.' After Church 'I sat in the sun all day but since then we have had roughish weather, misty and dull. The Atlantic is a cruel looking sea under such conditions … I am a bit bruised, the roll of the ship sent me to the floor when I was immersed in the *Personality of Britain*! But the only part of me that hit the floor was the part meant to cushion the shock so you need not waste your sympathy. The ship is very comfortable, the range of food on the menu marvellous… and the stewards a first class lot of men. I have not been *actually ill* but *queasy* and at times the thought of food is more than I can bear. Just as well perhaps for there's little to do on a ship but eat! Thank God I have my work. I have rewritten the Congress paper on Britain and at last see some shape and character in it. I have had a few games of Bridge in the evenings and deck games (very mild) when such were possible.' At the end of his letter he added a note 'Please keep *all Times and Observers* for me. I feel lost and should like to read about the elections.'

The *SS Letitia* arrived in Montreal early on the following Sunday morning 1 November; he was met by Mr E. L. Judah, McGill University Museums Curator. He was taken to the Berkeley Hotel, which he described in a letter to Olive as 'comfortable, I have a bath and lavatory *en-suite*, writing table, telephone, all conveniences but jolly expensive; bed and breakfast about 18/- a day at present rates of exchange. Lucky I have plenty of money to pay for it.' That first Sunday was spent walking in Mount Royal Park and assessing the work from the papers that were waiting for him in his room. As his return passage was booked for 13 November, there were just two working weeks to accomplish the task.

His proposals, based on a necessarily brief but nevertheless thorough survey of the 16 University Museums, were published by McGill in February 1932.[9] His recommendations, which included the building of a new museum and a complete reorganisation of the often duplicated and desperately overcrowded collections, were fully accepted by the Principal and his senior colleagues. In their preface to the report they wrote that the citizens of Montreal 'will be concerned to know that [the McGill Museums] high educational value in illustrating the history of Canada … is greatly reduced by the grave limitations that Dr Fox describes. …To put it quite bluntly, it is plain that further additions of material, so necessary for the growth and development of our museums, will embarrass rather than assist the work of our University unless proper facilities for housing and exhibition are at the same time provided.' Much of his report is a damning indictment of the organisation, or lack of it, 'Case after case contains material ill-labelled, ill arranged, with numerous duplicates…some not touched for forty years.' He could find no policy directive for the museums and since there were only Honorary Curators, no one with the necessary authority to implement University instructions.

One instance of this was the extraordinary custom, in a predominantly French speaking Province, of writing all labels in English. Coming from the National Museum of Wales Fox was well aware of the unnecessary antagonism that a tactless practice such as this could arouse. Another was the unexplained absence of any professionally produced Guidebooks for visitors. Before leaving, Fox briefed Sir Arthur Currie and his Museum Committee of his findings. One notable omission from the subsequent published report, which was written during the return voyage to England, was any criticism of the Associated Art Gallery and the Chateau de Ramezay, even though they had been specifically mentioned in the remit. An article in the *Montreal Herald* expressed considerable misgivings at this omission, though praising Sir Arthur Currie for publishing the rest of the report; suggesting that the City of Montreal might not have come out of the original survey in a very favourable light.

* * *

Back in Cardiff work on linking the new east wing to the existing Museum building with the inevitable domestic upheaval that this caused, was beginning to dominate his life. In his spare time he worked on the Congress address which, with an enlarged text and additional illustrations, would be published in book form by the Museum. At the turn of the year he wrote to Lal Chitty to tell her of his intentions and to ask if he might use her 'Methuen' maps for both purposes, to which she readily agreed. In late January 1932 he reported to the Council that the East Wing extension and, what was to become known as the Reardon Smith Lecture Theatre, were nearing completion (Fig. 50); the architects could guarantee a hand over in October. The Council resolved to invite HRH The Prince of Wales to perform the opening ceremony – in the event he was unable to accept and the invitation was accepted by his younger brother HRH The Prince George. At the same meeting Fox suggested that senior staff should be urged to take their vacations early, to ensure that displays in the new galleries were not held up by the absence of key personnel. He intended to take his full annual three weeks holiday at Easter; he would also be away in August on Wat's Dyke, but would be returning to the Museum each weekend.

In February Cyril joined his brother Norman and sisters Dorothy and Mary for a weekend at Bursledon, to celebrate their parent's Golden Wedding anniversary. For this event he had commissioned a silver Rose Bowl from H. G. Murphy, a leading jeweller and silversmith, who taught at the LCC School of Arts and Crafts. Fox was a great admirer of Murphy's beaten silver work; he later commissioned several other pieces for himself including a pair of silver ashtrays, the origins of which he loved to relate. Fox had had a very happy working relationship with Sir William Reardon Smith, initially as Treasurer and, since succeeding Lord Pontypridd in 1927, as President. Shortly after handing over the Presidency to the Earl of Plymouth, Sir William pressed an envelope into Fox's hand with the injunction 'Spend this on yourself my boy.' Utterly embarrassed and not knowing what to do with the Five Pound note he found inside, which he knew he should not accept but could not return, Fox decided to seek the advice of Mr Murphy. Many years before he had acquired two rare One Shilling silver tokens; one issued in Hampshire and the other in Newport, Isle of Wight. On his next trip to London he visited the studio and between them they designed an ashtray, with a token caught in the centre, on which he could knock out his pipe or

*Figure 50:　Naltional Museum of Wales. Top: Central Block and Entrance Hall from the south 1928.
Bottom: East Wing and Reardon Smith Lecture Theatre 1932 (National Museum of Wales)*

extinguish a cigarette. Around the rim of each of the two ashtrays was engraved the inscription *Sir William Reardon Smith dono dedit*. Sir William's Five-Pound note did not go far towards covering the cost but honour was satisfied.

The 1932 Easter break, his first proper holiday, had been 'arranged' by Olive, Louis Cobbett and W. M. Palmer. The latter was a General Practitioner and Antiquarian from Linton in Cambridgeshire, who had been associated with Fox when working on Fleam Dyke in 1921. He had now become a close friend and was known to all the family as 'Uncle' Palmer. Together, they had decided that the only way to ensure that Cyril had a complete rest was to separate him from his papers and take him abroad. Knowing him only too well, whatever their plans he might refuse to go with them, a carrot was required to tempt him away from his desk – surely an 'Hellenic Cruise' would prove irresistible. Departing from Victoria on Thursday 17 March, they would all embark in the *'Queen Mary'* at Venice three days later and spend a fortnight visiting all the most important archaeological sites; the schedule included Athens, Constantinople, Troy, Knossos and Mycenae. The ship was due to return to Venice on Thursday 5 April and they would arrive back at Victoria three weeks from departure to the day. The combination of a fortnight in the Mediterranean sun, seeing all the treasures he had read about and never seen, with Cobbett and Palmer to keep him company, did indeed prove irresistible; the bookings were confirmed.

Olive left Cardiff first, taking the children to her mother in Steyning and arranging to meet her husband for lunch at the Grosvenor. This extravagant start to their holiday arose from an invitation from Ralegh Radford, who needed to see Fox on Congress business. His chance invitation led indirectly to an encounter that was, in due course, to have far reaching consequences. Radford readily recalled the occasion for me.[10] 'In view of the train's early afternoon departure I suggested the Grosvenor rather than a restaurant. After lunch we went down into the station and across to the platform where we joined by Olive's sister [Mary]. Whilst we were standing there I saw Aileen Henderson with her father and two other young ladies I was shortly to learn were her sisters. She spotted me and waved. I knew Walter Scott Henderson slightly, we met at the Antiquaries, and although I knew that Cyril had met Aileen when we visited the excavations at Richborough [in 1929], I did the introductions and we all remained chatting together until it was time for the train to depart.'

Fox kept a diary of the trip starting with their arrival at Milan and ending with their final expedition from the ship to Split. It is mostly a series of personal notes on archaeological and architectural details for use at some future date; it also contains some vivid impressions of the scenery and the people he saw. That both he and Olive thoroughly enjoyed their holiday is evident. – he, with Cobbett and Palmer, rushed hither and thither missing nothing and enthusing over all that he saw; she, happy that her husband had at last been separated from his book, pottered and painted. The *Queen Mary* that they had joined at Venice turned out to be the *SS Kralica Marija*, with crew and food as Yugoslav as the name. This apparently irritated Walter Scott

Henderson, who was expecting a British ship and disliked Yugoslav food, but probably passed unnoticed by Fox – he was too involved in the sights. It was at Mycenae that he met up with Aileen again, as is recalled in her own memoirs; she clearly made little impression on him at the time, and is not mentioned in his diary.

The vignettes of this holiday of a lifetime are the personal memories. Sailing from Candia 'after a drink of heady Cretan wine taken at Olive's suggestion at a tavern by the harbour so that we only needed to fall into the ship's launch.' Being taken from Nauplia to Mycenae with a driver who 'drove like a Jehu over pot-holed roads and scattered a group of peasants at a cross-roads nearly running over two of them.' Driving past strings of camels at 40 mph on the road to Troy, causing one to 'wonder how long such archaic transport can survive' and on the return journey 'when our car got a puncture after going at 70 kph for a breathless spell, being entertained by a man playing a concertina' whilst the necessary repairs were completed. For their children, when recounting their experiences, the most memorable occasion took place at Delos. The ship had arrived at midday and there were only a few hours available before sailing for Crete, so only one opportunity to go ashore. Their mother wasn't ready and father was not prepared to abandon the trip, so left without her. He assumed she would spend the afternoon quietly onboard, but had reckoned without her charm and winning ways. As his boat neared the shore the Captain's launch swept past with a single passenger; Olive was on the jetty to greet them.

* * *

Four months later Fox was standing nervously at the lectern in a lecture theatre at King's College London awaiting the moment when he would be invited to speak. Like so many accomplished lecturers his nerves vanished as soon as he started to talk but until that moment he would feel physically ill; on an unique occasion such as this doubly so. The financial restrictions imposed after the *National Economy Act* were still in force. To the extreme disappointment of the Archaeology Department, the Museum would only allow their two contributors, Fox and Peate, to attend. Nevertheless, in this truly international gathering, Fox was surrounded by friends and colleagues willing him to achieve the success they knew was his due. Lal Chitty, Louis Clarke, Stuart Piggott, and my other godfather Professor Daryll Forde, who had come down from Aberystwyth with Fleure, are probably the names that would come most readily to his mind, excluding fellow members of the organising committee.

That the lecture was a success goes without saying; Piggott recalled it being the dominant topic of conversation at the Congress. For Fox it gave him international recognition as one of the great archaeologists of the twentieth century. For the Council of the National Museum of Wales there was the knowledge that they had a Director, whose influence and achievement was far greater than they could ever have imagined. The published version of *The Personality of Britain* became a 'best seller' in

Figure 51: Classic Peanuts by Schultz – Cyril Fox and the Beaker Folk (Knight Features)

four editions.[11] It became a standard school text book (Fig. 51), selling more copies for the Museum than any other publication, other than guide books, before or since. To those familiar with *Archaeology of the Cambridge Region* and his subsequent papers, there was nothing new in the framework of what he said, but for the first time his geographical concept was being applied to the whole country, and throughout the Neolithic to Iron Age periods. 'The climate resulting from the position of the islands and the soil derived from its structure, determined the vegetable life which she nourished, and the animal life she harboured. Her indented coastline offered convenient harbourage for invaders; her deep estuaries and slow moving rivers invited penetration.' Thus the scene was set for his thesis of the 'Highland and Lowland zones' which, since first appearing in 1926, had dominated his approach to pre-Roman archaeological problems to the south of the Forth-Clyde isthmus. Invaders easily overran the lowland areas of Britain adjacent to the Continent and they usually imposed their cultures. When they reached the Highland zones to the west their impetus was weakened and their cultures tended to be absorbed. The Lowlands provided the largest area of fertile and habitable ground; hence supporting wealthier populations than the Highlands. There was greater unity of culture in the Lowland Zone; greater continuity in the Highland Zone.

Fox developed this theme by discussing the influence of climate and geology upon the inhabitants of Britain, as he had done before for East Anglia. There, prehistoric man sought low hills and plateaux, with porous sub-soils or gravel terraces; shunning the densely forested claylands. In the Highland Zone, man could not comfortably live in our wet and cold winters above a certain level whatever the soil; 'Hence,' as Fox emphasised in a key sentence, 'soil character was the controlling factor in Lowland distribution, elevation in Highland distribution.' The printed version of the lecture was much expanded. It contained many more of the distribution maps upon which the thesis was founded. As Fox wrote in his introduction, these maps illustrate for us 'where in this island Early Man lived and laboured.' Archaeologists and geographers alike enthusiastically accepted his contention that the dominating factors connecting these distribution patterns were climate, elevation and geology.

Well over half a century later it is difficult to conceive the impact that this 'essay' had upon historical and geographical teaching in the early thirties. The co-operation of his senior colleagues from the Geological, Botanical and Zoological Departments, North, Hyde and Simpson's replacement Colin Matheson, a routine feature of Museum activity, provided a broad scientific basis for the thesis; they added considerably to its academic weight. Fox's predecessor Wheeler, writing in the *Archaeological Journal* wrote, 'the hackneyed phrase "epoch-making" can be used in a more than usually complete sense. For the work does in fact mark a definite epoch in the study of the prehistory and protohistory of these islands. ... The general importance, not only of the geographical position of the British Isles but also their geological structure, had been present in the minds of the principal archaeological scholars of this country during the first dozen years of the century. Haverfield, Thurlow Leeds, Professor Myres and Crawford, each in turn developed the theme but amongst those, who in the last decade have developed the principles underlying this impulse, Dr Fox stands without peer.' Fleure, reviewing the book for *Archaeologia Cambrensis* stated, 'With characteristic energy the Director of the National Museum of Wales has prepared this publication which is ... a contribution to knowledge that is of wide archaeological interest far beyond Wales ... [and] which relates to geographical studies in a way that has made him one of the foremost of archaeological geographers.'

There were inevitably many letters from archaeologists, historians and geographers, some known, some unknown. Amongst the former is that of Professor G. M. Trevelyan 'the amount of pleasure you have given me in life recently is great. It is twofold. First an extra zest to my walks in Cambridgeshire in following your splendid book about its archaeology. Secondly a mental bird's eye view of the early history of our island. The "Personality" recapitulates it all so well. Above all I like pp 82–3 [The Epilogue – a sketch of the 'essential Britain' in the dawn of the Iron Age] though I have read it all through at a sitting with delight.'

The enduring quality of this work is delightfully demonstrated by the geographer and historian Professor E. G. R. Taylor's review of the Fourth Edition in 1943.[12] 'When *The Personality of Britain* first appeared in 1932 it gave quite a shock to geographers, startling some into noise and motion rousing others from apathetic acceptance of neglect. This essay ... might be described as the focus of a minor earthquake corresponding to the number 6 on the Rossi-Forel scale. "General awakening of those asleep. General ringing of bells. Some startled persons leave their dwellings." Why did the bells ring? Because there appeared from the pen of a non-geographer, a geographical interpretation of the prehistory of Britain. Historians to be sure had always allowed that, insofar as contiguity and distance in the horizontal plane were geographical facts, geography was relevant to history. But here was an archaeologist of repute going the whole way, accepting the geographer's major thesis, namely that human settlement, migration, land use, transport, economic and social life, can only be understood in relation to the whole geographical sequence: position, shape, size, structure, relief, drainage, climate, soils, vegetation and the rest. True that a lead had earlier been given by Mr O. G. S. Crawford but he is "sui generis". In a second direction *The Personality of Britain* had an importance greater than its modest size and format would suggest. It demonstrated outside geographical circles that the distribution map is not merely a convenient method of factual illustration but may be a fruitful instrument of research through the relationships that the pattern upon it suggests. How freakish does the run of Roman roads about York appear until we plot it on the geological map.'

Of course there were critics. When the Highland-Lowland zone concept had first been suggested in 1926 in his Kilpaison Burrows paper,[13] there were those who thought his division too precise. As Grimes subsequently stated, 'with later knowledge we were to find that there was greater activity in the Highland zone than Fox envisaged, not as richly, but the same kind of activity and the same dates as the Lowland zone in England'. A second issue was raised by Grahame Clark, pointing out that there is 'a serious danger implicit in the use of [distribution] maps that has not always been fully appreciated by archaeologists. In so far as archaeological distributions are determined by geographical factors they are determined by the *contemporary* and not the *present* geographical environment. But geographical environment is no more static than climate or plant life. In so far as there has been geographical change since the period with which he is immediately dealing, the archaeologist who assumes the present state of affairs as a background for his map is thereby vitiating the very basis of his evidence.'[14] Fox had always accepted that with time further discoveries would be made. These might invalidate or require him to modify his theories, but as he made clear in the introduction to the fourth edition, 'the essay is to present principles and not to present the prehistory of Britain'. In that purpose its reputation must stand as high today as it did when first published seventy years ago.

One matter only dealt with in passing is the title. Although Wheeler in his Homage[15] has said that the *Personality of Britain* provided 'a pattern and a stimulus [that] has inspired emulation as far afield as India,'[16] the use of the word in this context was not original. It was first developed by the French geographer Paul Vidal de la Blanche, who in 1908 he wrote the first section of the great 'Histoire de la France' entitled 'La France: Tableau Geographique'. The English translation of this sub-title is 'The Personality of France.' When discussing this with me in 1986, Glyn Daniel said that, 'he had always been puzzled by the lack of recognition to La Blanche, and also to Sir Halford Mackinder, who taught at Oxford and had used the phrase "personality of Britain" in *Britain and the British Seas.*' Knowing that Fox had not read Mackinder and could not read French, Daniel said, 'these ideas were circulating generally in geographical circles in Wales and impinged upon sympathetic archaeologists through general conversation and lectures. Certainly I now realise there was no direct reflection of either French geographers or Mackinder in Cyril's work, but it was the overall concept of that time that affected him and thus produced both the content and title of "The Personality of Britain".'

* * *

Having already taken his annual holiday at Easter and with so much work to do in August, mostly away from home, Cyril and Olive had decided that she would take the children for a long summer break by the sea. Olive had reserved rooms for three weeks with the possibility of extending for a fourth at the Bell View, a guesthouse at Llangennith[17] on the western side of the Gower peninsula. Fox drove them down on the Saturday 30 July and left the following day to return to Cardiff. From there he went on by train to London for the Congress. It was at Llangennith on the following Thursday 4 August that Olive received a letter-card from her husband to tell her 'The lecture was a *glorious success*. I was *amazed* because I felt I had not done it as well as I had hoped. But nobody noticed the failure in certain parts.' By the same post she received a much longer letter from Harry Randall, a Bridgend solicitor, who was a well-known amateur archaeologist and close family friend, who had also attended the Congress. He had told her all the news and how her husband's address had been cheered at great length by the delegates.

Immediately after the Congress Fox had returned to Cardiff, spending Friday and Saturday nights with their architect neighbours Alwyn and Ethel Lloyd, before departing for Oswestry on Sunday. Olive wrote to him at home on the Thursday. 'Thank you for your short card! (Mousie expected a letter!!!) I am so very glad *the* lecture was such a huge success. I knew it would be. …I still have not quite recovered from not being there' and in a footnote she added 'I hope you will get this before leaving for Watt's Dyke [sic], I do not know any addresses in future.' Fox's intention had been to spend about ten days based upon Oswestry, staying at the Wynnstay Hotel, making his way back to Cardiff via Ludlow to see Bryan O'Neil's dig at Titterstone Clee Hill on Thursday 18 August and Kerry Hills Ridgeway the following day. After a week in Cardiff (22–26 August), which included an important reception and a committee meeting, it was back to the dyke where he would meet Wheeler (27–28 August). They had planned to go on together to Newtown, for the Annual General Meeting of the Cambrians, and then to York for the Yorkshire Philosophical Society. It was an extremely busy schedule. Most of the correspondence between Olive and himself was concerned with family arrangements; giving notice to Nanny Goode and arranging for her to leave with her luggage on 18 August, and collecting his family from Llangennith, before the next guests arrived to take over their rooms on Saturday 27 August.

On her arrival at Llangennith, Olive had almost immediately made herself known to the local Vicar, the Reverend (Father) W. H. A. Willmer. Olive frequently refers to him as 'Little Father'; he appears to have taken Olive and the children under his wing, accompanying them to the Blue Pool Bay beach on several occasions. Bell View was not as close to the beach as Olive would have wished, and without help to carry things up and down it was too much of a trek to undertake every day. On Friday 19 August Father Willmer had accompanied Olive and the children to the beach. They had all played together on the sands and swum in the shallows, when Olive told them she was going to swim out to the point to see the birds. Felicity told her mother not to go. She started to swim after her but felt the pull of the current and struggled back to the shore. Olive swam on. It was only a matter of a hundred yards but she was caught by the tidal stream, swept rapidly round Broughton Point and out to sea. The children could hear their mother crying and called frantically for help. Father Willmer went into the water but, realising the current was too strong, came back to raise the alarm. Leaving the children with some other holidaymakers, he ran to the other end of the beach and managed to attract the attention of a passing fishing boat. By the time Olive had been located and picked up it was too late.

'Gower Bathing Tragedy: Welsh Museum Director's Wife Drowned: Within Sight of Daughters' were the headlines to the article in Saturday's afternoon paper. 'Dr Fox receives the sad news at the National Museum, Cardiff.' With Phillips, he had spent the night at Ludlow and had just returned to Cardiff for an early and unscheduled meeting with the President of the Council, only to be told of the tragedy. Lord Plymouth insisted that Fox had to be accompanied by Archie Lee and that they were both driven in Lord Plymouth's car to Gower, to join the two girls and to attend the inquest. The inquest was held shortly after he arrived. The Coroner returned a verdict of 'Accidental Death' adding that 'no-one was in any way to blame for this tragedy.' Although not well known to holidaymakers Blue Pool Bay was known to be dangerous for bathing at certain states of the tide; it was unfortunate that Olive happened to be swimming in that particular place at that time.

Fox was an extremely emotional person and was totally overcome. It was left to Archie Lee and Father Willmer to make the necessary arrangements for the funeral at Steyning, and to take Olive's body from Wales to Sussex; he was, according to all reports, certainly incapable of doing anything himself. The children had spent the night at the Vicarage, their father joining them after the inquest. Father Willmer then accompanied them all on the train to Steyning and helped to officiate at the service. This was held in the Parish Church where her father had been Vicar for over thirty years. Fox forbade his children to attend but his goddaughter Rosalind, Olive's niece, was there and remembered the occasion vividly. 'I had never before seen a grown man weep unrestrainedly and he was quite shattered for a time. Rhiwbina was a happy household and Cyril and Olive were most devoted. We always called him Uncle Peter and when I asked my mother [Mary Congreve-Pridgeon] why, she said Olive calls him Peter because he holds the keys of heaven.'

After the service Olive was buried beside her father at the eastern end of the churchyard, where in due course her mother was to join them. A tall cross marks the grave and though the inscriptions are difficult to decipher, her own somewhat strange epitaph can be read with the help of the shadows of the midday sun. 'In memory of Olive Fox younger daughter of Arthur and Jesse Congreve-Pridgeon: Beloved wife of Cyril Fox Director of the National Museum of Wales, who passed suddenly into rest at Llangennydd Gower Glamorgan on August 19 1932. She served her master and her faith and was beloved by all who knew her. Her husband and daughters, Felicity and Penelope, have caused this record of her gracious personality to be inscribed. Faithful unto death.'

Her obituary in the *Western Morning News* had originated the latter phrase. 'She was a woman of gracious and outstanding personality, versatile and talented. Her particular interests were art and music and she also shared her husband's interest in archaeology. She was a patron of the National Orchestra of Wales' concerts at the City Hall… and was also intimately connected with the Cardiff Naturalists Society of which Dr Fox is an ex-President.' These interests and the churches with which she was connected, at nearby Llanishen where she worshipped, St Dyfrig's in Cardiff and Llangennith where she died, all were represented in a veritable host of floral tributes that flooded the graveside in a sea of blossom. In the curious way that tragedies of this nature so often reveal, whilst staying at Llangennith Olive had spoken to her younger daughter of death and her fear of dying in water. This is not a subject one would expect to raise with an eight-year-old, unless there was an overwhelming conviction that death was near at hand. It would be hard to challenge the view that her mother knew she was going to die.

After the funeral the children were taken to Ifield to stay with their father's sister Dorothy. Their future was 'arranged' by the clergy with whom Olive had been so closely associated; both of them were sent to the Convent of St Agnes and St Michael at East Grinstead. Their father was clearly quite incapable of looking after them and East Grinstead was very close to Steyning enabling their grandmother to visit them and take them 'home' for half-terms and holidays. Felicity found sufficient strength to endure this new life, she had had experience of school away from home, but Penelope was miserable, desperately missing her mother and unable to obtain from her father the comfort and love that she needed. He returned alone to Cardiff and to the empty house at Rhiwbina. For him the only consolation was work; he threw himself into the fray with a desperate intensity. Triumph and tragedy are frequent partners, separated for him by little more than a fortnight, but thankfully the dark days of loneliness were to be short lived and happiness would soon return to his life.

Notes

[1] President Museums Association 1928–1933 whom Fox succeeded in 1934

[2] Sleds, Carts and Wagons *Antiquity* V

[3] I. Peate *Rhwng dau fyd* (Between two worlds) pp. 102–107 *Ailargraffiad (Aberystwyth)* 1980 Translation of Welsh text arr. D. Bassett

[4] The National Museum of Wales: Museum's Affiliation Scheme *Mus.Journ.* 30

[5] E. M. Jope *Dictionary of National Biography* 1961–1970 p. 383–5

[6] *Br.Acad.* LIII p. 400

[7] Kidwelly Castle Carmarthenshire: including a survey of Polychrome Pottery found there and elsewhere in Britain. *Arch.* LXXXIII. G. C. (Gerald) Dunning, who was interested in polychrome

ware, provided the Appendix. The decision to include the Appendix with the paper delayed publication until 1933

[8] Wat's Dyke – A Field Survey *Arch.Camb.* LXXXIX

[9] *McGill University Report* 1932

[10] Interview with the author 1987

[11] The Fourth Edition was reprinted in 1959 with minor amendments.

[12] E. G. R. Taylor review of Fourth Edition 1943 *Antiquity* XVIII p. 103

[13] A Bronze Age Barrow on Kilpaison Burrows, Rhoscrowther, Pembrokeshire p. 28 *Arch.Camb.* LXXXI

[14] G. Clark review of Fourth Edition revised 1959 *Antiquity* XXXIV

[15] *Culture and Environment* 1963 p. 4

[16] B. Subbarao *The Personality of India*, Baroda 1956; Carl O. Sauer The Personality of Mexico, *American Geographical Review* July 1941; Roger Summers The Personality of Rhodesia, *Proceedings of the American Philosophical Society* 1960, E. E. Evans *The Personality of Wales BBC Wales Radio Lecture* 23 Nov 1973

[16] In some reports the alternative spelling Llangennech or Llangennydd is used

VIII

Fame But No Fortune 1932–1939
To the Pinnacle of Academe

That Fox was able to cope with the emotional pressures, in the period following Olive's funeral, was due to the unstinting support of his family and friends, as well as the sheer necessity to pick up the pieces of his life and to tackle his responsibilities as Director. The most urgent of these tasks was arranging the Royal opening of the East Wing extension in October. The daily administrative routine augmented by the detailed planning for the visit of HRH The Prince George (later Duke of Kent), more than filled his working hours. In the evenings and at weekends, it was the kindness and understanding extended by colleagues and friends, such as his next door neighbours, the solicitor Edward Lewis and his wife Amy (whom we all knew as Lulu), that prevented him from brooding over what might have been, and descending into despair. Since Nanny Goode had left in August, there was no one to keep him company or to look after the house. For the first few weeks his sisters, Dorothy and Babs, took it in turn to stay and help him come to terms with his loss. They made arrangements for the disposal of Olive's clothing and other personal possessions. Babs also managed to find a lady – described by Aileen as a prim elderly housekeeper[1] – to keep the house in order and do basic cooking, so that he was not left totally unsupported when she left. He drove down to Steyning to visit the children for the occasional weekend, but he was not able to give them a home, or the support that they needed; he devolved that heavy responsibility on their grandmother.

Although the Government's imposed financial restrictions took a little of the gloss off this second Royal occasion for which Fox had been responsible, it was nevertheless a well organised and entertaining occasion. The Prince, who was also receiving the Freedom of the City of Cardiff, found much of interest in the exhibits that he was taken to see, the whole visit being far less formal than that in 1927 (Fig. 52). Among the galleries opened by the Prince in the new East Wing, was the Circular Gallery. Situated above the main auditorium of the Lecture Theatre, it was purposely designed to be off the main sequence of galleries and kept for special exhibitions. As Douglas Bassett described, 'It was to provide room for displaying material from the Museum collections, which could not be permanently exhibited, and for loan collections from

Left: HRH visits the Folk Culture Gallery in the new East Wing with Fox and Dr Iowerth Peate before going on to open the Reardon Smith Lecture Theatre

Below: HRH accompanied by the Director, Secretary Captain 'Archie' Lee and President Sir William Reardon Smith

Figure 52: National Museum of Wales – Official Opening of the East Wing and Reardon Smith Lecture Theatre by HRH Prince George 1932 (Western Mail & Echo Ltd)

outside sources. The Lecture Theatre, named to commemorate the munificent benefactions of Sir William and Lady Reardon Smith, embodied in its structure the results of contemporary research in acoustics and was generally considered to be all that could be desired for lecturer and listener.[2] The inaugural lecture was given on 2nd November by Professor (later Sir) John Lloyd. This was followed by the first of a series of presentations that Fox gave to the schoolchildren of Cardiff on the aims and objects of the Museum.

At the AGM that followed the official opening, the Court of Governors gratefully acknowledged the extra work that had been undertaken by all Museum staff. Their rather stiff and formal resolution was typical of the period; clearly well intentioned and apparently well received. They expressed 'to the Director and Staff their appreciation of the completeness of the exhibits in the new galleries, and the excellence of the labelling; and of the efficient manner in which the arrangements in connexion [sic] with the Opening were carried out. The Court realises that only by a sustained effort was it possible to have carried through successfully, in so short a time, so heavy a task.'

With this official occasion now behind him, Fox found his diary being filled with a succession of Museums Association, Antiquaries, Royal Commission and Cambrian committee meetings, in London and throughout Wales. He had accepted the Presidency of the Cambrian Archaeological Association for 1933 and was determined to ensure that the Annual General Meeting was held in Cardiff. Wat's Dyke had been put off until next year and there were no other outstanding excavation or survey reports; this allowed him to give the four-day Cambrian programme rather more attention than usual. He had also agreed to accept the Presidency of the Prehistoric Society of East Anglia, but this only required a presidential address and attendance at their annual dinner. However both speeches were extremely important. Most leading archaeologists were attending one or the other, so though the topics to be covered had already been decided, he knew he would have to devote much time and effort to their content.

Although Nash-Williams took little interest in the work of his Assistant Keepers, Fox, as previously mentioned, was well aware of Peate's excellent work cataloguing and displaying the Museum's growing collection of folk material. He was also aware that old and dying Welsh rural industries needed to be identified; their buildings, tools and working practices *had* to be preserved. He therefore drew up a memorandum for the Council to formally establish a sub-department that would combine these two regimes; whilst retaining Nash-Williams' overall responsibility. The Council accepted his proposal at their meeting in January 1933. They resolved to 'establish in the Department of Archaeology a sub-department of Folk Culture and Industries in the charge of an Assistant Keeper, who shall have charge of the national Welsh Folk Collections.' This initiative paved the way for the declaration by the Council in 1934 of the need to provide an Open Air Museum as an annex to the National Museum, and two years later for the upgrading of this sub-department to full departmental status. Fox received considerable support in this enterprise from his friend Leonard Twiston-Davies, who took great interest in the sub-department and donated £500, a considerable sum in those days, towards research and for 'propaganda'.

* * *

One of the more difficult personal tasks was replying to the scores of letters of condolence, mostly from close family and professional friends but some from comparative strangers. Amongst the latter was one from Aileen Henderson, whom he had met briefly at Richborough in 1929 and who, with her father and sisters, had also been on that memorable Hellenic cruise in April. *Personality of Britain* had been published by the Museum at the beginning of September. Fox had already given the Secretary instructions to forward complimentary copies to the more important people, who had attended the Congress. In addition to this 'official' list, he had sent personal inscribed copies to family and friends and now added one to Aileen. Her acknowledgement was 'a cool response' but a subsequent invitation to meet him at the Antiquaries led to a working weekend at Cardiff, staying with his friends Joe and Barbara Blundell. He was a member of the Council and lived at Nottage Court, on the edge of the dunes at Merthyr Mawr, near Bridgend. After several other meetings in London Cyril was invited to meet her family at their home in Surrey.

Aileen's father, Walter Scott Henderson, whom he had met briefly on Victoria Station with Ralegh Radford, was a solicitor working in the city as a partner in the firm of Stephenson Harwood and Tatham. He specialised in company affairs, with a particular concern for the Hong Kong and Shanghai Banking Corporation in which his father Dr Edward Henderson had a considerable interest. This interest stemmed from Dr Henderson's appointment in 1869, as Medical Officer of Health for the British colony in Shanghai. Serving both as Government official and in private practice for thirty years, he was able to offer the British community the expertise of an Edinburgh trained GP and Surgeon. One of the leading figures of that community in the 1870s, with whom Dr Henderson established a life-long friendship, was David McLean. At the time he was manager of the Shanghai branch but later became a Director of the Hong Kong and Shanghai Bank.[3] The family friendship became even closer when, in 1905, Dr Henderson's second son Walter married David McLean's eldest daughter Alice. They lived in Cottesmore Gardens, Kensington, for fifteen years during which time they had three daughters: the eldest, Aileen, was born in 1907. Immediately after the Great War Walter Scott Henderson decided to move out of London. He bought a small property, which he subsequently greatly enlarged and renamed 'The Grange', on a four acre plot in Walton-on-the-Hill. On this site he and his wife created an extremely attractive garden, with an abundance of plants that he collected from all over Europe.

Although all three of their children were to pursue independent careers in archaeology, art and the ballet, Aileen was the only one to elect for University training. She had gone up to Cambridge in 1926 to read English at Newnham, but found that her real interest lay in archaeology. After graduating she had spent three seasons cataloguing and arranging the finds from the Bushe-Fox excavation at Richborough. She had also spent six months in Rome at the British School, studying the Roman and Etruscan civilisations, which led some fifteen years later to her special interest in Romano-British archaeology.

Fox found a warm welcome at The Grange; Walter and he had much in common and Alice took to him immediately. It soon became clear that Aileen was destined, not just to fill the void in Fox's life created by Olive's death, but to be an active partner in his professional activities. With 25 years between them it was not surprising that Aileen's parents had some misgivings, as to the suitability of Cyril as their future son-in-law, but they were short-lived; the engagement was announced in March and the wedding planned for July. All that remained was to introduce Aileen to Felicity and Penelope – a rather stilted occasion at London Zoo. Step relationships are never easy; the circumstances of their mother's death, combined with their ages of 13 and 9, made acceptance extremely hard. Their father, the only person who could have helped his daughters to accept his re-marriage, was as always totally immersed in his professional life and unable to provide the lead that was required. In time they all came to terms with the new situation; for the girls, life at Four Elms could never be the same; for Aileen, the letters CF OF over the front door, would be a constant reminder of her predecessor.

*   *   *

Fox planned to use most of his annual leave for their honeymoon in Spain but accepted an invitation from George Pitt-Rivers to join him for his Easter field meeting in Dorset. Glyn Daniel told me of his vivid memories of that group, 'George and I with Wheeler, Fox, Hemp, and the two babies Hawkes and Piggott, all reading one another lectures and visiting sites around the county. Fox was particularly thrilled to see Maiden Castle. Wheeler, leading him round with his long legs striding out along the ramparts, Fox struggling to keep up with twice as many steps and the rest of us following in their wake. A truly bizarre sight, both of them talking non-stop and full of enthusiasm and fun.'

There was also the Wat's Dyke survey to be completed for which Dudley Phillips, on leave from Canada for a month, had arranged to join him (Fig. 53). This survey covered the Dyke from Wrexham to its southern end at Pentrecoed Farm, in Shropshire. Fox, like those who had mapped it before him, was uncertain where it actually ended. There was no geographical reason for its termination at the Morda Brook and no trace of a line beyond this point, despite the apparently suitable terrain.

Figure 53: Wat's Dyke – Fox and Phillips (at the foot of the Dyke) near Oswestry 1933 (Cambrian Archaeological Association)

He found that the Dyke, being constructed almost entirely on lowland with flat or gentle gradients, was of fairly uniform design with a considerable bank and well made western ditch. This was all in marked contrast to Offa's work, a mile or two to the west, where steeper contours made for scarps and ditches could be found on either or both sides of the bank.

In completing his survey of all the dykes in this March land, Fox felt able to place Wat's Dyke in its historical context. He believed that it was a frontier designed to present a visible barrier to the highlanders when they reached the lowlands, whereas Offa's Dyke controlled access to those plains and incorporated defensible positions. No objects had ever been found in the ditch or on the bank that could provide firm dating, but being of similar design it was clearly of the near Offan period. Fox concluded that the balance of historical evidence pointed to the need for the construction of this boundary rampart by Offa's predecessor, Ethelbald. It, he assumed, 'thus precedes by not more than one generation the final effort to define the whole western frontier of Mercia undertaken by Offa. It may have been still a building when Offa came to the throne in 757 AD. If so the name of Wada, the Helper in time of need, was doubtless given it in compliment to the new king.' Fox ended by stating that the survey was laborious to perform and perhaps tedious to read.

Wat's Dyke was certainly far less dramatic than Offa's Dyke, and its publication did not produce so much correspondence or comment.[4] However the evidence of system and organisation in the northern Marches clearly impressed R. G. Collingwood. In his letter of 14 January 1935 he linked this survey with Fox's theories of highland and lowland cultures. He pondered the 'question whether the curious blend of poetry and practicality that makes up the historic character of the English people from the middle ages may not be a cross between the poetic, idealistic and somewhat slum minded Celt, who couldn't in the least assimilate the lessons in efficiency that Rome tried to teach him, and the dry, tough and persevering Low German temperament of these dyke building pioneers. For me, and I judge from your *Personality of Britain* for you too, it is this modern England that is the problem we archaeologists are trying to explain. This new paper of yours adds another quite important chunk of evidence towards the way in which the problem is more and more coming to present itself, to my mind, as the question of how exactly Celt and Germanic strains contributed to the final result.'

* * *

Cyril and Aileen were married in July; after a weekend near Farnham, they sailed from Tilbury for Vigo and a honeymoon in Santiago de Compostela. Both of them realised there was an understandable degree of resentment from the Congreve-Pridgeon family to Cyril's re-marriage within the year, and decided on a very quiet wedding. Walter and Alice Scott-Henderson must have assumed that the marriage of their eldest daughter would be a notable occasion in their local parish church, but it was not to be. The service was held at Chelsea Old Church in London, with only their immediate families – Felicity and Penelope were given the day off from school – and a few close friends (Fig. 54).

Returning to Museum duties at the beginning of August, Fox was immediately immersed in the programme for the Cambrian Archaeological Association AGM. This would be the Cambrians second visit to Cardiff but their first to the National Museum. The four excursions that he had planned included tours of Llandaff

Figure 54: Cyril and Aileen, Chelsea Old Church 6 July 1933

Cathedral and Palace, Cardiff and Caerphilly Castles and of the Museum, where Colin Matheson had prepared a special Zoology Department exhibition of 'Changes in the fauna of Wales within historic times.' The subject for Fox's presidential address was the prehistory and history of Wales, as illustrated by the objects preserved in the Department of Archaeology. In an apology at the start, he confessed that it was difficult to tell his audience anything new, since 'nearly everything in the collection has been published in one form of another.' As Bassett points out 'this was clearly a very different situation to any of the other departments' and was due 'in part to the systematic nature of the collecting of archaeological material, … and in part also to the availability of *Archaelogia Cambrensis*'[5] and other similar learned publications. Fox decided to use his distributional theories as the vehicle for his summary of the history of man in Wales, from the Upper Palaeolithic period through to the present day. Objects, from the Zoology and Archaeology Departments and the sub-department of Folk Culture and Industries, were used to illustrate the movement of successive cultures into Wales from England, or across the sea from Ireland.

Fox used a similar pattern for his address in November to the Prehistoric Society of East Anglia on the history of man in East Anglia. This time restricting himself to the Neolithic, Bronze and Early Iron Age periods, he selected objects from local museums to illustrate his theories on the movement of man within the region, and how soil and the environment had dictated this movement. It was in effect an extension of his Cambridge thesis, with the addition of the wider distributional patterns as set out in *Personality of Britain*.

Aileen found the transition from archaeological career girl of twenty-five to wife of a distinguished man of fifty with two schoolgirl stepdaughters a considerable challenge. She was fortunate to be given a private income by her father that allowed her to engage a Cook-Housekeeper and, when her children arrived, a Nanny to look after them. Until I was born in July 1934, Aileen was able to take part in most of the Museum's social activities. She also accompanied her husband on his frequent trips to London, as President-elect of the Museums Association and for meetings of the Wales and Monmouthshire Royal Commission. Felicity and Penelope remained at school in Sussex; they only came home to Cardiff for half the holidays, so there was little to keep Aileen at home. Many members of the Museum Council and the Royal Commission had become close friends of Cyril and Olive, they now welcomed Aileen in her place. Lord Raglan, Leonard Twiston-Davies, Wilfred Hemp and T. W. Proger are those that come most readily to mind to us as children, not forgetting the regular presence of 'Rik' Wheeler, who seemed to have a multitude of reasons to return to Cardiff, bouncing in and out of Four Elms at will. All of us had a particularly soft spot for 'Uncle' Proger, who was always good for Christmas presents.

Aileen's independence also ensured her full participation in her husband's archaeological work. From November 1933, with their contributions to the Board of Celtic Studies on early cultivation and a fortified hamlet near Llanfrynach, in south

Fig. 55: Margam Mountain Farm (reconstruction) 1934

Glamorgan, the initials C. and A .F. were to become as familiar to archaeologists as C. F. had been before. Their first joint paper was 'Forts and Farms on Margam Mountain'. Published in *Antiquity* in December 1934 it reported fieldwork from the winter of 1933/34 (Fig. 55). The remains of 'three peculiar hill forts and four sites of platform houses new to Welsh archaeology' were examined and interpreted 'as being of post-Roman date mainly because of the nearby "Bodvoc" stone.' However, as Aileen acknowledges, they were wrong; excavation in 1938 of a similar earthwork in Devon, established that Margam Mountain was almost certainly an Early Iron Age site.[6] This, the first of many such reports, was undertaken as part of a survey for the prehistory section of a projected Glamorgan County History. It was abandoned during the war, but subsequently edited by Hubert Savory and published as *Early Glamorgan,* in 1984.

Fox's work for the Royal Commission involved a mass of correspondence with their Secretary, Wilfred Hemp, but his other commitments had made visits to Anglesey, and now to Caernarfonshire, extremely rare. Unlike most of the other commissioners, who tended to restrict their visits to an annual pilgrimage, Fox tried to see most of the important houses and monuments that were being recorded. Piggott, who left the Commission at the end of 1933, was very much a prehistorian with little interest in later periods or architecture, but found that work with the Commission required a broader outlook. In particular Piggott recalled for me how Fox had encouraged him to view the development of architecture as exciting and fun. Walking together through Beaumaris, past an 18th century terrace with one house untouched and its neighbour 'victorianised', he 'had felt a hand on his shoulder – a very characteristic gesture of his – and a loud and excited voice decry, "Look at that – one half perfect and the other buggered up." He always did call a spade a spade. Now Hemp was a preposterous and extraordinary little man and the greatest social snob I have ever met, but it seemed to me, when I started, that here's a chap who is an archaeologist and I thought I must learn something from him – I didn't learn a thing! Then Dr Fox arrived and within a matter of ten minutes ... I realised that this chap *was* an archaeologist.'[7] On leaving, Piggott wrote, 'My regret at leaving the Commission is that I shall miss the opportunity of working with you in the field. From you during your all too brief visits with us in Anglesey I have learnt more archaeology than from anyone I know and from you I have gained some of that sense of historical and geographical perspective so essential to an archaeologist.' His successor with the Commission was Williamson but, as his field visits became less frequent, Fox was never able to establish the same close relationship with him as he had had with his predecessor.

*   *   *

The New Year started well and Fox began work for Methuen on *Neolithic Britain* with renewed enthusiasm. His salary had been restored in 1933 to £950 and in April was increased to £1100. Thus, after thirty years he finally managed to pass the £1000 a year that Mr Gaye had promised would be his income from the Norfolk Market Garden. Aileen was determined that she should have a holiday before their first child was born, due at the end of July, and arranged a ten day break in Normandy for the end of April. Staying at a hotel in Caen they enjoyed a week of visits to museums and cathedrals, but the highlight for Fox was the Bayeux Tapestry. It was revelation to him that became the inspiration for a series of drawings, illustrating holidays and visits abroad, for many years to come (Fig. 56).

As President elect of the Museums Association Fox's attention was focussed on the forthcoming conference in Bristol, at the beginning of July. Not surprisingly, in view of his support for the new sub-department in his own Museum, he chose to bring conference attention to the 'importance of creating and developing collections illustrating the conditions of life and work of the peoples of Britain' or Folk Culture and Industry.[8] It was a strong plea for funds, both from Government and philanthropists, to follow the Scandinavian lead to create both national and regional Open Air Museums. Recognising regretfully that so far, he had been 'unable to create any effective interest in the idea of a National Open Air Museum for Wales', he suggested ways for regional museums to prepare the way. Preservation of redundant buildings was important: More important were their contents, domestic and occupational, and the establishment of provenance. His predecessor, Sir Henry Miers, had been President for five years. It had been a hard act to follow, but Fox had chosen a theme for which he was an enthusiast and which his colleagues welcomed.

Figure 56: Beachlea-Aust Ferry 'Tapestry' – Return from Bayeux 1933

With Government funding for museums still tight there was no immediate response. However, the seed had been sown and many artefacts in folk museums and galleries across the country today can be said, indirectly, to owe their salvation to this plea. Although Aileen returned home to Walton-on-the-Hill after I was born, her husband stayed on in Cardiff to catch up on Museum duties. In mid-August he left for a series of visits with colleagues, to excavations and other sites around the country: Radford took him on a tour of Devon and Cornwall; Murray-Threipland and Forde escorted him around their excavations in mid-Wales: Gordon Childe and Wheeler entertained him at their excavations at Sherborne and Maiden Castle, Dorchester. At the end of this gruelling three weeks he went on to Steyning, for a long weekend with Felicity and Penelope. A week later he was off again, to Cambridge to join Lethbridge and Clarke to see the latest developments in their work in the Cambridge fens, before returning to Walton-on-the-Hill for my christening. Despite these all too frequent absences from the Museum, it was clear that his leadership, and the work that he was undertaking, had the full support of both the Council and the Court of Governors. On 27 October, the *Western Mail* reporting on a lecture by S. F. Markham to the 1933 Museums Association Conference on Museums of the Empire wrote, 'that the National Museum of Wales has got a reputation not merely within these islands but throughout the Empire and the world. ... The knowledge, ability and enthusiasm [of the Director] were an inspiration to all who worked with and for him.'

But the pace of life, combined with the stress of the past two years, was about to catch up with him. At the beginning of December he became extremely ill with what was eventually diagnosed as Norwegian dysentery; for a few days there were serious concerns for his life. His slow recovery was helped by the arrival of a confidential letter, from the Prime Minister's office, with the news that he was to receive a knighthood, for services to archaeology and the National Museum of Wales. Unfortunately, as Aileen recalled, his recovery was temporary. 'Soon after Christmas ... Cyril was still very languid, unable to concentrate, sleeping badly and quite unable

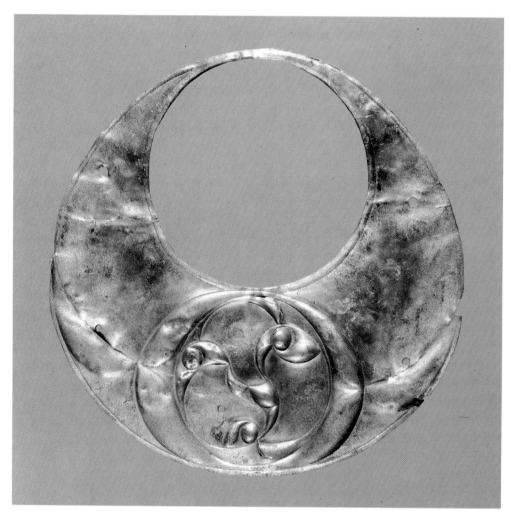

Plate 1: Llyn Cerrig Bach – Crescentic bronze plaque (see page 169)

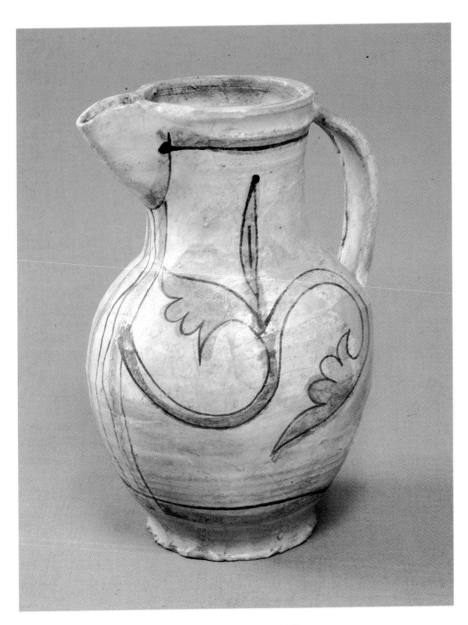

Plate 2: Kidwelly Castle – Polychrome Ewer (see page 112)

to enjoy the flood of congratulatory letters which arrived in the New Year. It became apparent that he was having what was then called a nervous breakdown and that the local doctors could nothing for him.'[9] He spent nearly three months in a Surrey Nursing Home, a further four months convalescence at home and completed his recovery at the Twiston-Davies family holiday home at Tenby.

Aileen's initials or acknowledgement appears on most letters of this period, as she took charge of her husband's affairs. Since he was unable to attend his investiture, he was never dubbed. His Knighthood was awarded by Letters Patent dated 20th February 1935, and published in the London Gazette two days later. By March it was apparent that he would be unable to continue as President of the Museums Association, and Aileen wrote to tender his resignation. At their General Meeting on the 2nd April this was accepted 'with deep regret and sincere appreciation of his services. The Association also recorded their 'gratitude for the unceasing zeal and sympathy with which he has directed its affairs … and their earnest hope for his speedy and complete recovery.'

Clearly one of the root causes of this illness was the continual pressure of having to produce his text for Methuen. In July 1935 Methuen wrote to Fox at the Museum to ask if 'the handbook could now be included in their list of forthcoming publications for Summer 1938.' Lee replied that this was very unlikely, his Director was still recovering and had not yet been given a date when he could return to work. This official reply was followed by a letter from Aileen, with a copy to Lal Chitty, to inform Methuen, with regret, that her husband would now have to withdraw from the project. Lal Chitty was clearly incensed; her response indicating her resentment at having to discuss matters with the woman whom she considered had taken Cyril from her after Olive's death. 'Methuen's contract is my sole potential guarantee against the waste of my best working years. … I should be foolish to become a party to letting Methuen down when I hope some day they will publish my Archaeology of Shropshire, which I more or less laid aside when I began whole time work for Cyril in June 1927.' But both parties had to accept the situation when Fox visited Methuen in January, and the book was never published. Commenting on her reaction Grimes informed me, ' I hadn't realised until recently that Lal was never paid. She had a very deep love for him which was reciprocated but as it was [by Fox] for all people.'[7] It is perhaps significant that Chitty's name was added to the title page of the 1938 (third) edition of *Personality of Britain,* and the typeset for this tribute to her contribution was enlarged and expanded in the subsequent 1943 and 1959 editions.

After a short holiday at Southerndown with all the children, Fox returned to the Museum in mid-August to pick up the threads of his working life. Apart from his duties as Director, and his continuing membership of the Royal Commission for Ancient Monuments in Wales and Monmouthshire, he was free of all responsibilities. This was an almost unique situation for him and Aileen was determined to keep it that way. That his health never seriously let him down again until well into retirement is proof that she was right. By the end of the year everyone in the Museum was aware that his recovery was complete and that he was exercising his authority over all aspects of Museum activities. Keeper's duties and monthly reports were scrutinised and instructions issued to remind them of the format to be used as well as the need to keep him fully informed.

In April 1936 Folk Culture and Industry was formally separated from its parent, the Archaeology Department. Apart from the generous donation from Twiston-Davies, this change in status had been given a considerable boost by an extended visit to the sub-department in October 1934, of three internationally renowned experts; the ethnologist Professor Åke Campbell of Uppsala, the folklorist Professor Carl Von Sydow of Lund and Professor Seamus O'Duilearga, the head of the Irish Folk Institute in Dublin. Peate, in his autobiography, emphasised the importance of this visit and of his Director'support for the department. 'The biggest kindness of the three was their preaching at Cyril Fox regarding the importance, indeed the necessity of developing folk-life studies in the Museum. They succeeded, and it was their message during these three days, that made Fox enthusiastic about that development; from that developed the Department in 1936 and the Welsh Folk Museum in 1947. I pay my most generous homage to Cyril Fox for his generous help and his consistent and untiring support in our effort to secure a Welsh Folk Museum for Wales.'[10] In view of Fox's long standing interest in 'bygones' and exhibition of folk material, the visitors were probably preaching to the converted, but the outcome was clearly welcomed by all concerned. There had been an earlier disagreement between Fox and Peate, now appointed as the department's first Keeper, on the name. 'The Director insists on using the term bygones and adding the phrase "old-fashioned life" (A Victorian idea)',[11] but this had been amicably resolved by the use of Peate's phrase 'Folk Culture', to which 'Industry' was subsequently added. This name was retained when the sub-department achieved full departmental status. Shortly after the visitors left, Peate submitted a memorandum to the Director on the need for Welsh speaking lecturers. Fox had given this memorandum his full support and agreed that Peate's Assistant must be similarly qualified. Peate described the appointment in his autobiography. 'There were a large number of applications, including some candidates who became national figures in other fields later on. Fox met me to choose a short list of three. When we came across Ffransis George Payne, Fox threw him to one side saying he had no degree. I suggested boldly that if he, Cyril Fox, had been an applicant, he would not have been appointed. "Why do you say that?" he asked, "Because at that time you were not a graduate". Without further word, Mr Payne's name was included on the short list of three, … [and] when the three appeared before the appointments committee it was realised at once that Mr Payne had particular qualifications for the post and he was chosen unanimously.'[12] It is perhaps evident, from this and other extracts from Peate's autobiography, that there was a certain 'frisson' in his relationship with his Director. Probably originating with the selection of Grimes, for the position of Assistant Keeper in 1926, it seems that Peate's determination to press his nationalist and pacifist views, on his English and conservative Director, and vice versa, resulted in these occasional and sometimes determined differences of opinion. There is certainly no evidence that I have come across of continuous or outright hostility. As Peate's extensive bibliography illustrates, he was an extremely able academic and renowned writer of Welsh prose and poetry; in later years his work was to be acknowledged by the award of Honorary Doctorates from the Universities of Wales and Ireland and of the prestigious Cymmrodorion Medal. Fox certainly recognised and readily acknowledged Peate's ability and scholastic achievements, but he was never able to enjoy the same friendly relationship with him that he had with his other Keepers.

The only outstanding report, from work undertaken in 1934, was the survey of an Early Iron Age Hill Fort at Caer Dynaf. According to Aileen's autobiography, the brief report, which appeared in *Archaelogia Cambrensis* in June 1936, was a joint undertaking. However, it appears under his name, with no mention of her participation, and there is no amendment on his personal copy of the reprint to indicate any error. It now seems likely that at the time this was a jointly agreed and deliberate tactic to re-establish his credentials after his illness. All entries in the *Bulletin of the Board for Celtic Studies* on work for the Field Survey of Glamorgan for the same period and extending into 1936 are credited to both of them, although the work undertaken in 1935 and 1936 is A and CF rather than the other way round (Fig. 57). In July they both attended the wedding in London of his sister-in-law, Mari Henderson, to the architect Peter Bicknell and three weeks later left for Stockholm for the Second Prehistoric Congress. This was a more relaxed occasion, with no responsibilities, and included a short break based on Uppsala (Fig. 58). There he was able to see the exhibits in the Folk Museum at greater leisure than had been possible on his previous visit in 1930, and with the guidance of Professor S. Lindquist, to tour the magnificent royal grave mounds and see the artefacts in Uppsala Museum.

Figure 57: Cyril and Aileen working together on Carn Goch for the Field Survey of Glamorgan 1936

Fox had not accepted any official outside engagements, nor had he undertaken any excavations, for eighteen months. He had planned to make the Cambrian's meeting at Abergavenny in August the occasion for his return to public life; he was programmed to speak on their excursions to Llanfihangel Court and Tretower Court, but in the event he was still not fully fit. The following month he received an invitation from the

MONDAY TVESDAY WEDNESDAY

FRIDAY SATVRDAY

THVRSDAY MONDAY

STOCICHOLM July 27–Aug 3 1936

Figure 58: Stockholm and Uppsala 'Tapestry' 1936

President of the Cambridge and County Folk Museum Committee to open their new museum in November; this time he was determined to be there. This was the first obvious fruit of his Presidential address to the Museums Association and an appropriate recognition of his leading role in advocating this new branch of museum activities. Fox was obviously delighted to be back in Cambridge, if only for a day, and for his first address to be on 'the collecting of folk material, a branch of museum work in which I have for many years taken a particular interest.' As in 1934, he was able to use a public occasion to stress the pre-eminent position of the National Museum of Wales with 'probably the most extensive folk collection in Britain and the first National Museum to create a special department dealing with folk culture and primitive industries.'[13]

The reason for such a brief return to Cambridge was another Royal visit. The Duke of Kent, as Prior of the Order of St. John of Jerusalem, was holding an investiture in the Reardon Smith Lecture Theatre. Fox was there to welcome him to the Museum and to escort him to the Theatre. All in all it made for a successful conclusion to the year and gave him the encouragement he needed to resume his active academic life.

* * *

After this two-year break Fox was back in demand as one of the nation's foremost museum directors and as a working archaeologist. He was a popular and successful lecturer, and an effective and enthusiastic committeeman; an ideal candidate for Vice-

President of the Society of Antiquaries. Between the start of 1937 and the outbreak of war in September 1939, Nash-Williams and his Assistant Keepers Grimes and Dr Hubert Savory, who was appointed to replace Peate, undertook most excavation work for the Museum. However the situation in Europe had forced the Government to overhaul its defence capability; sites for new military depots and airfields were being identified and evaluated all over the country. Under the 1937 Defence Scheme rescue excavations were required, often at very short notice, when these sites were known to have features of archaeological interest. The first of these was at Bridgend, where surveyors had noted two unrecorded mounds and asked the Museum to investigate. Nash-Williams apparently showed little if any interest. As the War Ministry urgently needed the site for construction of an Ordnance factory, Fox, with the help of his wife, decided to excavate it himself. This was the first of several such excavations and surveys, some of great importance others less so, but it was work that should have been allocated by Nash-Williams to his prehistorian, Grimes. Whatever the reasons for Fox volunteering himself for this work, Grimes told me that it fuelled comments within the Museum that the Director was interfering; undertaking field work clearly the responsibility of the Archaeology Department.

Simondston was the earlier of these two Bronze Age barrows. It was of standard construction except, being on a slight slope, the mound was buttressed by thrust blocks in the outer stone ring. There was no evidence of ritual treading and the only item of note was that coal had been used as part of the fuel for the pyre – at that time the earliest recorded use in Wales.[14] F. J. North, Keeper of the Geology Department, was an archaeological enthusiast. He provided a geological assessment of the stones and coal found on the site (Appendix V) and followed this up with his own more detailed analysis for *Antiquity* two years later.[15] Pond Cairn was of much greater interest being more akin to a disc barrow, a rarer type of prehistoric burial place in comparison with the ubiquitous round barrow design of the adjacent Simondston Cairn. Furthermore the centre was a cylindrical turf pile, the like of which had not previously been recorded, with clear evidence of ritual treading in the ditch between the pile and the outer stone ring (Fig. 59). Aileen added to the interest, finding grains of wheat and barley – the earliest recorded use of the latter – for which her husband was later to write a very formal letter of appreciation. The disc shape of the barrow was by no means new to archaeologists; earlier examples had been found in many southern counties from Berkshire to Devon. Similarly the ritual of circular treading or ceremonial dance, associated with some barrows, was also well established. A ritual of this nature had been first suggested by Professor (later Sir) William Boyd Dawkins of Manchester, some forty years earlier, as an explanation for the compacted earth ring around the outer perimeter of a round barrow at Whatcombe, Dorset,[16] but the turf pile at Pond Cairn was unique. Correspondence shows that Grinsell and Piggott took a particular interest in this barrow, providing Fox with comments and suggestions of similar sites. Lord Raglan, a member and future President of the Museum Court,

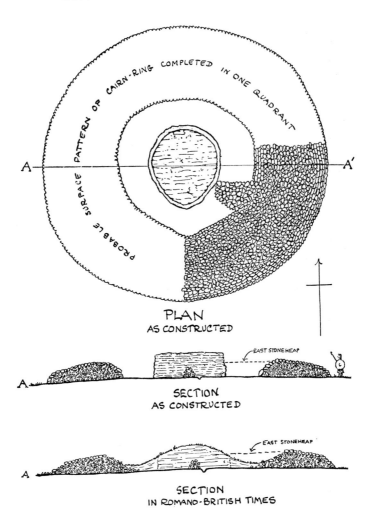

Figure 59: Pond Cairn (Society of Antiquaries of London)

questioned the shape of the pile; he advocated a hemispherical rather than cylindrical shape, to represent the earth of a sacred mountain. But once again it was Fox's imaginative reconstruction of events that caused comment. Savory wrote to tell me that in 1938 'stories were being told of Fox behaving or speaking rather strangely or being too subjective in his reconstruction of Bronze Age burial ceremonies. My own view is that creative imagination has a role in prehistoric research even if one's reconstruction ultimately turns out to be not quite correct. Without it progress towards understanding the remote past is slower and the public on whom one depends for support gets bored.'[17] But whatever the rights and wrongs of ceremonial imagery, these valuable sites had been photographed and fully recorded before the land was levelled; the Commissioners for the Ministry of Works duly wrote to acknowledge their appreciation for 'coming to our rescue in this noble fashion.' In addition to the geological appendix, which covered both sites, there were equally comprehensive contributions from Professor John Percival, who identified the seeds, H. A. Hyde, Keeper of Botany, on other forms of plant life and L. F. Cowley, Assistant Keeper of Zoology, on osseous remains.

In June 1938 Fox undertook a second Ministry task, this time a survey for the Admiralty of an extensive area of land to be used as an Armament Depot at Trecwn, five miles south of Fishguard. His report describing the 18 cottages, none of which was more than 300 years old, is of note in that it provides for the first time his approach to the study of regional architectural practice. This detailed examination was to be the model for his later work with Lord Raglan on a wide range of houses in Monmouthshire. The paper concludes with yet another plea for preservation of this heritage. 'The reader may think that the plans and descriptions of a Llanychaer cottage are unnecessarily detailed. I would plead that this is done as some defence against the march of time. Such a cottage … ought long ago to have taken its place in a series of primitive dwellings of Wales in a national open-air museum, but such a folk museum seems as far from realisation as ever. The best that can be done today is to make a record sufficiently detailed, to permit students, in a more enlightened age, to reconstitute a ruined or altered example.'[18] Mortimer Wheeler was highly appreciative of this foray into new territory. 'The sureness with which you get to the heart of the matter, the conciseness of statement and the perfection of illustration knocks me off my feet. It does show incidentally how much material of first class interest there still is amongst the remains of Welsh peasant architecture.'

Back at work in Cardiff, Fox was able to report to the Council that the financial position of the Museum had improved steadily; the overdraft on the building fund having been cleared in August 1937. The Council was therefore in a position to discuss further enlargement of the building by constructing the West Wing, for which they were given an estimated cost of £88,000. Bassett records, 'After the response in Wales to earlier appeals there was little chance of raising this sum at home. It was therefore decided to "turn to the generosity of America" and an appeal was launched for a Welsh American Wing.' The Council prepared an attractive illustrated booklet *A matter of great interest to Welsh Americans* describing the Museum and the purpose of the new gallery. This was sent to America for distribution by the local appeal committee, which was based in New York and under the chairmanship of a Cardiff expatriate Mr Aubrey Morgan. The committee proposed a series of fund raising activities including 'a four week tour of America in 1939 by Lord Harlech [President] and Cyril Fox.'[19]

* * *

Cyril and Aileen had decided that his eldest daughter Felicity should stay on at St Agnes and St Michael's in Sussex, until she completed her education in July, but had moved Penelope to Howells School, Denbigh, in North Wales, for her last four years. Her father had given a lecture there and was impressed both by the buildings and the Head Mistress. Penelope continued to do well academically, but she was most unhappy and to a certain extent frightened of her Victorian father, so never really settled. Although always very affectionate with his children, he was not at all paternal. Having made these decisions about their education, he virtually ignored them, until they appeared at home for part of the holidays – they still spent half of the time at Steyning with their grandmother. He never visited them at school, nor enquired as to their treatment, merely presiding over the reading of their school reports, which were taken as the only true measure of their abilities, academic or otherwise. He was rarely able to relate to children and had little affinity with them until they were adult; the occasional expedition with one of us, when we were treated as equals, remains etched in the memory.

One such was with Felicity in the summer of 1937. Schooldays over and before going to Lyme Regis for a Domestic Science course, he took her on a four day tour of Cathedrals, churches and other monuments staying in Family and Commercial Hotels and having lunch in the local markets. 'I will always remember that long weekend when my father put out all that brilliance and sense of humour just for me.' Her stepmother Aileen, who was about to have her second child, was neither naturally maternal nor overtly affectionate. Like her husband she was for much of the time immersed in her own archaeological career, initially as an amateur and later as a professional, so was unable to make up for his lack of intimate support. That both of them were distant rather than close supporters of their children had its affect on us all, but particularly on the girls, who were ill prepared for the move from school to independence and later for marriage.

Felicity had done well at school and horrified the family when she then refused to go to Cambridge, preferring Oxford, and then insisted on trying for a career on the stage. She stayed with Fox's sister Babs at Oxford, working for a year at the Oxford Playhouse, before going into the WRNS. There she met and later married Lieutenant Patrick Redgrave RCNVR and in due course emigrated to Canada. After her schooling Penelope went to Cardiff Technical College to study art but, to the intense fury of her father, she left after a year to join the WRAF. She qualified as a radar operator and was stationed at Beachy Head No. 1 Experimental Radar Station, controlling Beaufighters for night interceptions over the Channel. That both of his daughters were eventually to go to University and pursue academic careers would have been so satisfying for him; sadly he did not live long enough to be aware of their considerable achievements.[20]

Over the next two years, as preparations for war intensified on both sides of the Channel, Fox was involved in a series of rescue excavations on the site of a new airfield at St Athan in Glamorgan and subsequently at Milford Haven in

Figure 60: Sutton 268' – The excavated Barrow 1940 (Society of Antiquaries of London)

Pembrokeshire.[21] These excavations, together with others that have already been described and two more that were undertaken later in the war, provided the material for his book *Life and Death in the Bronze Age* that consolidated his researches on Bronze Age culture. The airfield site included six barrows, five of them turf barrows and one, known as Sutton 268, with an unusual grave pit (Fig. 60). As Fox records 'most of the features of the Beaker burial and its attendant constructions are elsewhere on record but seldom is the known setting of such an interment so spacious, so dignified, so monumental. … The ditch too is interesting. Though not interrupted it had two bridges or causeways on opposite sides.' Comparisons with other sites in Dorset and his own excavation at Ysceifiog provide some similarities but not with so large a pit and the presence of arrowheads and broken arrows around the inhumation together with a deliberately broken beaker made this site of particular interest. As usual there were secondary interments of cremated remains of progressively later dates with some unusual grave goods and a subsequent enlargement of the mound in which a final interment had been made. The principal interment of the second phase was a child of the Middle Bronze Age and introduced the overhanging rim urn culture (Fig. 61). It was accompanied by three contemporary cremations, which Fox concluded must be 'regarded as sacrificial deposits … of four children selected to accompany the noble child to the other world.'

Dating and sequencing of these interments then led Fox to analyse overhanging-rim funerary urns that he and others had found in Bronze Age Barrows. This turned his paper from a routine report into yet another milestone in Bronze Age research. Again there were detailed appendices written by Cowley, Hyde and North on the zoological, botanical and geological aspects of this site to add to its academic weight. The summary provided Fox with another opportunity to give his interpretation of the burial sequence – words in italics are his own pencil amendments to his text. 'Not later than 1500 BC a chieftain of the conquering beaker folk, who had colonised a patch of territory in the Vale of Glamorgan, died, and was buried with appropriate

Grave Pit

Rock-cut Ditch

The Urn disclosed

The Overhanging Rim Urn

Figure 61: Excavation of the Barrow at Sutton 268' 1940 (Society of Antiquaries of London)

grave goods near his dwelling. … The culture, which this man had inherited, was of Breton origin; it had lasted in southern Britain some *200* years when he practised it on the northern side of the Bristol Channel and was in decay. *The land controlled by successors* of this archer adopted new conventions and ideas, one of which was related to the disposal of the dead – by cremation instead of inhumation. Pygmy cups and thereafter overhanging rim urns, replaced beakers and metal knives were in use. … When he died, probably not later than 1450 BC, his ashes, with bronze knife and pottery cup, rested in the founder's barrow; its construction was still in the memory, and a position of dignity was chosen for the interment exactly at the base of the hidden cairn. A child's body, reminiscent of the ancient burial rite, was inserted at the foot of the cairn, overlapping this cremation: human sacrifice was evidently part of the new ritual. The interest then shifts to the outside of the ditch on the north. The death of a child presumably of the same gens, but after an interval of one or two centuries, was the occasion for another cremation, in an inverted overhanging rim urn; a finely flaked arrow-head, perhaps symbolic of the craft the noble youngster would have mastered, lay beside it. ... [This] cremation was associated with elaborate ritual, for the ground in the neighbourhood was cleared down to the rock ... Again child sacrifice is in evidence for three adjacent cremations placed in hollows between the stones without grave goods can hardly be natural deaths. ... They are certainly contemporary for at this stage enlargement of the barrow was undertaken. ... This formed a ring ... surrounding the ancient barrow. ... The turf slope (and the turf flat on the northern side) were then heavily trampled; we may envisage a ritual dance, which completed the ceremonial of the cremation and had some reference to the older interments.' Excavation of the remaining barrows on this site was presumably not so urgent as the work was not carried out until after the outbreak of war.

Although the report on this and other rescue fieldwork appears under Fox's name, he fully acknowledged the assistance of his wife. In her autobiography Aileen discusses the collaboration between the two of them during this period. 'Initially Cyril was the leader' but clearly as the years passed it became more of a joint effort as for instance during this excavation. 'We employed two or three workmen with pick and shovel whilst Cyril and I did the fine trowelling (Fig. 62). He planned the features and the general layout (and wrote up the reports), whilst I recorded the finds and supervised their packing and transport to the museum.'[22]

Throughout this period in the late thirties Fox was extremely busy and often away. Savory wrote to tell me of his early days as a newly appointed Assistant Keeper for the Archaeology Department. 'The times immediately before the war were difficult at the Museum because your father was absent a great deal on fieldwork or carrying out his duties at the Society of Antiquaries, and much administration had to be delegated to the Museum Secretary. Archie Lee, rather a sharp character, who had been an Army Adjutant in World War I and was suspected (rightly or wrongly) of forming his ideas of what was going on in the Department partly from the malicious gossip of female staff. The atmosphere was further spoilt by the activities of the Peace Pledge Union, supported by at least two of the Keepers and infiltrated by Welsh Nationalists.'[23] This activity was of little import at the time but was to have dramatic consequences in 1940 and 1941, bringing the Director, Secretary and several members of the Council to the brink of resignation.

Despite his many commitments Fox still found time, mostly at weekends at home, to comment on items in the Museum's collection that interested him and which

Figure 62: Simondston – Cyril and Aileen at work 19 April 1937 (Western Mail & Echo Ltd)

he considered deserved further examination. The Llyn Fawr hoard of bronze and iron had been found in 1910, when a small lake was being drained prior to the construction of a reservoir, and presented to the Museum by Rhondda Urban District Council. It was described and analysed by Crawford and Wheeler in 1921.[24] In 1936, the engineer responsible for that work sent two further items that he had found at the time and kept – a second bronze cauldron and an iron sword – which he now wanted placed with the rest of the hoard in the Museum. They were sent to the British Museum for repair and cleaning; on their return they aroused the interest of the Director and acted as a catalyst for further study of the hoard.[25]

The cauldron and sword were imports, one from Ireland and the other from France. How did they and the rest of this hoard, which included bronze and iron sickles and axes, end up in a peaty tarn on the high ground overlooking the Neath valley and thirteen miles from the sea? This was another cultural question with Fox's response being based on soil and settlement. He used the now familiar distribution maps for the cauldrons, sickles and axes to argue for likely routes along the heads of the valleys and down to the trading rivers; the Ely being the most favoured. His interest in this hoard, and in particular the sickles, was further developed in papers for the Prehistoric Society[26] and the *Cambrian Archaeological Association*[27] which set out to define and typify all socketed and non-socketed Bronze Age sickles. All three of these papers were clearly well received, by fellow archaeologists and geographers alike. Professor E. Estyn Evans writing from Belfast wrote, 'I am moved to say that your treatment of the Llyn Fawr hoard is a most exciting argument of real geographic interest… I feel grateful to you for relieving me (and the archaeological world) of my stumbling examination of the sickles.' That Gordon Childe would still be writing to Fox in 1953, to add new finds to the lists, is indicative of the thoroughness and lasting value of this work.

Holidays, which Aileen insisted he must have, had to be work-related expeditions: Cyril could not abide sitting on a beach with the children or whiling away the hours in a hotel. Despite the threat to his health if he did not take his full entitlement to leave, he still insisted on holidays with an archaeological or historical interest, if he was to be included. Aileen had given birth to their second son Derek, in September 1937 and she was determined that both of them should have an overseas break. Cyril agreed and so in the spring of 1938 they went to Italy, staying with Ralegh Radford, now the Director of the British School in Rome, and in late summer joined Mortimer Wheeler and Peter Murray-Threipland in Brittany to see their excavations of Iron Age sites at Huelgoat and Quimper.

In March 1939 with Lord Harlech they crossed the Atlantic in the *Queen Mary* for the long planned tour of the eastern seaboard of America to raise funds for the proposed Welsh-American Galleries. This four-week tour, which was timed to include the St. David's Day celebrations, consisted of a series of receptions and lectures with a film showing the work of the Museum. However, as Douglas Bassett succinctly states 'the time was unpropitious and the result, despite considerable efforts, disappointing. When the war came in the autumn of that year the fund closed when it stood at about £13,600.'[28] Cyril and Aileen were able to combine business with pleasure at the end of the tour; taking a short holiday in Virginia. This included a visit to the former colonial capital Williamsburg, purchased and restored at enormous expense by John D. Rockefeller, and then opened to the public. 'It was a new concept of an open air museum designed to teach history in its broadest sense, based on thorough detailed and documentary research.... As we wandered from building to building it certainly gave us new ideas about museum developments and how to cater for an intelligent public, ideas that were later to be incorporated by Cyril in the Welsh Folk Museum at St Fagans. ... Reflecting during the voyage home Cyril and I concluded that, all in all, it had been an enjoyable trip, even if it had not achieved its purpose of raising enough money for the museum. ... Now we were returning to Cardiff to face the growing tension of an approaching war.'[29]

Notes

[1] A. Fox *Aileen – A Pioneering Archaeologist* p. 73
[2] D. Bassett, The making of a National Museum Part III *Soc.Cym.* 1984 p. 23–4
[3] This connection enabled Dr Henderson to be an influence in the selection of Stephenson Harwood & Tatham as a suitable firm of London solicitors for the bank, an association which has been retained to the present day
[4] Wat's Dyke – A field survey *Arch.Camb.* December 1934
[5] D. Bassett, The making of a National Museum Part IV *Soc.Cym.* 1992 p. 252
[6] A. Fox *Aileen – A Pioneering Archaeologist* p. 77 and 82
[7] Discussions with the author 1986
[8] Museums Association Presidential Address *Mus.Journ.* 34
[9] A. Fox *Aileen – A Pioneering Archaeologist* p. 84
[10] I. Peate *Rhwng dau fyd, Darn o hunangofiant* p. 135 Translation arr. D. Bassett
[11] *Op cit* p. 131 Translation arr. D. Bassett
[12] *Op cit* p. 111 It should be emphasised that both of the other candidates were Welsh speakers with Honours degrees in Welsh from Cardiff.

[13] The new Cambridge and County Folk Museum *Mus.Journ.* 36

[14] The Bridgend site was initially reported in the *Bulletin of the Board of Celtic Studies* 9 Part iii and the paper read to the Society of Antiquaries in March 1938. This was published as Simondston and Pond Cairns in *Archaelogia* LXXXVII later that year. It was also summarised in *Man* June 1938 p. 90–91

[15] F. North, A Geologist amongst the Cairns *Antiquity* XIV

[16] *Proceedings of the Lancashire and Cheshire Antiquarian Society* XVIII

[17] Letter to the author dated 25 May 1986.

[18] Peasant Crofts in North Pembrokeshire *Antiquity* December 1937

[19] D. Bassett, The making of a National Museum Part III *Soc.Cym.* 1984 p. 36. A matter of great interest to Welsh Americans. An appeal for funds to erect Welsh-American Galleries. *National Museum of Wales* 1937

[20] Assistant Professor Felicity Redgrave Hon BA B.Ed.; Dr Penelope Eames MA Ph.D. FSA

[21] Bronze Age Barrow (Sutton 268) *Arch.* LXXXIX: A Beaker Barrow enlarged in the Middle Bronze Age, at South Hill, Talbenny, Pembrokeshire *Arch.J.* XCIX

[22] A. Fox *Aileen – A Pioneering Archaeologist* p. 85

[23] Letter to the author dated 25 May 1986. The nationalists included a small number, who favoured direct action, as well as true pacifists like Peate. It seems unlikely that the former would have joined the Peace Pledge Union

[24] The Llynfawr and other Hoards of the Bronze Age *Arch.* LXXI

[25] A second Cauldron and an Iron Sword from the Llyn Fawr Hoard *Ant.J.* XIX

[26] Socketed Bronze Sickles of the British Isles *Prehist.Soc.* 1939

[27] The Non-socketed Bronze Sickles of the British Isles *Arch.Camb.* XCVI

[28] D. Bassett, The Making of a National Museum Part III *Soc.Cym.* 1984 p. 36

[29] A. Fox *Aileen – A Pioneering Archaeologist* p. 92

IX

The Crowning Glory 1939–1948
Wartime Discoveries and The Welsh Folk Museum

The start of the Second World War had been heralded on 24th August 1939 by a declaration from the Government of a State of Emergency. For institutions like the Museum, this had initiated action to safeguard their national treasures (Figs 63 and 64). Whilst Fox had been away in America the situation in Europe had deteriorated further; the invasion of Czechoslovakia on March 18th providing irrefutable evidence that the Munich Agreement had failed. The Council arranged for the construction of 'strong rooms' in the basement and departments were required to list all objects of national importance for preservation. Savory readily recalled his Director's efforts through that summer and his reaction to the imminence of war. 'Fox, being a highly conscientious as well as intelligent man under strain sometimes became over excited. ... I had been on a cycling holiday in North Wales, largely out of touch with developments, and got back to Cardiff a bit late ... and found that the archaeological collections were being dismantled and stored in the sub-basement in a great hurry until nothing was left on display but replicas and photographs.'[1] The Museum was temporarily closed, but reopened a month later and remained open for the rest of the war.

Over the next six months life in the Museum had a semblance of normality and Fox was able to resume his 'rescue' excavations. Working against time through the hard winter of 1939–40, excavation was frequently held up by the weather. 'Frost and thaw played havoc with sections as in frost a floor cannot be studied for stake holes or other features. ... In a thaw the floor (with its stake holes)

Figure 63: Museum preparations for war August 1939 (Western Mail & Echo Ltd)

Figure 64: Dispersal of national treasures – Henry VIII's armour in the National Museum Entrance Hall with Fox and Sir William Goscombe John 1940 (National Museum of Wales)

comes away on one's boots.'[2] Despite the conditions, excavation of these turf barrows yielded new evidence of Middle Bronze Age barrow construction. Although one of the three was a ritual barrow, with no primary or secondary interment, all had a domed central pit surmounted by a turf stack and surrounded by remarkably regular circles of closely driven wooden stakes. In one, known as 'Sheeplays 293', there were a series of these stake rings at 10 foot intervals from 18 to 58 feet from the centre: the 28 foot ring probably formed the supports for a wattle walled ceremonial hut.[3] The ritual that took place around this interment was most unusual since the floor of the hut had not been trodden down but had been carefully filled with and surrounded by turf, and finally buried under the mound. This paper was read to the Antiquaries in April 1941 and his great friend Tom Kendrick wrote 'it was a revelation to me that such a dramatic story could be made of a small group of poverty stricken barrows of that sort. It is really grim to think how much evidence has been missed or destroyed by dear old boys who lacked your amazing gift for reconstructing ceremony and the religious background.'

The last of the barrows on this site, excavated in October 1940,[4] had a stone cist that formed part of the 28-foot stake circle (Fig. 65). The cremation urn was very rare (Fig. 66), with only one other flared rim example being found – Elworthy in Somerset. This evidence, with the support of interments from the other Cowbridge barrows, established for Fox a progressive movement of Beaker and Bronze Age folk across the Severn by

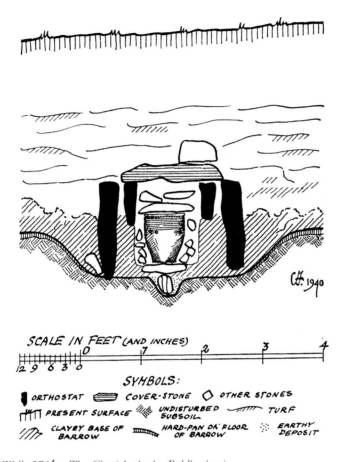

SCALE IN FEET (AND INCHES)

SYMBOLS:

Figure 65: Six Wells 271' – The Cist (Antiquity Publications)

land and sea into the Glamorgan plain. This movement was extended westwards in 1941 by another 'rescue' excavation at Talbenny near Milford Haven in Pembrokeshire.[5] Bryan O'Neil had located a barrow on an Air Ministry site and wrote to Fox to suggest that Grimes should undertake the excavation. In the event Fox found that Grimes was fully committed at Chedworth, so volunteered Aileen and himself to do the work. Fox contended that the discovery of a stake circle in this beaker barrow, which had been enlarged in the Middle Bronze Age, was of more than chronological importance. 'The beaker folk must have brought this forest or parkland technique with them' he wrote. Comparisons with Woodhenge or Overton were not relevant

Figure 66: Six Wells 271' – Flared Rim Urn (Antiquity Publications)

Figure 67: Six Wells 271' – The Libation in the Pit

for the close 'intervals of driven stakes of the South Wales circles represent the hurdle makers' technique while the Wiltshire structures – basically tree trunks set up in dug holes – represent carpenters' or axe-men's technique'. This last excavation was also notable for using a mechanical excavator to complete the total excavation of the site; an experiment that Fox did not care to repeat, but which he clearly enjoyed both at the time and in the telling. The audience at the Archaeological Institute must have found his enthusiasm in presenting his findings both instructive and enjoyable. His ability to breathe life into the cold dry analysis of archaeological excavations was by now legendary (Fig. 67); the reaction of his audience was typified by Jacquetta Hawkes who wrote 'What a marvellous lecturer you are, no-one else could make a barrow so enthralling.'

*   *   *

The long winter forced him to put off further excavation until the spring, but he and Aileen were able to continue their Glamorgan field survey. In the hills above Neath she drew his attention to a ruined croft. From his earliest days in Cambridge Fox had been interested in regional development of dwellings; he had read Iorwerth Peate's article in *Antiquity* and had recently been asked to review his subsequent book *The Welsh House*.[6] As Peate records, his book 'had a princely response by specialists such as Professor A. E. Richardson and Sir John Summers and a number of other scholars, but it was reviewed quite unfavourably by my Director, Cyril Fox'.[7] Fox was later to acknowledge the valuable contribution of this work in the study of regional architecture; apparently he did not recognise its importance at the time. However it was clearly in his mind and this ruined croft seemed to be a primitive form of long house, such as Peate had described. Surprisingly, he found that there were also features that he recognised from his work with Aileen, on mediaeval moorland platform houses at Gelligaer.[8] The ensuing paper, describing both this croft and a similar but later and still occupied house in Carmarthenshire, suggested to him that these rural dwellings known as long houses, with farming families and their cattle living under the same roof, had evolved from primitive beginnings.[9] From my evaluation of his work on the regional architectural evolutionary process, this paper was probably the catalyst for his work with Lord Raglan that they started together in 1941. Certainly it was recognised by both Wheeler and Piggott 'as the beginning of a new archaeology,'[10] though neither could have anticipated that in time it would become a new subject for academic study known as *vernacular architecture*. On receiving his copy of *Antiquity*, Professor Forde wrote to Fox proclaiming his paper as magnificent; he described Peate's dismissal of this [evolutionary] theory in a footnote in his book as 'purblind'. This mutual academic criticism was unfortunate; it probably elevated minor matters to major issues and led to challenges to authority and the polarisation of Museum committees partly on nationalist lines. Peate's account of the Art, Archaeology and Folk Culture and Industry Committee's decision to congratulate him on the publication of *The Welsh House,* and Fox's reluctance to incorporate this in the minutes, typifies this personality and cultural clash. Regrettably it was just the prelude to a greater and more public disagreement.

The strange situation that had existed nationally since the outbreak of the Second World War came to an end in May with the dramatic events at Dunkirk and the start of the Battle of Britain. Although one or two members of staff were in the Reserves and had been called up almost immediately, the majority were awaiting events. Unlike other national museums, staff of the National Museum of Wales were not classified as civil servants; therefore they were not given automatic reserved status. The Council had publicly stated that its policy was 'to release for service in the Armed Forces of the Crown members of its staff, without exception, as and when they volunteered or were called up for such service' and this was apparently accepted without question.

Nash-Williams, Keeper of Archaeology, was the first to go and Fox took over the Department at the beginning of the year. It was well known that three Keepers, Kighley Baxandall (Art), Hyde (Botany) and Peate, as well as some of the junior members of staff, held pacifist views but this was held to be a matter of individual principle and not thought to be of concern to the Museum. Unfortunately it was brought to the Council's attention by the actions of Peate who, in the words of the Council briefing notes, 'made use of his personal friendship with a high official in the Ministry of Labour and National Service to place privately ... a case for the inclusion of members of staff of this National Museum in the List of Reserved Occupations. On receiving ... private intimation by letter that the staff of the museum was included ... he made known this information to a number of members of staff without the permission of the Council or the Director and before any official communication was received by the Council from the Ministry.' The Museum's Emergency Committee felt that Peate had 'usurped the authority of the Council, deliberately involving the Museum in his personal effort to avoid service and obtained the reversal of the Council's present policy of full support for the national war effort.' Mr Hyde, acting on this information, 'visited an official of the Cardiff office of the Ministry of Labour with a view to the postponement of the medical examination of a member of the Museum staff (Departmental Attendant Mr J. W. Davies), who had registered with official approval, for service with the Royal Air Force.'[11] Both Keepers were suspended until the full Council meeting the following week.

Fox had divided loyalties. As the Council's Chief Executive he was responsible for implementing Council policy, but as Director he was concerned for the welfare and morale of his staff. He was aware that this issue, with its nationalist undertones, might divide the Council and therefore proposed a compromise solution. Both Keepers should be severely censured, but they would be reinstated subject to written apologies and guarantees to him of future loyalty. This was agreed by the Council and in due course by the individuals concerned. Council members were clearly grateful. Robert Richards MP wrote 'a personal note of thanks to you for the very generous and statesmanlike way in which you got us out of the impasse into which we were drifting. As my friend [Professor] Ifor Williams pointed out we might have been discussing the situation still but for your very courageous intervention. I think we all realised how difficult such a gesture must have been to you – as the person most immediately affected by the affront which had been done to the Council and on that account we one and all appreciated it all the more.' Peate's own account adds little to the official record except, surprisingly, to state that neither he nor Hyde was given any opportunity to state their case. 'The Council met and Harold Hyde and I were told to sit in the Director's room. We were there all afternoon but were not called. A vote of censure was pronounced on us, and that without giving us an opportunity to appear before the Council to place the facts before the members. We were ordered to apologise and promise to behave in future as a pair of boys caught stealing apples. In my "apology" I purposely noted that I would at all times do my duty to my country.'[12]

On a happier note the Council had cordially congratulated their Director on his election to a Fellowship of the British Academy. He was of course delighted; he was particularly pleased when the Academy then asked him to deliver the Sir John Rhys Memorial Lecture in October. He chose as his subject the 'Boundary Line of Cymru', a phrase taken from Sir John Rhys' book *The Welsh People* when referring to Offa's Dyke. Although the results of Fox's surveys of Offa's Dyke, Wat's Dyke and the Short Dykes had all been published sector by sector, no summary of general conclusions had been offered except the initial statement in *Antiquity* 1929, and a short lecture to the Yorkshire Society for Celtic Studies in 1937.[13] Having described the dykes, their routing, construction and presumed purpose, Fox compared this ancient boundary line of Cymru with the modern political map. For around 60 of the 149 miles the boundaries correspond, for another 60 the modern boundary is on the Welsh side of the Dyke and the balance is to the east on the English side. In his conclusion, Fox attributes this extraordinarily close relationship to the mountainous nature of the Principality and his theory that in prehistoric times cultures were imposed in the lowlands but absorbed, transformed or lost in the highlands. Thus, despite the Roman and Norman conquests, the high country that is the heartland of Wales remained in the hands of the Welsh. Here the native traditions, customs and language were retained. In times of peace they returned to the valleys and so were able to shape the political map of the Marches in the sixteenth century as effectively as Offa had done eight hundred years before.

Wartime restrictions notwithstanding, the lecture was well attended and was duly published by the Academy in August 1941. Five years later it was adjudged to have been the most important contribution of the decade to the Archaeology of Wales and the Marches, for the period AD 43 to AD 1100, and Fox was awarded the Cambrian Archaeological Association's GT Clark Trust Prize. Ian Richmond in his assessment wrote 'The study of Offa's Dyke and kindred earthworks covered by the survey has a highly important bearing not only upon the Welsh and Saxon relations but upon the very genesis of the Marches. Its scholarship is as outstanding as its value as a topographical, geographical and political study and it represents the breadth and sweep of archaeological study in the hands of one of its acknowledged masters.'[14]

The pressures of Fox's wartime routine, acting as Director and Keeper, meant that much of his writing and research was carried out at home. He would wake early, make himself a cup of tea and then shut himself in his study until breakfast was on the table. His secretary would type out his manuscript and this would then be revised and amended in the evening. The Museum remained busy; attendance figures standing up remarkably well. Tours were arranged for troops stationed in the local area and the Director and Keepers gave lectures on a wide variety of subjects for units further afield. The Commanding Officer of a Canadian Battery stationed at Castlemartin Range in Pembrokeshire wrote to thank Fox for his lecture and the presentation of books that all contributed to the education of 'rude soldiery'. 'I now realise' he added 'that a Cromlech is not after all a kind of Welsh Cake.'

The start of the blitzkrieg on London, and other key provincial cities, persuaded Fox that the Museum had to institute its own measures to reduce the risk of damage, especially from incendiary attack. He had a camp bed installed in an office at the top of the building, insisting that a senior member of Museum staff slept there every night with junior staff patrolling the building until the threat to the city was lifted.[15] He was incensed that, due to a lack of similar precautions, several great London churches were gutted when a warning from someone on the spot might have saved them. His love of architecture made the loss of these buildings especially poignant; he was determined that his own museum would not suffer a similar fate. This duty was apparently resented by some members of staff and in the event proved unnecessary, as the building emerged unscathed from the bombing, but looking at the devastation in nearby Queen Street made everyone realise what might have been and complaints evaporated. There was a reward for this voluntary duty; salaried staff were paid a subsistence allowance of 3/- a night with the following morning off, and wages staff were given sixpence an hour with a minimum of 5/- a night. Fifteen months later in September 1941, under the Fire Prevention (Business Premises) Order, this duty became compulsory, and the Government's pay rates of 3/- up to 12 hours and 4/6 for periods in excess of 12 hours were imposed.

Fox was a gregarious character and related easily to people of all kinds and all walks of life. He wore his great scholarship lightly, never seeming to be superior or unapproachable; a characteristic vouched for by virtually all of the younger generation of archaeologists with whom he came in contact. There was however one group, with whom he usually felt there was little rapport – the aristocracy. James Lees-Milne's diary records that Fox felt that Lord Bute was quite impossible, as was Lord Tredegar. In fact 'the aristocracy are all the same. They keep to themselves and are afraid of outside contacts. I do not expect them to fraternise with a mere ordinary citizen like myself, but they might discuss cultural matters with me on a common level.'[16] There were of course exceptions; the Museum President was invariably a peer, as were some members of the Council. The President, for the first three years of the war, was Lord Harlech, though he was abroad in South Africa for most of his period in office. Lord Plymouth, the immediate Past-President, with whom Fox had always had an excellent working relationship, stood in until the end of 1942, when Lord Howard de Walden took over. But of all the peers that he knew there was only one, Lord Raglan, with whom he established a close family friendship, firstly with Olive and subsequently with Aileen.

Lord (Roy) Raglan was a Fellow of the Society of Antiquaries, with a particular interest in architectural history and the academic training to appreciate Fox's archaeological achievements; they had much in common and enjoyed each others company. Fox didn't really approve of the way that Lord Raglan and his wife Julia brought up their children. As his younger daughter Penelope remembers, 'on returning home he would inveigh against the indulgence accorded to these sprigs of the noble house for interrupting serious conversation and interfering in the logical flow of informed argument. It would never be permitted in his house, but he did not allow this minor irritant to mar his friendship!' Lord Raglan had enjoyed reading Peate's book *The Welsh House,* and Fox's papers on crofts in Brecknockshire and Glamorgan as well as his booklet on Six Wells, Llantwit Major, A *Country House of the Elizabethan period in Wales.* He considered that this evolutionary process that Fox had identified merited further study. The demolition in 1941 of Upper Wern Hir, a seventeenth century farmhouse near Usk (Fig. 68), prompted him to suggest his own county Monmouthshire as being particularly suitable for a regional study of rural architectural development. Fox agreed and readily accepted this invitation. Over the next eight years, whenever they could mutually spare the time, they undertook the necessary research and fieldwork. As I remember him telling me 'His Lordship provided the means of entry and I wrote up the results.'

Figure 68: Upper Wern Hir, Llanbadoc – Elizabethan Hall House demolished 1941 (National Museum of Wales)

* * *

Although the Ministry of Labour had decided that staff of the National Museum of Wales would be given reserved status, this did not prevent the issue of call-up papers; nor did it change Council policy to release those who wished to serve. The Museum also undertook to make up salary or wages as necessary and to guarantee reinstatement once the war was over. Unless the Museum was prepared to state that the position of a member of staff was essential, an objection to service had to be investigated by the South Wales Tribunal. If an application was accepted as genuine, formal registration as a Conscientious Objector (CO) would then be issued.

Baxandall, Keeper of Art, who was known to have pacifist views and had made provisional application for CO registration, changed his mind in January 1941 and was accepted for service in the Royal Air Force. The Council agreed to make up his service salary and that Fox should add Art to his Keepership of Archaeology for the duration with Ffransis Payne being temporarily transferred from Folk Culture to Art to assist him in that Department. Hyde, Keeper of Botany had also made a provisional application, but he was older and was never called up.

Peate, the most deeply involved member of staff in the dispute with the Council in 1940, had given a written undertaking 'that if not reserved [by the Museum] he was prepared to do his duty to his country.' On the basis of that undertaking he had been reinstated, but on being called up in July it was learnt from the press[17] that Peate had avoided service by registering as a CO. Fox wrote to Lord Harlech in Pretoria to summarise the position for him.[18] 'The Council promptly dismissed him for telling untruths and making misleading statements. He issued a very tendentious pamphlet, which brought a large attendance at the October Court meeting,[19] including 11 MPs, who were determined to bring him back as a victim of the Council's determination to get rid of the only Welsh-speaking Welshman on the senior staff. ... The age-old suspicion and prejudice that has embittered relations between Welsh and English was revived and in the most deplorable and disgraceful manner. ... Of course if an English member of the Staff had behaved as Peate behaved, *he* would have been sacked. ... The Court, by a large majority, approved a resolution requesting the Council to reinstate Peate. The Council, it is certain, has legal power of appointment and dismissal of staff but it is difficult to sustain a veto in the face of the "sovereign body". Lord Plymouth has borne the brunt of the business and I am sorry for him.' Peate's description of these events makes no mention of 'call-up papers' or of any pamphlet issued in his defence, nor does he comment on the Emergency Committee's interpretation of his statement in 1940 as being willing to serve in the Armed Forces. W. J. Gruffydd, Professor of Welsh at Cardiff and a member of the Court, wrote to the press in support of 'Dr Peate's thought about duty to his country,' but this could not by any stretch of the imagination be termed tendentious. Furthermore it was far too short to be re-issued as a pamphlet. Nevertheless the evidence of Fox's letter to the Museum President would seem to establish that such a pamphlet must have existed. One can only presume that Peate did not wish or think it necessary to refer to it in his autobiography. Interestingly Peate considered Lee to be the 'eminence grise' and the driving force behind his suspension and dismissal. 'No plotting was beyond him in order to achieve his aims. I believe sincerely that he prepared the bullets, and Cyril Fox, a weak man, fired them innocently enough, and he like every "servant whilst reigning" felt insecure and that firing the bullets reinforced his ego.'

The Council was placed in an unenviable position – were they or the Court ultimately responsible for the running the Museum. Lord Plymouth, as acting Chairman, undertook negotiations with the Secretary of State and spoke to the Press, but behind the scenes it was Fox, who was most personally affected and who, with Lee, was required to brief Council members with the background information they required. He discussed resignation with Lee, Frank Treharne James and possibly others but was persuaded to await developments. He then produced a series of draft resolutions for Lord Plymouth, all of which underlined the determination of the Council to stand its ground. This was reinforced by Lee's reminder of the unrecorded suggestion at the November meeting of the Council, that if the Court voted again for reinstatement, many of them would have to resign; by inference so would the Director and Secretary. Fox finally provided Lord Plymouth with a solution that Peate was prepared to accept. His dismissal in October would stand, but he would be appointed as a Senior Assistant Keeper on 1st March for a probationary period with the prospect of subsequent re-appointment. Peate was duly re-appointed as Keeper on 1st September but subsequent relations were somewhat strained. It also caused Fox considerable distress, for he prided himself on relations with his staff and could not understand why Peate had never attempted to discuss matters with him. But Fox's attitude to service, engendered in the 1914–18 War, made it most unlikely that anything constructive could have been achieved; doubtless Peate was well aware of this when deciding to apply for registration without informing his Director. Looking back it is clear that Peate had no lasting animosity towards his Director. His account concludes, 'Cyril Fox was rather bashful if not suspicious of me for some months but he soon realised that I was not one for holding a grudge, and for the years that followed up to his retirement in 1948 we worked together very amicably.'[20] If any good came out of this episode it was that it established the right of the Council to run the Museum and the authority of the Director over its staff.

* * *

By the end of 1942 the fortunes of the allies seemed to be on the turn. In North Africa Rommel's armies were being forced to retreat and in Russia Von Paulus was almost surrounded at Stalingrad. Unfortunately the battle of the Atlantic was still a constant source of depressing news, but at least there was a glimmer of hope that there would be a favourable end to the war and plans could be made for the future. In January Aileen had given her husband a third son, George, and so it was with some cheer that Fox drafted his plans for the future of the National Museum of Wales and the Welsh Museums with which it was affiliated.

The Memorandum was published in February 1943 and forwarded to the Welsh Reconstruction Advisory Council with five recommendations. Bassett considers this Memorandum 'was in many ways as important as the Charter of Incorporation of 1907' by setting out for the first time 'the functions of museums and art galleries in relation to the community.'[21] It was recommended that: extension of the Cathays Park building be on the official list for post war reconstruction: financial provision be made for an open-air museum; favourable consideration be given to applications for building and reparations by local museum committees: a Grants Committee be set up for Welsh local museums and that an annual grant of at least £1500 be provided by the Government for technical assistance. Very little direct action came of this except that the principle of an open-air museum was agreed, though no financial commitment was forthcoming. However the Museum Council had provided a blueprint for the future; in time most of their recommendations would be fulfilled.

Archaeologists were also looking forward to life after the war and those who were not on service, or otherwise committed to the war effort, attended a conference to discuss the future of British archaeology at the London University Institute of Archaeology in Regent's Park. Fox represented the Museum and Aileen joined him on behalf of the University College. She had been appointed to a temporary lectureship for the duration, when Nash-Williams had been called up, and was by this time a key member of the faculty. Fox was also one of the principal speakers, advocating a National Archaeological Register with a permanent staff to set up and maintain it. Although this was not to be implemented nationally, the County Council Sites and Monuments records, that were created instead, do ensure ready access for scholars to local records. They also go some way to satisfying his plea for 'the record and preservation of knowledge and preservation of research.' In her autobiography Aileen recalled the exhilarating atmosphere and sense of missionary zeal that inspired the delegates, and the new mood and sense of purpose that it gave to British archaeology.

As a direct result of this Conference the Society of Antiquaries took the lead in establishing a new Council for British Archaeology, with central and regional committees to plan and oversee all aspects of archaeological activity throughout the country. Important though this was for the profession, and for the preservation of our heritage, it was perhaps of equal merit that delegates generally recognised the need for the public to have an understanding of the subject, and to involve them in their work. Over the succeeding years the success of this policy has been remarkable. Although some spectacular finds, such as the excavation at Sutton Hoo in 1939, had aroused widespread interest, archaeology was still a somewhat erudite university subject for the few. Sixty years later it has almost become mainstream for many schoolchildren and university undergraduates.

The summer of 1943 brought another remarkable find. Not as spectacular as Sutton Hoo, being of iron and bronze instead of gold and silver, it was of almost equal importance and required an immense amount of correspondence with colleagues and research before publication could be achieved.[22] The Air Ministry was constructing an Air Station (RAF Valley) on the island of Anglesey. Peat, from the margins of a nearby lake at Llyn Cerrig Bach, was being used as top dressing for the airfield. Mr J. Jones, the Resident Engineer, wrote to the Museum in early July enclosing a sketch 'of metal weapons and chain, which together with one or two smaller articles … and some human remains, have been dredged by us from a bog.'[23] The peat had been extracted in 1942; having dried out, it was being spread on the sandy surface of the airfield when a chain, subsequently identified as a gang chain, was caught in a harrow and other metal objects were then spotted. Mr Jones was immediately informed of the importance of his discovery, and the metal pieces and bones were recovered.

Fox visited the site in August to inspect the collection, including the bones, about which he subsequently wrote 'masses of which were left and only a few collected.' He also had the good fortune to pick up a currency bar from the surface of the field, and several objects were later recovered from the edge of the lake, where the peat had been dried. Some damage had been incurred during extraction and spreading, one of the gang chains being used for towing, but not irredeemably. In all ninety metal objects and a small collection of bones were forwarded to the Museum for analysis; most of the metal pieces being sent to Dr Plenderleith at the British Museum for cleaning and preservation. In January 1945 Mr Jones sent a box by train to Cardiff with 'the remaining metal relics and one sack of bones', but no other items have been found since.[24]

The nature of this discovery, artefacts unknowingly dug up and subsequently arbitrarily spread over a wide area with no possibility of site examination, led Fox to a detailed study of each object to establish likely dating and provenance. 'The make up of the collection,' he wrote, 'is predominantly masculine, a bracelet being probably the only thing which might have belonged to a woman; it is moreover overwhelmingly military in character. More than half the finds are metal fittings from chariot or pony harness. The numerous swords and spears – which are the two weapons shown by continental burials to be carried by the warrior in his chariot – are consistent with the probability that the deposit, in its military aspect, is solely concerned with this form of warfare.' Distribution maps were used for a wide variety of objects, ranging from horse and chariot furniture to gang chains and currency bars, to establish their origins (Fig. 69). Northwest Wales had no known source of such fine and artistic pieces, and Fox contended that the majority of the hoard had probably come from the Bristol Channel region, the land of the Dobunni, with its iron deposits and metalworking in the Forest of Dean. Other sources were East Anglia and Southeast England, but two items, the bronze war trumpet and a bridle bit, had been imported from Ireland.

The most striking object, a crescentic bronze plaque with an oval ornamented panel in low relief, probably came from Yorkshire. Looking somewhat like a small

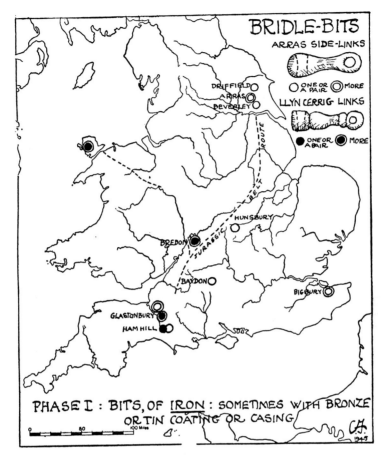

Figure 69: Llyn Cerrig Bach – Distribution of Bridle Bits (Phase I) (National Museum of Wales)

torque but with a closed loop, the purpose or fitting of this plaque has never been established. It is the subject of the single colour plate in the Final Report and was described by Jacquetta Hawkes as 'Celtic decorative genius at its most accomplished. It has an asymmetry, which is subtly balanced and succeeds in making the matrix of space as powerfully effective as the design itself. It is wholly abstract, yet there is some strange movement in it; simple to austerity, yet the curved surfaces of the repousse work lend a certain voluptuousness'[25] (see Colour Plate 1). Some of the iron metalwork was local, a blacksmith's tongs gave evidence to that, and the high quality of the steel used for the wheel tires pointed to the technical skills of local smiths.

As well as being fully illustrated, each of the 36 different categories of object was provided with a documented list of similar finds in Great Britain and Ireland. These tables, that took weeks of work to produce, were practical examples of the national register that he had so forcibly advocated at the 1943 Conference. They had been a regular feature of much of his work and were invaluable to fellow archaeologists and museum curators alike. Many of these objects, such as military weapons, harness fittings, domestic items like cauldrons or water clocks and currency bars were familiar, others like chariot horn caps had not been previously identified in this country. This book was considered by D. B. Harden to be of especial value to museum curators, most of whom were unfamiliar with such amorphous bits of iron and bronze, by providing them with a ready reference to assist them in recognising objects brought in for identification. Fox assessed the finds as being dated between the early part of the 1st century BC and the arrival of the Romans in Anglesey in 61 AD.

Recently some of the animal bones have been subjected to carbon dating. This suggests that 'there was a rite of animal sacrifice at Llyn Cerrig Bach, which continued from at least the 4th to the 2nd century BC and possibly later. This raises the question of whether some of the metalwork can be given an earlier date or whether the deposition of metal artefacts was a later development of the rite which complemented or replaced the earlier custom of animal sacrifice.'[26] L. F. Cowley, Assistant Keeper of Zoology had described the bones in an Appendix, as being Ox, Horse, Pig, Sheep and Dog. Although Mr Jones in his original letter had referred to human remains, none were found and it must be concluded that he was mistaken. Fox was very familiar with human sacrifice, his *Archaeologia* paper on the barrow at Sutton 268 that included child sacrifice had only just been published, and he would not have been at all surprised to find human remains at Llyn Cerrig Bach. He, it will be recalled, had visited the site in August and inspected all the objects that Mr Jones had collected. If human bones existed there can be little doubt that they would have been recognised and forwarded to Cardiff for analysis.

The most spectacular result of this research was his reconstruction of the Celtic war cart and the model that Fred Gay produced in the Archaeological Department workshop. I have the most vivid memory of my father working at his study desk in Cardiff telling me how he had recreated this 'chariot' from the metallic pieces and the small quantity of wood (mostly Ash) that had survived. His enthusiastic description of the drawing that he was doing of this military vehicle will always be with me (Fig. 70). D. B. Harden was clearly of the same mind. Describing this reconstruction of the chariot he wrote, 'This is modern archaeological method at its best; a standard at which so many aim and which so few attain.'[27]

In his conclusions, Fox assesses the likely reasons for this rich hoard of militaria that had been garnered from all parts of southern Britain and Northern Ireland. 'Anglesey,' he wrote, 'has rich cornlands but they are of limited extent and could hardly, at so early a period, have secured for its warrior class such rich panoply as was deposited in the lake.' Although most of the metal objects recovered had bright blue patches of vivianite, a hydrous phosphate of iron due to being in contact with animal phosphates, Fox does not attempt to link the military equipment deposited in the lake with the animal remains. This could well have been a much older and continuing rite; it does not affect

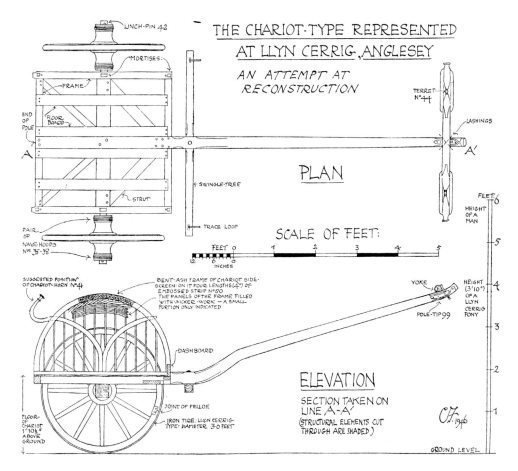

THE CHARIOT·TYPE REPRESENTED
AT LLYN CERRIG, ANGLESEY

AN ATTEMPT AT
RECONSTRUCTION

PLAN

SCALE OF FEET:

ELEVATION

SECTION TAKEN ON
LINE A–A'
(STRUCTURAL ELEMENTS CUT
THROUGH ARE SHADED)

Figure 70: Llyn Cerrig Bach – Chariot (reconstruction) (National Museum of Wales)

his conclusions. Since his dating brought him into the middle of the 1st century AD, with many of the weapons clearly damaged before deposition, he suggests a possible link with the Druids and Suetonius. Christopher Hawkes, commenting on this, wrote, 'Whether the depositing was done piecemeal or all at once, it is impossible not to join Sir Cyril in connecting it with the famous Druids of this sacred island. They will have been the magnet which drew such a diversity of material hither from so far afield, whether as offerings or presents over a long period of time, or as a single oblation e.g. of battle spoils. At present the former seems the more likely, but the wealth long in gathering may yet all have been committed to the lake together as a supreme sacrifice, perhaps in panic, or by the hand of a victorious and destroying enemy. For read the puzzle how one will, the imagination cannot shut out the thought of the sack of the island's Druid groves by Suetonius Paulinus in the fateful year 61.'[28]

Both the interim and final reports were enthusiastically received by his colleagues. Wheeler cabled from Simla 'Your Anglesey book just arrived. It's tremendous. A new firm base for Celtic studies,'[29] and Radford described it as 'a publication of such moment ... that has your characteristic quality of learning lightly worn.' However it was his friend Stuart Piggott, by this time Professor of Prehistoric Archaeology at Edinburgh, who wrote the most telling and perceptive comment. 'Praise is impertinent, but how I've enjoyed it all. I am now quite enthralled by the Iron Age in Britain in a way I never was before. Why did nobody before you appreciate the essential excitement and interest in the metalwork and its connections in carpentry and coach builder's craft? Because nobody before took the craftsman's viewpoint and I believe because most of our revered seniors and some contemporary colleagues are townsmen first and last. You (and I) had the enormous good fortune to be brought up as countrymen and spent our boyhood smelling round cow byres and blacksmith's shops; knew a bit about farming; saw good thatching done; got earwigs up our short pants riding in harvest wagons and knew the tilt and set of a dung cart. You've got all this and more into the interpretation of archaeology and I hope that I have taken at least some steps on the same road.'[30]

*   *   *

Throughout these war years Fox was frequently called upon to vet a wide range of sites that were commandeered for both military and civil purposes. Most of these trips were by car for which the Ministry of Works might, on request, provide the petrol. 'I wonder if the Office could let me have a few gallons,' he wrote to Bryan O'Neil 'The distance is 250 miles there and back and I am very short ... 4 gallons would make me happy, 2 gallons would make all the difference to my peace of mind!' Though most journeys were to sites in South Wales, there were occasional carefully planned expeditions covering half a dozen or so places in Central and North Wales.

As well as his own work, for which he would sometimes be accompanied by Aileen, he was also asked to visit Ministry excavations being undertaken by Audrey Williams, Leslie Murray-Threipland and occasionally Grimes. Having visited the site he would then report back on the need for scheduling, delaying operations or excavation. Typical of the latter was his inspection of the preliminary work for a new open cast mine at Blaenavon. He found that this threatened three cairns and his request to stop surface soil removal provoked a confrontation with the contractors anxious to complete their work to time. Fox reported that he was equally anxious that the cairns should be properly examined before being destroyed, but was 'concerned that the blame would fall on him *personally* for holding up this vital coal production.' Grimes was diverted from Plymouth and the cairns were duly recorded for posterity. Towards the end of 1943 the Government decided that the western end of the Gower Peninsula would be made available to US Forces as a Battle Training Ground. Though live ammunition was not to be used, concern was expressed locally for the security of their ancient monuments; Fox was asked to visit the area and produce a list of antiquities that needed protection. Having forwarded his list to O'Neil at the Ministry of Works it seems that no action was taken and the Americans were never told of the 'risk' that they posed to Welsh heritage. Perhaps this was just as well, they might not have appreciated an academic concern for earthen mounds and old stones when they were trying to win a war.

From mid 1944 until the end of the war there was little activity that involved possible destruction or damage to scheduled sites, except for the extension of open-cast mining.[31] With peace and the emergency housing programme on bombed-out town and city sites, Fox was again in demand until local councils took over responsibility from central Government. Debates at the Council for British Archaeology, for which Fox was in the chair, questioned the effectiveness of this latest work. O'Neil wrote in reply to say that the Inspectorate of Ancient Monuments had vetted 36,000 sites, mostly on paper, examined 110 of which 50 needed supervision and 8 full excavation. It was a 'very considerable effort for comparatively little reward, but any one of those could have been another Caerleon or Exeter and heritage destroyed is lost forever'.

During the war Bryan O'Neil was a fairly frequent visitor to Four Elms; like others he needed to come provided. 'We shall be very pleased to see you,' Fox wrote, '… Aileen says that she needs no ration foods for one night but since you are staying two it would be helpful if you brought some bits and pieces.' In her autobiography Aileen describes these efforts to keep her family fed and to cater for friends, who came to stay. Although I was away for most of the time, either at boarding school or with my grandparents in Walton-on-the-Hill, my memories of moving around also involved taking little bits of paper from the ration cards, or being given a package of rationed food to take with me. We were fortunate as a family having friends in America. Occasionally parcels would arrive with little luxuries, a few packets of Passing Cloud cigarettes for father (he gave up smoking after the war), tins of ham and dried fruits for the house, chocolate for the adults and sweets for the children. Rabbit from the market was a regular dish and as enjoyable now as it was then. I cannot say the same of scrambled egg made with dried egg powder, but it was better than nothing, and no-one, family or guests, went hungry.

In this latter part of the war Fox was very much involved in discussions with the Welsh Department of the Ministry of Education to set up a museum school service. The Museum had been undertaking work in schools since the early twenties but this activity was now to be expanded and given national status under R. A. Butler's 1944 *Education Bill.* Fox's memorandum *A Proposal for a National Museum Schools Service* was published in December and formed the basis for a service that was to be inaugurated by his successor in 1948. Although not accountable to the Museum Council, the Director was nominated as Chief Executive of the service and it was to be housed within the Museum building. All operating expenses, including a vehicle that would take the necessary facilities for museum lectures and exhibitions to schools all over the Principality, were to be paid for by the Local Education Authorities. Subsequently this highly successful pioneering initiative was expanded to include training colleges and university education departments, and was internationally recognised as setting the standard for intra- and extra-mural schools services.

Fox's pre-eminent position, as museum director and field archaeologist, had been recognised by colleagues at the Antiquaries in 1944, when he was unanimously elected to succeed Sir Alfred Clapham as President. It was to be a difficult five-year period, as the nation tackled the shortages and difficulties that typify transition from war to peace. As their first 'provincial' President, with pressing commitments in Wales, he devolved many of his committee duties to his Vice-Presidents. Previously this had been almost an honorary position, which one acknowledged with gratitude and pride and from which one might be elevated to the Presidency, but as he recalled in his final Anniversary Address, the office demanded little if anything in the way of duty. With the pressures of today it is inconceivable that one person could fulfil all presidential responsibilities alone, but at the time the concept was new and encountered some comment and objections on principle from the older members.

With no lessening of his duties in Cardiff, or for the Ministry, Fox found little time for any new work. Research on houses in Monmouthshire with Lord Raglan was a means of escape, and his only relaxation at home was in his work on the Llyn Cerrig Bach finds. His presidential duties at the Antiquaries, meetings at the British Academy and the Council for British Archaeology, of which he was ex-officio Chairman, took him more and more frequently to London. There were some benefits however; he could meet friends and colleagues to discuss his latest ideas on chariot furniture and Celtic weapons face to face rather than dealing with it all on paper. It was on one such visit to London, shortly after the end of the war, when the British Museum was starting to recover its antiquities from store that he was reminded of national treasures hidden for the duration but now to be returned to public view. Glyn Daniel recounted to me how Christopher Hawkes, who had been serving with the Ministry of Aircraft Production, had returned to the Museum 'to find the forecourt filled with lorries with a horde of stalwart porters lugging green packing cases up to the galleries. He contacted Fox at the Antiquaries who told him "I must come and see, I must be there when these treasures are opened up," and wrote to Kendrick to ask his permission.' As he arrived Hawkes had just unpacked the Thames Helmet[32] and had it in his hand (Fig. 71). 'Cyril was thrilled, but could not accept that it needed a leather lining until he tried it on. He looked so ridiculous. "You're right, you're right, you're right," he said, "there must have been a leather cap inside. It started as a leather helmet with tusks and the sheet metal was added later." This was typical of Cyril, he had a mind like quicksilver and was never afraid to revise his opinion.'

The National Museum had also been recovering its treasures from the basements;

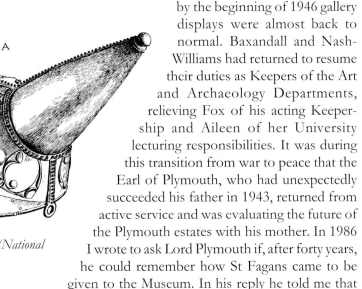

Figure 71: Thames Helmet (National Museum of Wales)

by the beginning of 1946 gallery displays were almost back to normal. Baxandall and Nash-Williams had returned to resume their duties as Keepers of the Art and Archaeology Departments, relieving Fox of his acting Keeper-ship and Aileen of her University lecturing responsibilities. It was during this transition from war to peace that the Earl of Plymouth, who had unexpectedly succeeded his father in 1943, returned from active service and was evaluating the future of the Plymouth estates with his mother. In 1986 I wrote to ask Lord Plymouth if, after forty years, he could remember how St Fagans came to be given to the Museum. In his reply he told me that they 'had decided to give up St Fagans Castle, but made no decision about its future, when they received a timely word from the Director of the National Museum of Wales ... that it would be welcomed as a Folk Museum.'[33] The idea was obviously well received by the family. On 4 February 1946 the Earl of Plymouth with his mother, Irene Countess of Plymouth, called on the Director to inform him that he wished to offer St Fagans Castle and its immediate grounds to the Museum as an open-air museum. On 18 February 1946 he wrote to confirm this offer, stating that he understood 'that for many years there has been a desire to secure a Field Museum as an adjunct to the National Museum of Wales. I am writing therefore to say that I am prepared to place St Fagans Castle and gardens at the disposal of the National Museum if, and so long as, they should be required by the Council for museum purposes. I know only too well the great interest which my father and grandfather took in the National Museum of Wales. I believe that it would have been their wish that, since the family will no longer be living there, the house and grounds should be given to the museum for such a much desired extension of its services to the public' (Fig. 72).

For Fox, this was to herald the crowning achievement of over twenty years service to the Museum, and was the end of a personal crusade for a folk museum for Wales. Basset records, 'almost immediately ... an informal meeting of the Museum officers was called ... to consider the offer and visit St Fagans. As a result the Director prepared a report on the site for the Council in which he argued among other things, that if the proposal was to be seriously considered it would be essential to provide enough space for the reconstruction of buildings from all over Wales.' On 15 March the Council minutes recorded their 'high appreciation of the most generous offer.' They resolved to gratefully accept Lord Plymouth's offer provided the Council was able to get reasonable assurances that maintenance funds would be available and that suitable arrangements could be made with Plymouth Estates Ltd to purchase or lease not less than 80 acreas of adjacent woodland to add to the 18 acres that Lord Plymouth was intending to hand over. Two month's later the Council had received the necessary assurances from the Treasury and from Plymouth Estates and were able to ratify their acceptance of St Fagans

Figure 72: St Fagan's Castle (National Museums and Galleries of Wales)

Castle. Bassett records that 'work started almost immediately on the task of transforming the Castle into a museum and of opening it to the public … and the decision was made that the [full bilingual] title of the new annex should be Amgueddfa Genedlaethol Cymru – Amgueddfa Werin Cymru or National Museum of Wales – The Welsh Folk Museum.' The Department under Iorwerth Peate took the lead in this work. Following a visit to museums in Sweden, he 'prepared at the Director's request … a long memorandum on the policy, of acquisition, siting and reconstructing of buildings as a national folk museum. This memorandum was accepted in its entirety by the Council in October 1946 and has formed the basis of the development of the site from then on.'[34] Although the gardens were opened briefly to the public in July 1947, alterations to the Elizabethan House and its surrounding buildings delayed the opening until the following year. Subsequently representations were made to turn the Welsh Folk Museum into an independent institution. The Council resisted the change, they gave it considerable autonomy but insisted that it remained an annex of the National Museum. Peate was initially appointed Keeper-in-Charge and in 1953 as Curator, but he still remained responsible to the Director.

*   *   *

Being born in 1882 Fox was due to retire in December 1947 but willingly agreed to continue in office for a further year to oversee the completion of the first phase of the St Fagans Castle project. The present Lord Raglan recently told me that his father was most disappointed that Fox had not accepted the Council's informal offer to continue beyond this date but it is clear that he was concerned that his wife's career should not be jeopardised.[35] In 1945, Aileen had been asked by Professor Ian Richmond to undertake trial excavations in the war-damaged areas of Exeter. This work was to continue for three seasons and lead to the invitation in August 1947 of a Special Lectureship at the University College of the South-west, now Exeter University. Together with her Honorary Curatorship of Cirencester Museum, where she was responsible for rearranging the archaeological collection, this showed how she was building her own career and could feel confident that she was 'accepted by the professionals and no longer considered as Cyril's shadow.'

In the summer of 1946 they had their first holiday since touring America in 1939. They went by train to Fishguard, took the ferry to Cork and toured the antiquities of the southern Irish counties by train and country bus. They enjoyed a typical Irish blend of rain and warm sunshine but above all a seemingly unlimited supply of fresh food. Their first breakfast, of two eggs and bacon, was more than their ration for a week! This was to be their last holiday before he left the Museum, although he did make one or two extended trips to Exeter to see Aileen's excavations in the city.

They had been discussing his forthcoming retirement for some time and were still undecided on his next move. Monmouthshire, Cirencester and even Cambridge (where there were firm indications that a Chair would be on offer) were considered, until the decision was made for them by Aileen's acceptance of the lectureship at Exeter.[36] The University College agreed that this appointment should be part time for the first year, whilst her husband was completing his service at the Museum. Aileen found a house in Exeter in St Leonard's Road, which they both liked, and arranged to move in the late summer of 1948.

Fox's last year at Cardiff was a busy one. In addition to the routine work at the Museum, there were regular meetings to discuss the conversion of St Fagans Castle, and its associated fund raising projects. He was also regularly commuting to London on Antiquaries and Royal Commission business, as well as trying to complete as many of his Monmouthshire house surveys as possible. In July 1947 the University of Wales awarded him an Honorary Doctorate of Literature at a colourful ceremony in the Brangwyn Hall in Swansea. In his address the Cardiff historian, Professor William Rees, praised Fox for his contribution to Welsh archaeology with his 'deep imaginative insight and unerring instinct. Equally versed in archaeology, architecture and geography he exemplifies that rare combination of humanist and scientist. ...Wales owes a debt to Sir Cyril Fox,' he continued, ' for his successful and sympathetic treatment of her past and for his part in making this available for her people. ... The conception of a Folk Museum for Wales, about to be realised at St Fagans under his guidance, is a pioneer effort in museum development in these islands. It is for these reasons that the University today desires to pay its tribute to his work and to set its seal on his labours.'

There were many other tributes paid for his administrative work at the Museum and his research work throughout the Principality, culminating in a presentation by the Court and Council of a fine Welsh landscape by Cedric Morris. Looking across the water from the rural landscape of the Gower peninsula, with memories of that survey to protect its antiquities from the 'ravages of our American allies', there are the smoking chimneys of the steelworks at Llanelli. He had chosen the subject himself as typifying the extremes of Welsh activities in the twentieth century. It hung above the fireplace in his sitting room in Exeter and gave him immense pleasure for the rest of his life.

The Council had also been responsible for recording a tribute that formed part of the local news on the Welsh Home Service, thus ensuring that it would be heard throughout the Principality. The broadcast drew attention to his ability to inspire the devoted co-operation of all staff and the Council's high regard and sincere affection for him. It was noted how he had always borne in mind the need to bring the resources of the Museum to the most distant parts of Wales, by the Affiliated Museum Scheme, the Museums School Service and the extension lectures by his staff. Now the idea of an Open-Air Folk Museum, which he had advocated for so long and so persistently, had come to fruition during his directorate.

There were innumerable letters from members of the Council, Museum staff, friends and neighbours that lent added further credence to this tribute. As one commentator wrote about his forthcoming retirement, 'There are other archaeologists, who can claim a high degree of scholarship and achievement, but few who can inspire and charm as does Sir Cyril Fox! To be with him is indeed an inspiration.'[37] Lord Raglan added, 'a lot of the zest will have gone out of our Council meetings with your departure.' It was the end of an era for the Museum, but he had achieved so much of what he had set out to do and his successor, Dr Dilwyn John and others would take it on from there. For him there were mixed memories, of personal achievement and success, as well as of those tragic days in 1932. He had the greatest affection for the Museum, for its staff and for the building itself, whose growth he had overseen and fought for funding for the past twenty-two years, but with one minor reservation. Glyn Daniel, a frequent visitor and lifelong friend many years later remembered him commenting on the 'stone circle' outside the main entrance 'Isn't it disgusting that outside this magnificent Museum there is this bogus antiquity and I have to walk through it every day.' At least he would be spared that embarrassment in the future. Aileen wrote 'we left Cardiff with few regrets though retaining happy memories. … Cyril was now convinced that it was best to make a break and that to hang around in South Wales, watching a new Director at work, would be a mistake.'[38] I am sure that he would not have quarrelled with that assessment as he came to enjoy and feel at home in the Devon countryside and its capital city Exeter. But fame and international recognition notwithstanding, when assessing his achievements it would surely have been that summer day in July when his ambition of an open air museum for Wales was finally realised that was for him the crowning glory.[39] Whether it was due to Fox's age and his natural diffidence, or his departure from the Welsh scene as soon as the Castle was open to visitors, the impression gained over the past forty years is that the establishment of this Welsh Folk Museum was entirely due to Iorwerth Peate. Little if any mention is made of the contribution of his Director Cyril Fox. This view is summarised by Catrin Stevens in the opening paragraph of her biographical summary of Peate's life and work for the *Writers of Wales* series. 'On 1st July 1948, both the Castle and gardens of *Amgueddfa Werin Cymru*, the Welsh Folk Museum at St Fagans, Cardiff, were opened to the public and became a tangible memorial to his vision and mission throughout his life. As the Museum's prime mover, creator and first Curator, Iorwerth Peate remains synonymous with the reputation of perhaps our most internationally esteemed national institution.'[40] Whilst no one should deny Peate his place in the forefront of twentieth century Welsh scholarship, both as an academic and poet, it is invidious to credit him alone with the achievement of a Folk Museum for Wales. Throughout his career as Keeper and Director at the Museum, and nationally as President of both the Museum's Association and the Society of Antiquaries, and many other stages, Fox was persistently advancing the cause of galleries and museums to house and display collections of folk material. It was Fox, who in 1926 persuaded his financially hard pressed Museum Council to build a special gallery to house the 'bygones' collection, who in 1933 proposed the creation of a sub-department of Folk Culture and three years later raised it to full departmental status and finally it was he, who made that suggestion to Lord Plymouth that St Fagans would be welcomed by the Museum as a folk museum. Fox's role as the driving force behind this project is best summarised by Sir William Goscombe John (RA and former member of the Museum Court), who wrote in October 1949. 'Those of us, who heard your first suggestion that such an addition to the National Museum of Wales was desirable, will remember how it was looked upon as quixotic and impossible to achieve. Well thanks to your faith and enthusiasm, and the great and unexpected generosity of Lord Plymouth, it is a going concern having had its first hundred thousand visitors. May I therefore offer you my sincere congratulations upon the result, for to you alone is entirely due the credit of the great achievement.'

Notes

1 Letter to the author dated 25 May 1986
2 Stake Circles in Turf Barrows: a record of excavation in Glamorgan 1939–40 *Ant.J.* XXI
3 Fox noted that Mortimer in *Forty Years Researches* had suggested that two Early Bronze Age barrows in Yorkshire were of similar construction.
4 A Datable Ritual Barrow in Glamorganshire *Antiquity* XV
5 A Beaker Barrow, enlarged in the Middle Bronze Age, at South Hill, Talbenny, Pembrokeshire *Arch.J.* XCIX. This paper and that on Sutton 268 read to the Antiquaries 31 Oct. 40, provoked considerable correspondence with Piggott, Childe, Tratman, Forde and Hawkes and enabled Fox to incorporate recorded finds from across the country.
6 *Y Cymmrodor* XLVII p. 65–66 and *Antiquity* X p. 445
7 I. Peate *Rhwng dau fyd, Darn o hunangofiant* p. 115–6 Translation by D. Bassett
8 Forts and Farms on Margam Mountain *Antiquity* VIII
9 A Croft in the Upper Nedd Valley, Ystradfellte *Antiquity* XIV
10 Letter from Mortimer Wheeler 27 June 1941
11 National Museum of Wales Council Emergency Committee Minutes 20 July 1940 and Council Minutes 26 July 1940.
12 I. Peate *Rhwang dau fyd, Darn o hunangofiant* p. 116–120 Translation by D. Bassett

[13] The Boundary Line of Cymru – Sir John Rhys Memorial Lecture 1940 *Br.Acad.* XXVI incorporating earlier reports in *Antiquity* (1929) and *Yorkshire Society for Celtic Studies* (1937)

[14] The GT Clark Trust Prize assessor's report to the Secretary of the Cambrian Archaeological Association dated 24 January 1946

[15] The roster included the Director, Secretary, Keepers and Assistant Keepers

[16] J. Lees-Milne *Prophesying Peace* p. 125

[17] *South Wales Echo* 24 July with Headline 'Regards Hitler as Brother' and *Western Mail* 25 July 'Dr Iorwerth C. Peate Registered a CO'

[18] Fox letter to H. E. Lord Harlech dated 19 December 1941

[19] The Charter of Incorporation, signed 19 March 1907, makes provision for a Court of Governors as the supreme governing body representing all parts and interests in the Principality, a Council to act as the executive body and a Director as the Chief Administration Officer – Douglas Bassett, The Making of a National Museum Part I *Soc.Cym.* 1982 p. 17

[20] I. Peate *Rhwang dau fyd, Darn o hunangofiant* p 116–128 Translation by D. Bassett

[21] D. Bassett, The Making of a National Museum Part III *Soc.Cym.* 1984 p. 41

[22] *A Find of the Early Iron Age from Anglesey.* An initial report was published in 1944 *Arch.Camb.* and *Trans.Anglesey Ant.Soc.& Field Club.* A comprehensive Interim Report was published by the National Museum of Wales in May 1945 and a Final Report in March 1947 (reprinted 1959).

[23] Letter to The Curator, National Museum of Wales dated 8 July 1943

[24] One of these relics, which arrived too late to be included in the Interim Report, was the subject of a special report – A Shield Boss of the Early Iron Age from Anglesey *Arch.Camb.* XCVIII

[25] Review of the Interim Report in the *Spectator* – 4 July 1945. Although not stated it is assumed that this initial sentence refers to British Celtic art since it cannot be compared to the glories of late La Tène metalwork

[26] Radiocarbon dates from the Oxford AMS system *Archaeometry* 40 Part 1

[27] *Mus.Journ.* 47

[28] *Ant. J.* XXVI

[29] Fox and Wheeler were in regular touch throughout the war. Wheeler's letters from the North African campaign were read out to the family at breakfast with delight at the vivid descriptions of the action and his surreptitious archaeological expeditions. Fox expressed pleasure and surprise that he should have been chosen as the recipient of such fascinating historical material. However Aileen was more percipient commenting 'he's written them for publication knowing that you'll keep them' which proved to be the case.

[30] Letter dated 5 March 1947

[31] Fox wrote a summary of his war work for the *Bulletin of the Board of Celtic Studies* entitled 'Field Archaeology in South Wales 1939–45 – Personal reflections and record' *BBCS* XII p. 52

[32] See *Pattern and Purpose* p. 49 and Fig. 36a

[33] Letter to the author dated 28 April 1986

[34] D. Bassett, The Making of a National Museum Part III *Soc.Cym.* 1984 pp. 44–47

[35] According to Lord Raglan Fox was asked to stay on as Director for a further term of 5 Years to his seventieth birthday.

[36] Fox also told his younger daughter that he had been asked by Exeter's Vice Chancellor if he would consider a part-time position at the University College but refused since he did not wish to compromise or undermine his wife's position.

[37] *Nature* 29 May 1948

[38] A. Fox *Aileen – A Pioneering Archaeologist* p. 110

[39] The doors of the house were opened on 17 July 1948 without any ceremony. In January 1949 the St Fagans Committee discussed a formal opening but decided to defer it. The deferment was permanent and St Fagans has never been formally opened.

[40] C. Stevens *Writers of Wales – Iowerth C. Peate* p.1

X

An Extraordinary Archaeologist 1949–1959
Monmouthshire Houses and Celtic Art

The house that Aileen had found was a typical Regency town house (Fig. 73). On a quiet road, surrounded by similar detached period properties, it was within easy walking distance of Exeter City centre and the University College in Gandy Street. With four floors, including an attic and semi-basement, there was ample room for each of them to have their own study, as well as a playroom and accommodation for all the family. A small walled garden ensured total privacy; in these congenial surroundings Fox quickly settled down to his new life in Devon. Over the years he became more accessible to the younger members of his family; seemingly less irritated when his study was invaded, and even open to persuasion to join one of his sons for a walk along the river, canal bank or into the city.

Though the pressure of day to day administration had been lifted, he was kept extremely busy writing and with regular trips to London, Wales and archaeological sites that friends and colleagues thought would interest him (Figs 74, 75). Shortly after retiring from the Museum, he had been asked by the Chancellor of the Exchequer, Sir

Figure 73: 28 St Leonard's Road Exeter 1948. Left, Viewed from the road. Right, Aileen in the garden

Figure 74: Visiting an excavation near Shrewsbury with Lal Chitty 1949

Figure 75: Fund raising for preservation of Tretower Court 1949

Stafford Cripps, to serve on a Committee investigating the management and funding of privately owned country houses. The Committee, which was chaired by Sir Ernest Gowers, presented its report *Houses of Outstanding Historic or Architectural Interest* to Parliament in June 1950. Most of the evidence was heard at a series of meetings in Whitehall from Government Departments, Public and Local Authorities and some sixty private individuals. Members of the Committee also visited twenty-six houses throughout the United Kingdom. These provided a cross-section of the properties they were assessing, ranging from mansions like Hatfield House, to smaller country estates such as Montacute and town houses in Edinburgh and London. Fox found much enjoyment and fascination in this work, not least in assessing the degrees of commitment and realism exhibited by the cross section of owners who came to express their difficulties and concerns.

His daughter Penelope recalled that 'all his love of architecture and history, together with a museum director's keen appreciation of the enormous value and responsibility of the movable furnishings within such houses, combined to make this sideline of his professional activities a wonderfully rewarding experience. He [with the other members of the Committee] was convinced that the only way forward to preserve the unique character of individual properties was to subsidise their owners to continue to live in them:' This, and some of their other recommendations, must have seemed to be at odds with the socialist doctrines of a Labour Government. The Chancellor wrote to thank each of the members for their work, but the Government, with its small majority, was in no position to do anything. It was to be many years, and at least one more Commission, before the recommendations of this report were re-examined and some assistance provided through tax relief.

On his retirement the Council of the National Museum of Wales appointed Fox a

'Research Associate in Archaeology' for five years. Whilst this position was unpaid the Council agreed to take responsibility for all his work and expenses for *Monmouthshire Houses*. Subsequently they were to invite him, on similar terms, to supplement his study of the Llyn Cerrig Bach finds by producing a complete survey of Celtic achievements in Britain. In addition the Antiquaries and all Government appointments covered any expenses made on their behalf, which meant that his changed financial circumstances, coming down from a final salary of £1400 to less than half that sum, had little immediate impact. Towards the end of his life, as inflation reduced the purchasing power of his income and working expenses had to be provided from his own pocket, he became increasingly concerned.

Following their move to Exeter Aileen's salary provided the means for all household bills, although my grandmother continued to pay for most of my school fees at Bryanston. On retirement, Fox's superannuation payments produced a sum of about £20,000. He had never had more than a few hundred pounds to his name and little interest in money, so sought the advice of his Bank and his brother Norman. Norman had had a successful career in the motor business; he had retired at the age of 50 to become a Golf Club Secretary, supplementing his living by astute financial investment. He advised his brother to invest in a broad range of equities but the Bank strongly recommended purchasing Government Stock, to ensure a secure income. Conscious of his need to provide for his wife in the longer term, and being chary of the risk that equities entailed, he chose the latter; his retirement income was funded by the Bank's investment of his money in 3.5% War Loan. Nineteen years later this income was unchanged and his total financial assets came to £8000. Over this same period his brother had trebled his income and the value of his investments – a sad reflection on the merits of Bank advice.

Fox's term as President of the Antiquaries came to an end on 23rd April 1949. His five Anniversary Addresses to the Society had covered a wide range of topics. Initially, they had been dominated by the war and his hopes for the future of British archaeology, but then he took the opportunity to introduce other aspects of research and the need for archaeological reconstruction. In 1946, he expressed his concern for the absence of such reconstruction in the work of previous generations. As an example he cited the nineteenth century excavation of Yorkshire chariot graves that surely would have provided enough detailed information to enable a modern craftsman to build a replica. In similar vein, he was concerned that knowledge of traditional styles of building in mediaeval and renaissance Britain was totally inadequate. In his opinion, there was no more interesting constructional form visible in ancient houses than the cruck truss. But how did it originate; were there distinct types; and did wooden constructional technique, of say the Midlands and eastern Wales, spread from the south-east or had it an independent western origin? 'Here is a great and largely unexplored field of study. ... It demands an archaeological approach; while we cannot do without the technical skill and knowledge of our friends the architects, we must not expect them to solve our problems for us [and] while the survey work on the yeoman's houses of Britain is going on, we can address ourselves to the fascinating and complex problems of origins – social, economic, environmental and cultural – of the several styles.'[1] In April 1947, he followed this up with a detailed description of the Llyn Cerrig Bach chariot; demonstrating to his audience what might have been achieved if the Yorkshire chariots had been found half a century or so later. For his final two addresses, he dwelt on the need to preserve our ancient monuments and antiquities from damage by weather, vandalism, accidental or even scheduled destruction and theft. Then, in the conclusion of his final address in April 1949, he once again urged members to take part in a 'national survey, archaeological and architectural of our local building techniques and house planning, treating each region separately and determining, insofar as surviving examples permit, its origin and evolution.'[2]

Here is the first recorded occasion when Fox refers to this subject as 'vernacular'. He used it again in October 1949, in his introduction to the 'Rhind' lectures for the Society of Antiquaries of Scotland on regional house styles, in his contribution to Crawford's Festschrift, *Aspects of Archaeology*, and in his introduction to the first volume of *Monmouthshire Houses*.[3] Although vernacular[4] usually refers to an indigenous people, or more commonly their language, the Oxford English Dictionary records usage relating to cottage building in 1857. Whether forgotten in this context or ignored, it certainly had no general acceptance or usage by anyone else until the founding of the Vernacular Architecture Group in 1952.

Fox's work on 'yeoman' houses in Monmouthshire, with his close friend and colleague Lord (Roy) Raglan, was a labour of love. Now free of both Museum and Antiquaries responsibilities, Fox was a regular visitor to Cefntilla Court, checking the surveys and discussing his text. Apart from easing entry to many of the remote and sometimes derelict properties that they had recorded over the past eight years, the general impression given to me by his contemporaries was that Lord Raglan was just a tape holder and a portable six foot measuring pole for many of the photographs (Fig. 76). Although he might have happily described his participation in such terms, this would grossly underrate his contribution and his achievements. He was a former President of the Royal Anthro-

Figure 76: Lord (Roy) Raglan – the 6ft measuring pole at work 1949 (National Museum of Wales)

pological Institute and, as his paper *The origin of Vernacular Architecture*[5] demonstrates, was a knowledgeable, erudite and companionable host with whom Fox could fruitfully argue the detailed points of his text. This admixture of local gentry and practical intelligentsia produced a volume that over ten years later John Smith would still describe as, 'the most important book on vernacular building that has yet appeared in English ... a work, which has revolutionised the outlook towards such studies.'[6]

The Fox and Raglan survey of around 470 houses, originally suggested by Lord Raglan in 1941, was stimulated by wartime security demands for the demolition of the late seventeenth century Upper Wern Hir farmhouse, near Usk (see Fig. 68). Starting in the vicinity of Usk, their survey gradually extended into the rural hinterland of Monmouthshire; eventually it included all the area to the north and east of Newport. Dr. Peter Smith records an interview with Lord Raglan who, told him 'that their method of working was for him to discover the houses of interest, obtain permission to enter and then call in Fox to complete the survey. They discussed the interpretation of the site together, after which Fox took the notes back to Cardiff to write up and draw out.' Since much of the work had to be 'accomplished at weekends and under pressure from other duties [Lord Raglan was Lord Lieutenant of Monmouthshire apart from his other responsibilities] ... it was a remarkable achievement for two men working in their leisure hours.'[7]

The authors acknowledged that giving dates to many of the early houses was difficult; the time lag for recognisable architectural features, in a district manifestly outside the mainstream of progress, could be considerable. However they avoided controversy by giving as their starting point the Owain Glyn Dwr rebellion. 'The vivid account included in the Chronicle of Adam of Usk (1377–1421) of the fighting, pillage and destruction ... suggests that when opinion hovers between the late fourteenth and early fifteenth century ... a date after the end of the Revolt (1415) is much more probable than one before it.'[8] The survey ends with the death of Queen Anne in 1714, which was the finishing point of the contemporary Royal Commission surveys. Their work in these old and often dilapidated buildings was sometimes hazardous. Geoffrey Somerset, Lord Raglan's younger son, who accompanied them on several of their expeditions, remembers the two of them falling through the floor of a barn, fortunately onto a pile of hay, with Fox still clutching his precious camera in his hand and roaring with laughter at their escape.

The first of their three volumes, entitled *Mediaeval Houses c.1415–1560,* describes the group of houses of mediaeval character that have, or had, one or more rooms, usually the hall or living room, open to the roof. Primarily of timber construction with cruck trusses[9] and one, two or occasionally three bays, they were the standard house of the arable farmer of the period. Unfortunately, by the mid-twentieth century, many of these buildings had become semi-derelict or decaying outhouses and barns. As the authors say of one such house, Cwrt-y-Brychan, Llansoy, 'it is sad to think that our generation is likely to be the last to see ... any example of this ancient and utterly outmoded technique in the splendid prime of its achievement.' The continuing development of the St Fagans programme has of course preserved some examples of such construction for posterity but no longer in their original situation.

The survey analyses the design, origins and development of cruck types in houses and barns, together with the associated features such as sill beams, doorways, windows, framing and mouldings (Fig. 77). Studies of the patterns of annual rings established, for the first time, a possible method of obtaining cruck blades from the trunk and one of the branches of selected oak trees. These angled blades were then installed upside down; secured by sill beams at the foot and tie beams at the top (Fig. 78) Archaeological interpretation of the remains of bay panels produced a pattern of interlaced riven oak slats, inserted into holes on the underside of the upper frame and a groove on the lower frame, to provide the necessary support for wattle and daub walls (Fig. 79).

For the more prosperous farmer walls were of stone; here the cruck was mounted into the wall or supported on a cornice (Fig. 80). One or more bays were ceiled to

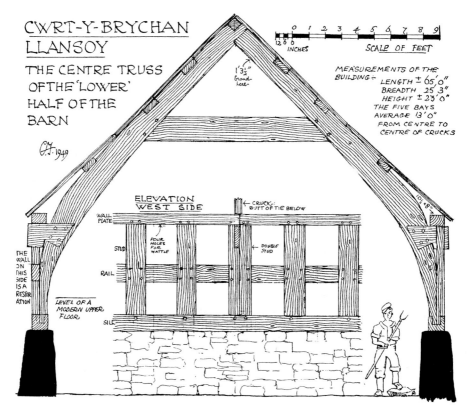

Figure 77: Cwrt-y-Brychan, Llansoy – Section with centre truss (National Museum of Wales)

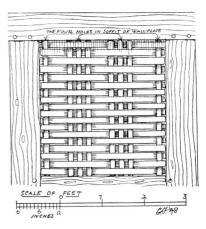

Figure 79: Great Trerihew, Llantilio Crossenny – Oak slat panel (National Museum of Wales)

Figure 78: Pit Cottage, Llanarth – Cruck truss, sill and tie beams (National Museum of Wales)

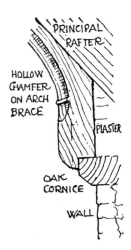

provide a Solar, or other family rooms, but in houses like Hendy Hall, the principal room or Hall remains open to the roof. In its review the *Times Literary Supplement* (20 Jul. 51) records, 'there is probably no type of architecture on which more vague generalisation has been expended than the late mediaeval timbered house. It is therefore particularly satisfying to come across a work in which the sponge is not thrown in nor are questions allowed to go by default; problems are squarely faced and theories are supported by weighed evidence.'

The story continues in the second volume, *Sub-Mediaeval Houses c.1550–1610;* most ground floor rooms are now ceiled and there are rubble walls. Particular attention is paid to mouldings, stops and chamfers. John Smith describes this volume as dealing 'with that crucial period when the social developments of the Renaissance were rapidly changing the

Figure 80: Llwyn-Celyn, Lower Cwmyoy – Cornice detail (National Museum of Wales)

open mediaeval hall, with its basic communal life, into a house offering the greater privacy of several rooms on two or three storeys, such as Upper Wern Hir. For the first time this process, as it affected smaller houses, is described in detail and the large number of buildings examined – 165 – guarantees the soundness of the author's conclusions. An archaeological technique applied to the study … caused them to

THE 'REGIONAL STYLE': DIAGRAMS OF HOUSE-TYPES

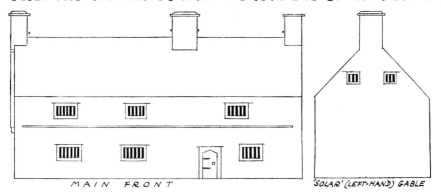

MAIN FRONT   'SOLAR' (LEFT-HAND) GABLE

TYPE III HOUSE : THREE GROUND-FLOOR ROOMS

MAIN FRONT   HALL (RIGHT-HAND) GABLE   'SOLAR' GABLE OF ANOTHER TYPE II HOUSE

TYPE II (A) HOUSE: TWO GROUND-FLOOR ROOMS

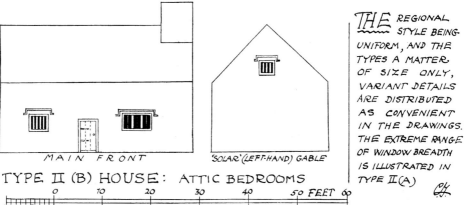

MAIN FRONT   'SOLAR' (LEFT-HAND) GABLE

TYPE II (B) HOUSE: ATTIC BEDROOMS

THE REGIONAL STYLE BEING UNIFORM, AND THE TYPES A MATTER OF SIZE ONLY, VARIANT DETAILS ARE DISTRIBUTED AS CONVENIENT IN THE DRAWINGS. THE EXTREME RANGE OF WINDOW BREADTH IS ILLUSTRATED IN TYPE II(A)

0   10   20   30   40   50 FEET 60

Figure 81: Regional Style – Diagrams of House Types (National Museum of Wales)

notice details often taken for granted by architectural historians. Thus they illustrate a dozen
sorts of chamfer stop – a feature scarcely
noticed in print before.' Society in Elizabethan
rural Monmouthshire was prosperous, but its
relative isolation and natural conservatism
meant that new ideas took time to become
established. Nevertheless 'the interaction of
cultures produced a basic house plan which
could be enlarged into either a modified long
house plan of the highland zone or a normal
lowland form with a buttery wing'[10] (Fig. 81).

In the final volume, *Renaissance Houses
c.1590–1714,* new features include framed
staircases, hipped roofs, bolection-moulded

Figure 82: Lhwyn-y-Gaer, Tregaer – Ovolo moulded window (National Museum of Wales)

panelling and the occasional use of brick. For the first time three window types are
recognised; the plain chamfered mullion, the reserved chamfer and the ovolo mould
(Fig. 82). Shaped doorheads and glazed windows appear and there is easy recognition
of dating features (Fig. 83). W. G. Hoskins regretted that the authors 'of this important
study, which has already established itself as a model of research and presentation,' ...
had chosen Monmouthshire, a county so influenced by Wales, as he would have

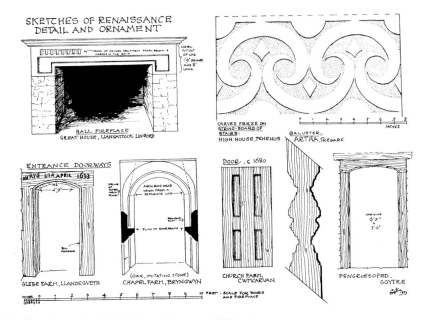

Figure 83: Renaissance details (National Museum of Wales)

'welcomed more warmly a purely English county with a more typically native vernacular. … The sooner we make comparable surveys of half a dozen other English counties the better they will be, for the rate of destruction or of substantial structural change is now so great that we are losing irreplaceable evidence every year, even possibly rare types of houses.'[11] In a footnote to the introduction of this third volume the authors agree stating that 'some of the houses revisited for checking earlier accounts have been found extensively modernised and the details on which conclusions were drawn are no longer available.'

Nearly fifty years later with so many cottages, farmhouses and outbuildings becoming redundant, being either sold as second homes and 'gentrified' or allowed to fall into total decay, this process has accelerated to the point where a survey as comprehensive as this would be virtually impossible. Throughout all three volumes Fox provided illustrations and architectural drawings of superb quality. As the *Times Literary Supplement* (20 Jul. 51) commented, 'the clarity and style of [the architectural details] suggests that the architectural profession has lost a distinguished draughtsman in the artist.' In 1994 the Museum reprinted the three volumes as one with an introduction by Dr Peter Smith. He concludes, 'Here revealed for the first time in its totality is the wealth of architectural detail that may be found in an unassuming farmhouse: that is the great contribution that Fox and Raglan made to the advancement of science; that is the justification for republishing this landmark in the history of scholarship, a landmark, in its own field, as significant as Darwin's *Origin of Species*.'[12] Grant Muter, writing in the Spring 2001 issue of the *Building Conservation Journal*, echoes this extraordinarily generous praise by noting the timeless nature of the work. 'This landmark publication is now widely regarded as the first truly comprehensive regional study of vernacular architecture in Britain. … [With] fieldwork carried out with an archaeological precision, it is hardly surprising that *Monmouthshire Houses* has stood the test of time.'

The value of these volumes to archaeologists and architects interested in domestic architecture cannot be overstated. Not only did they form a prototype and oft quoted reference for future publications, such as *Houses of the Welsh Countryside*,[13] but they also established nomenclature that still exists. Even more important was the stimulus that they provided for vernacular architecture, as a subject in its own right, and the founding in April 1954 of the Vernacular Architecture Group (VAG).

The origins of this group were fully described in a paper, read by the President Sir Robert de Zouche Hall, at the VAG 1973 Spring Conference.[14] It was conceived at a meeting in April 1952 in the house of N. Teulon Porter with L. F. Salzman, James Walton and Tom French. Fox had intended to be present. Unfortunately he had slipped when boarding a bus outside his home in Exeter, injured his leg, and was unable to attend. He did however send a letter warmly supporting the project and giving his comments on the subjects suggested for discussion. At the meeting French was appointed Secretary and it was decided to ask Fox to be President. He initially refused, but members were anxious to have his name on their headed paper and, under pressure, he agreed to be President for the formative period. Recalling this first meeting Tom French wrote, 'Fox was a very great scholar with the human touch, which so many others have lacked and with a lovely lack of self-importance. Characteristically his first move was to send me a cheque to pay for some properly printed stationery. His name was of enormous survival value to the VAG; there were not many first rate and well-known scholars amongst the Establishment, who had much sympathy with the study of domestic architecture. He remained President long enough to see the group firmly established, sending an unsolicited cheque periodically for administrative expenses.'[15]

Fox was also responsible for the name of the group, and that of the subject that subsequently became established as a university course in its own right. French had circulated the minutes of that first meeting, which included the proposal by James Walton of the name 'Domestic Architecture Group.' Sir Robert Hall, as Secretary after French, wrote to me 'CFs only amendment was the writing in of the defining word "Vernacular" in place of [Walton's] "Domestic".' Hall added in some indignation that 'by now the proposer was at sea on his way back to Southern Africa and his response, silent at the time, was to adopt – and he later claimed – the title as his own.'[15]

*   *   *

It would have been surprising if Fox's move to the Southwest had gone unnoticed by local archaeological societies; indeed, it was barely six months before he was approached by the Somerset Archaeological and Natural History Society, to accept their Presidency in 1950. His initial disinclination to undertake any commitment until his work on Monmouthshire Houses was ready for the publishers, was overcome by an abiding interest in the cultural links between South Wales and the Southwest.

His address centred on this theme of cultural interaction across the Bristol Channel of which, he affirmed, the southern shore was the dominant partner. He illustrated this interaction and movement of peoples, from Gloucester and Somerset into the South Glamorgan plain, with parallel examples of ritual pits and stake circles in Bronze Age Barrows and Iron Age Celtic art work, tracked across southern Britain into the Southwest peninsula, before crossing the Severn. This movement of cultural ideas even extended into the mediaeval period. He told his audience that if one found a novel technique or cultural feature of mediaeval or renaissance date in South Wales, to look first for parallels on the southern side of the Severn. An interesting example of this, was the previously unpublished scarfed cruck that he had found in a Long House at Maes-y-bidiau, Carmarthenshire; a form of construction he subsequently found in an earlier house (by then a Barn) at Burrow, Wootton Courtney. Concluding his address, he was concerned that insufficient attention had been paid by historians to the influence of terrain, in this part of the country, on our nation's history, drawing particular attention to the events of 878 AD. He invited the Society to press for completion of the Somerset edition of the national 'Drift' survey; accurate geological mapping of the limits of the peat moor, the dry peninsulas and ancient islands, was essential for a proper understanding of their historical role.[16]

Fox's disappointment that neither of his daughters had decided on an academic career had been greatly relieved when, in 1948, Penelope was appointed Assistant Secretary of the Griffith Institute in Oxford. There she was responsible for Egyptological records, including those of Howard Carter donated to the Institute by his niece. He was naturally understandably proud when, in 1951, she published her first book, *Tutankhamun's Treasure,* an illustrated appreciation of Carter's discoveries based on this material.[17] In the following year she resigned to marry John Eames, a Lecturer in Classical Archaeology at Liverpool University where she subsequently obtained her MA and Ph.D. in Medieval History.

Felicity's interest in an academic career was not to be fulfilled until long after his death, she was busy raising a family in Canada, but our father was very hopeful that I would opt for university training when I completed my education at Bryanston. He was especially pleased to be told by the Master, on the basis of a report from my Headmaster, that I would be offered a provisional place at Magdalene. Unfortunately his own father had other ideas, firing my imagination with tales of our family's naval forbears that included Charles Hammond, sometime Secretary to Captain Nelson. To my father's acute disappointment, I turned my back on Cambridge and chose instead to sit the Civil Service Examination. A high grade from this exam enabled me in the Spring of 1952 to enter the Royal Naval College at Dartmouth. Grandfather Fox, who died in 1953, lived long enough to see me in my Midshipman's uniform and to express his satisfaction at the return of the family to the Navy List. My father's initial regrets were eventually forgotten when, in 1961, he was able to join me on the bridge of my own ship, *HMS Tilford,* as we made our way up the Exe and the Exeter Ship Canal for an official visit and reception by the City of Exeter.

Since moving to Devon in 1948, Cyril had been very supportive of Aileen's work at the University College; in particular of her efforts to raise the profile of archaeology in the Southwest. He regularly visited her excavations, offering his views on her conclusions and providing practical assistance when asked. As his work on the last two volumes of Monmouthshire Houses became less demanding, indeed almost routine, he looked forward to these trips onto Dartmoor where Aileen was excavating stone circle huts at Kestor (Fig. 84). Cyril provided reconstruction drawings for this excavation and subsequently at Round Pond and Dean Moor. In 1951 he accepted the Dean of Exeter Cathedral's invitation to join both the Diocesan Advisory Committee and the Friends' Council, as one of their professional advisers. In the following year, working on behalf of the Chapter, he undertook a small excavation under the south wall of the Chancel, to determine the probable site of the Monastery

Figure 84: Aileen excavating at Kestor on Dartmoor 1951

of St Mary and St Peter. Two years later he successfully urged Dean Wallace to wash the West Front, removing the grime of centuries to reveal the glory of its original stonework.[18]

He found much of interest in the rebuilding of Exeter, admiring some of the new buildings in the High Street, such as Barclays Bank, whilst deploring the infilling and lack of architectural merit of Princess Hay. As Aileen records 'he was also concerned about the destruction of late mediaeval merchant houses in the city and together with W. G. Hoskins protested at several public enquiries. It was a triumph when an exceptional timber-framed house in Frog Street, on the line of the inner by-pass, was bodily moved to a new site and so preserved intact. It is still popularly known as "The House That Moved",[19] but his leading role in this conservation of Exeter's heritage seems to have been almost forgotten.

*   *   *

Fox's second remit from the Council of the National Museum of Wales 'to supplement his study of the Llyn Cerrig Bach finds by producing a complete survey of Celtic achievements in Britain' was now providing him with a wealth of fascinating research. It invoked a mass of correspondence, particularly with Stuart Piggott, and formed the topic of his address as President of Section H (Anthropology), to the British Association meeting in Edinburgh.[20] With Aileen, he took the opportunity to continue north to Caithness, joining Peter and Leslie Murray-Threipland at Dale near Halkirk. It had been two years since they had last stayed at their friends' holiday home on the Thurso River; Fox knew there would be plenty to keep himself amused – investigating the local stone towers, brochs and two-roomed crofts. He found total relaxation in this wild countryside. He delighted in the company of his hosts and the stimulation of investigating croft construction in this bare landscape, where wood was at a premium and gales the main enemy for a roof.

In the course of his research, Fox visited many museums across the country; seeing for himself the wide variety of Celtic remains that had been found or dug up and placed in their custody over the years. This gave him the opportunity to see more of his family; he frequently stayed with his brother initially in Bournemouth and then in Wareham, his sisters in the Isle of Wight and Oxford, and his ageing father in

Figure 85: Father Fox aged 93, Bursledon 1951

Bursledon (Fig. 85). He became a regular and welcome visitor for many of his professional friends, Daryll Forde, Tom Kendrick and Rik Wheeler in London, Gordon Childe, Glyn Daniel, Christopher and Jacquetta Hawkes, Tom Lethbridge, Nowell Myres and, whenever he was at home in Rockbourne, Stuart Piggott. He also kept in touch with his friends in Ireland, Professor O'Kelly and Professor Sean O'Riordain; exchanging information on Irish Celtic artefacts. He produced a short paper on the Lough Gur bronze mounts that was of particular interest for them.[21] These mounts, from County Limerick, had been acquired by the British Museum in 1850; they had always been considered to be chariot handholds. Fox's researches into the Llyn Cerrig Bach hoard convinced him that these were Pole-tip sheaths; his arguments certainly convinced O'Kelly, who wrote to 'congratulate him on the acuteness and brilliance of [his] observations and findings' and the importance of his work for his fellow archaeologists in Ireland. At the same time he produced a short paper on a group of five Early Iron Age bronze rings in the museum at Yeovil. These had almost certainly came from the Roman Villa at nearby West Coker, excavated by Haverfield in 1861. He found that one, of these totally unrecognised artefacts, was a highly decorated pony bridle bit ring; a delightful example of Celtic decoration of working equipment. It was most unusual, being the only known example in Britain from the second century BC with scrollwork of Marnian origin (Fig. 86).[22]

As his notes and correspondence on Celtic Art built up, Fox cleared his desk of earlier fieldwork, forwarding his last contribution to *Archaeologia Cambrensis*. He described it as an 'imperfect survey of three stonewalled houses in Carmarthenshire with rounded corners to their upper gables' that he had visited in 1940 and 1945; one of them had been featured by Peate in *The Welsh House*. This otherwise unremarkable paper illustrates the contrasting approach of Peate and himself, when investigating mediaeval houses with unusual features. Although in broad terms Peate was writing about peasant houses of this period, whereas Fox and Raglan were more concerned with yeoman properties, these were houses where their interests clearly overlapped. Fox was gently critical that Peate had failed to give building technique, like the scarfed

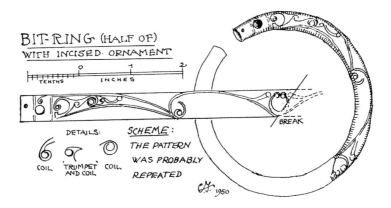

BIT-RING (HALF OF)
WITH INCISED·ORNAMENT

TENTHS   INCHES

DETAILS: *SCHEME*:
THE PATTERN
WAS PROBABLY
REPEATED

COIL   TRUMPET   COIL
AND COIL

BREAK

Figure 86: Celtic Pony Bit-ring from West Coker (Somerset Archaeological & Natural History Society)

cruck, the attention it deserved. He was also sceptical of Peate's assertion that the upper end of a long house was always paved, ending in the cross passage; when absent it must have been removed. However, it was in his conclusion, where Fox sought to elicit a valid purpose for these round gable ends, that he drew particular attention to Peate's indifference to historical origins to which he 'attached no cultural significance.' Peate's patently illogical explanations were successively dismissed by Fox, who wrote 'on this it may be said, without discourtesy to my kind helpers, that to rationalise the inexplicable is a well known habit of mankind.' As if to emphasise the difference between them, when unable to provide a logical answer himself, he sought solutions from his readers.[23]

In the Spring of 1952 Fox was successively honoured by The Society of Antiquaries, who awarded him their highest honour the Gold Medal, and his alma mater Magdalene College, which elected him an Honorary Fellow. Both of these honours gave him very great pleasure; particularly the privilege of dining in College, where he established a close friendship with the Master, Sir Henry Willink and his wife. Another happy occasion was Penelope's wedding: This took place at the end of May, in the small village church at Pusey near Oxford. In the succeeding years her father would be a frequent visitor to John and Penelope's home on the Wirral, and a proud grandfather to their two children.

Earlier that month Fox had attended the Spring Conference of the Prehistoric Society where he spoke on the development of triskele design. This art form, that in modern terms seems to resemble the blades of a propeller, provides the foundation for so many Celtic objects, especially mirrors (Fig. 87). Drawing on his intimate knowledge of horse and chariot fittings, he identified the design and purpose of three horse brooches from the Polden Hoard in Somerset that he had seen in the British Museum. His suggestion that the character of a triskele design on a First Century AD bronze

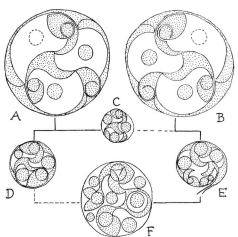

Figure 87: Triquetral patterns (National Museum of Wales)

Figure 88: Embossed Bronze Plate, Moel Hiraddug, Flintshire (National Museum of Wales)

plate, found by W. J. Hemp at Moel Hiraddug in Flintshire in 1927 (Fig. 88), indicated that this was an exact copy of a Celtic wood carving, aroused considerable interest. 'The central button was cut on a turntable' he wrote, 'the rest is freehand chisel work by a master craftsman. It suggests what we have lost; the range and quality of creative work of the period in wood may well have equalled that of metalwork.'[24] Ian Richmond writing from Durham commented 'what an exciting theory. How you think of these things baffles me. It is glorious.' O'Kelly took his theory further, agreeing that it was based on a woodcarving but adding, 'I see no reason why the carved wood itself shouldn't have been used for a die for such a thin plate.'

The following year was a busy one. Fox had just despatched the final volume of *Monmouthshire Houses* to the printers, when he received a letter from Mortimer Wheeler, Secretary to the British Academy. Wheeler told him that the Academy would like to reprint the reports in *Archaeologia Cambrensis* of his Offa's Dyke survey, together with his summary to the Academy – the 1940 Sir John Rhys Memorial Lecture – as a single volume. To bring this monumental work up to date, Wheeler asked Fox to write the introduction, which appears as the Author's Preface (1953), and Sir Frank Stenton was invited to provide a foreword. The resultant volume, published in 1955 in an enlarged format, had a handsome cover with an illustration of the obverse and reverse of an Offa silver penny. This publication was warmly welcomed. All those involved were praised for producing such an attractive and useful book for the new generation of archaeologists seeking to research this pioneering fieldwork.

At the same time D. B. Harden asked Fox for help, hoping he could provide a contribution for a *Festschrift* for E. T. Leeds. Having just written a short article, on the siting of the Monastery of St Mary and St Peter in Exeter for the Friends of Exeter Cathedral, Fox felt that an expanded paper on this subject would be a suitable topic. Bearing in mind the pressure of work at the time, he was certainly pleased and probably relieved when this was accepted. He had contributed to a *Festschrift* on two previous occasions and had mixed views on these publications. For his former mentor, Professor Chadwick, he had written an article on 'Burial Ritual and Custom in the Bronze Age', foreshadowing his book on this subject. Unfortunately Chadwick died before *The Early Cultures of North-west Europe* could be published; the essays were issued as Memorial Studies. His second contribution to a *Festschrift* was a paper on 'Round Chimneyed Farmhouses in Pembrokeshire' for Crawford. It was in correspondence in 1946 with Grimes, who was editing *Aspects of Archaeology in Britain and Beyond* for Crawford, that he indicated his reservations. Whilst recognising that a *Festschrift* was immensely rewarding for the recipient he, with Gordon Childe, felt that they 'tended to be forgotten because their contents are so varied that few people are interested enough to buy them for the single paper or perhaps two that are in their line.' They suggested that these tributes be published in an appropriate professional journal, in Crawford's case *Antiquity*. On this occasion editorial problems made this eminently sensible proposal unacceptable; the collection of essays had to be published separately.

Fox's father, Charles Fox, died in September aged 94; he had been infirm and was virtually confined to a wheelchair but totally mentally active to the end and was immensely proud of all that his eldest son had achieved. He had lived at The Lawn in Bursledon for over 50 years, so it took until the end of the year for Cyril and Norman to distribute family possessions between their sisters and themselves and to wind up the estate. Most of the Nelson memorabilia that had been given to Charles Hammond, including one of his swords and his Captain's Cocked Hat, had long since gone; stolen from Frederick Fox, Charles Fox's father, in the late 1800s. The only items that remained (inherited by my father and now in my possession) were a miniature locket, stated to be of Emma Lady Hamilton, and an anonymous biography of Nelson published two months after his death and signed by Charles Hammond on the title page. My grandfather told me that the family had always been convinced that Hammond was the author, but no one will ever know. My father also inherited the Fox family papers that included one of his forebear's Glebe Account Book, which recorded the '1685–1692 Harvest Accounts' of the Reverend John Crakanthorp, Rector of Fowlmere, Cambridgeshire 1667–1719. I deposited this detailed record of glebe income and expenditure in the late seventeenth century in the Cambridge County Record Office in 1974. Two of the other three or four books that made up the complete accounts had been located previously and they were all published in 1988.[25]

Throughout the fifties Fox was frequently asked to lecture and to take part in local archaeological society field days. In 1955 he was invited to address the Council for British Archaeology's first Field Survey School, at Urchfont near Devizes, and subsequently to deliver the O'Donnell lecture at the University of Oxford on the subject of early frontier dykes. Having studied the other two major dyke systems, in East Anglia and the Welsh Marches, his excursion with the Field Survey group to Wansdyke at Morgan's Hill stimulated his interest in the origin, purpose and construction of the third of the three great dykes (Fig. 89)

Wansdyke, which runs from Savernake Forest to Maes Knoll in Somerset, was considered at the time to be a continuous post-Roman frontier. Differences, between the Wiltshire and Somerset sections, suggested to Fox that further research was needed. Apart

Figure 89: Council for British Archaeology Field Day on Wansdyke, near Urchfont, Wiltshire 1955

from his minor excavation in the Palace garden beside Exeter Cathedral, Fox had not undertaken any archaeological fieldwork since he left Wales. Over the next three years Aileen and he surveyed the dyke and reported their findings to the Archaeological Institute.[26] Their work has been fully described by Aileen in her autobiography, where she records that 'our report was closely modelled on that for Offa's Dyke. It fell to me to draft much of the text, whilst Cyril concentrated on the illustrations. He also assessed the evidence of the local Saxon charter boundaries … the related entries in the Anglo-Saxon Chronicle, … and realised the significance of the unusual Woden place names.'[27] Their conclusions, that East and West Wansdyke were not linked and were constructed nearly a century apart for different purposes, have now been generally accepted. Earlier assessments may be said to stem from Saxon times, when the name Wansdyke was ascribed to both dykes, and inadequate research undertaken in the 1920s by Albany Major and E. J. Burrows for their book *The Mystery of Wansdyke*.

*   *   *

Fox's 'Survey of Early Celtic Art in Britain' was published in 1958 and received international acclaim. In his foreword he succinctly summarises his enthusiasm for his subject and his love of craftsmanship. 'Early Celtic Art is distinctive … the incised patterns and the relief ornaments are on purposeful things – torcs and brooches and bracelets, weapons and drinking vessels for example. It was not only a decorative art; useful things were well shaped with a sense of style, so a beautiful or well balanced form often sufficed, satisfying the bronze worker's critical sense, as it does ours. When the Council of the National Museum of Wales invited me to write a book on the subject, therefore, I had a title ready *"Pattern and Purpose"*. Fox's style of working is particularly distinctive; he treats his reader as though he was there to lead through the text. As Stuart Piggott described it, there 'is the elegance and clarity of his prose set off by the racy bravura of his own drawings'[28] (Fig. 90).

The introduction places the Celts in their European historical context, as they moved from the northern slopes of the Austrian Alps (Hallstatt), to the Rhine (La Tène) and Marne, in the Early Iron Age. From thence they spread through Gaul into northern Italy and north-west Spain, and from the French and Spanish Atlantic seaboard came to Britain and Ireland in the third century BC. Fox also uses this introduction to outline his theme; 'the development of art styles and techniques.' As Glyn Daniel wrote of his friend in the *Sunday Times* (21 Feb. 59) 'He lovingly lists and describes the patterns which the Celtic craftsmen used – palmettes, lyres, trumpets, spirals, circles, segments, triskeles – and gives us a grammar of Celtic art in Britain.'

Most of the artefacts that illustrate this developing history of British Celtic Art were well known. Many were included in Dr Jacobsthal's *Early Celtic Art* and E. T. Leeds' *Celtic Ornament*, but here Fox took the subject to greater depth. He examined links in their pattern and detail; suggesting schools of crafts-manship and districts where this art flourished. He maintained that the earliest artefacts were imported and that this led initially, to the estab-lishment of two or three centres of excellence, and later, to a much wider distribution of the manufacturing art.

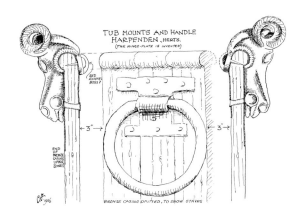

Figure 90: Tub Mounts and Handles, Harpenden (National Museum of Wales)

This thesis was not universally supported. E. M. Jope, a notable expert in this field, wrote, 'Much attention is given to locating the workshop area … it is questionable how far this can really be done for material much of which was the accoutrement of a mobile nobility with their own craftsmen in their retinues.' Jope also challenged the concept of "imported" art – 'how many really were? Few would pass unobtrusively among continental grave groups.'[29] F. R. Hodson was critical of his dating. 'British Celtic Art is controversial not only on artistic standards. Problems of stylistic groupings are inevitably linked with other fundamental problems of the early Celtic settlement in Britain, cultural groupings, chronology, relations with continental groups and so forth. Here Fox's opinions may not be readily acceptable to all archaeologists. … Dates before 50 BC are more speculative than Fox implies … [and] the whole fibula typology expounded in this volume and the reliance on the continental La Tène typology for absolute dating of British material could be seriously challenged.' Notwithstanding this criticism Hodson concluded 'But, after all, this book is not intended to provide a list of facts and dates. What it does provide is far more – a brilliant and highly sensitive interpretation of a whole epoch of art and artists in early Britain.'[30]

International interest in British Celtic Art was reflected in entries in archaeological journals in Belgium and America. Philip Lozinski, writing from New Haven Connecticut, must have provided Fox with his most rewarding review. 'This thorough survey ... is a masterpiece of its kind. The author's keen scholarly enthusiasm ... profound knowledge and the astonishing scope of his thinking are reflected in the ease with which he treats the subject. ... This type of research, method of approach and thinking can scarcely be carried further. As an apex of one period's achievement it is a most brilliant work. The author does not purport to solve all the problems, and when suggesting a solution never speaks ex-cathedra, but marshals his evidence to state his opinion as such, not as an established fact.'[31] Lozinski's comments were particularly noteworthy for the final part of his analysis that both Jope and Hodson had chosen to overlook. In nearly all his work, where there is an element of uncertainty or speculation, Fox allows facts to speak for themselves. He readily acknowledges the need for further research, which might well prove some of his conclusions to be wrong. His personal copy of *Pattern and Purpose* is full of amendments and references to later discoveries and analysis. It is evident that his love of Celtic art continued to the end of his life, and that he clearly took pleasure from the knowledge that others were continuing to research this fascinating period in our island's story.

Although Celtic Art had dominated his life for the past five or six years, Fox had also been reviewing his excavations of Bronze Age barrows and his interpretation of the last rites of Beaker folk. Results of these excavations had been published in a variety of professional journals over a period of twenty-five years; there had been little opportunity to comment on the subject in its totality. In his contribution to the Chadwick Memorial Essays (*Burial Ritual and Custom in the Bronze Age*), Fox had provided a short summary of the eight wartime 'rescue' excavations, undertaken between 1937 and 1943, and the insight they provided to ritual associated with death at that time. Now in a full-length book entitled *Life and Death in the Bronze Age,* he expanded this theme by adding his 1925 excavation at Ysceifiog in Flintshire and two, undertaken by colleagues, in Glamorgan and North Yorkshire. He also included some important funerary urns and artefacts from several other sources. "Death", as he explains in his Preface, 'represents persons important enough in the life of a tribe ... for the distinction of burial in a barrow or cairn; "Life" the evident pleasure the leaders and commonalty concerned took in elaborate funeral ceremonies.' His enthusiasm for this subject is also made clear. 'In this field-work I took great pleasure. I like measuring and plotting complex structures as their pattern gradually develops; I like the isolation of a thinly populated countryside to which such work usually takes the archaeologist and the friendly contact with a couple of workmen such as one employs for the heavy work.'

Much of the book and nearly of all the illustrations are taken from his previous reports; repeating assessments of the time and giving rise to uncharacteristic criticism. Although Fox had added a short commentary at the end of his book, admitting his dating of burial urns by form is in question, Humphrey Case was disappointed that he 'did not amend his statements of background archaeology to present day views. No one could place this book in the hands of students without qualification. Tellingly, Case continued, it was 'most unlikely that A-Beaker people came from Brittany (p. xvii) or that Spain was the principal source of copper (p. 22). Few could now feel reasonably confident in the post-Beaker chronology of the monuments, based on pottery typology – a change of view to which Fox alludes only in afterthought (p. 184–5).' Case was also one of many archaeologists who could not support Fox's enthusiasm for imagined ritual, expressing the view that the 'ecstatic was too little balanced by the mundane'. But he attached no such qualification to 'Fox's achievements in the hard act of excavation. He has already seen his influence inspire a host of barrow diggers eager to emulate him.'[32] Others, like Atkinson writing in the *Listener* (21 May 59), were far more supportive. 'From its very beginning, nearly forty years ago, Fox's fieldwork has exemplified his belief that a mere record of things seen is not enough. The evidence must not only be recorded. It must also be interpreted, not merely as a sequence of events, but as the tangible expression of specific human purposes and within the framework of a code of established behaviour, which is no less real or compelling even if its details must remain for ever beyond our grasp. As Sir Mortimer Wheeler has truly said "Cyril Fox has revealed and lit up the mumbo-jumbo of Bronze Age burials with the fires of unresting imagination." To specialists these excavations have long served as familiar and inspiring models; to the wider public, for which they are now presented afresh, they will be a revelation of the degree to which, in the hands of a master, archaeology can claim to reconstruct the past.' But for the layman it was left to Harry Green, a reporter for the *Western Mail* (7 Mar 59), to provide the most telling and succinct commentary on this work. 'Like a mourner from afar, less interested in the departed than "in the ham upon the sideboard standing by" Sir Cyril Fox is more concerned with life than death, though he digs into graves for his material. It is true of all his work as an archaeologist, what interests him is the men behind the monument.'

Since retiring in 1948 Fox's writings had focused on the environment, activities and craftsmanship of his fellow man; from the Early Bronze Age to the seventeenth century; from burial sites to major defensive or boundary dykes; from metal craft working to house building technique. In all these fields he was to the forefront of understanding and knowledge. His expertise was accepted throughout the profession. For one man to encompass so wide a range of archaeological interests and to be acknowledged as eminent in them all must, by any qualification, be considered an extraordinary achievement.

Notes

[1] Anniversary Address 2nd May 1946 – *Ant.J.* XXVI
[2] Anniversary Address 28th April 1949 – *Ant.J.* XXIX
[3] Fox and Raglan *Monmouthshire Houses* in 3 volumes – National Museum of Wales 1951, 1953 and 1954
[4] '*Verna*' is Latin for a native slave. When applied first to language it combined the meaning 'local' with 'lower class'
[5] *Culture and the Environment* Chapter XV
[6] *Culture and the Environment* Chapter XVI. Apart from publications in Germany and Sweden, other milestones include *The Evolution of the English House* by Sidney Addy (published 1898), *The Development of English Building Construction by* Thomas Kenworthy (published 1916) and *The Welsh House* by Iowerth Peate (published 1940).
[7] Fox and Raglan *Monmouthshire Houses* 2nd Edition – Foreword p. iv
[8] Fox and Raglan *Monmouthshire Houses* Vol. I p. 11
[9] This term has been used since 1278 to describe the timber blade that with its matching pair forms the main support or framework for a house but was brought into modern architectural parlance by Sidney Addy in 1890 (OED). In 1948 the South African architect James Walton, who was living in this country at the time, wrote a paper on 'The Development of the Cruck Framework' *Antiquity* XXII
[10] *Arch.J.* CX
[11] *Arch.J.* CXI
[12] P. Smith *Houses of the Welsh Countryside*
[13] Fox and Raglan *Monmouthshire Houses* 2nd Edition – Foreword p. xi
[14] *Vernacular Architecture Journal* 5
[15] Letter to the author 1986
[16] Somerset from a South Wales Viewpoint, Presidential Address 1950 *Som.Arch.* XCV
[17] P. Fox *Tutankhamun's Treasure* – Oxford University Press 1951. Her subsequent publications for the Furniture History Society, *Furniture History* Vols.VII and XIII were issued in 1971 and 1977
[18] Siting of the Monastery of St Mary and St Peter in Exeter *Friends of Exeter Cathedral 23rd Annual Report* to 31 March 1953 and The cleaning of the Image Wall and Porches of the West Front *Friends of Exeter Cathedral 26th Annual Report* to 31 March 1956
[19] A. Fox *Aileen – A Pioneering Archaeologist* p. 121–123
[20] The Study of Early Celtic Metalwork in Britain *The Advancement of Science* 50
[21] *Ant.J.* XXX p. 190
[22] A Group of Bronzes from the Early Iron Age in Yeovil Museum *Som.Arch.* Vol. XCVI
[23] Three Rounded Gable Houses in Carmarthenshire *Arch.Camb.* CI
[24] Triskeles, Palmettes and Horse Brooches *Prehist.Soc.* 1952 – Part I
[25] Accounts of the Reverend John Crakanthorp of Fowlmere 1682–1710 *The Cambridgeshire Records Society* 8
[26] Wansdyke Reconsidered – *Arch.J.* CXV
[27] A. Fox *Aileen – A Pioneering Archaeologist* p. 121–123
[28] *Antiquity* XXXIII p. 155
[29] *Ant.J.* XXXIX p. 127–129
[30] *Prehist.Soc.* Vol. XXVI 1960 p. 358
[31] *American Journal of Archaeology* 1960 p. 375. Lozinski was presumably not too familiar with our island's history as he queries the reason why this Celtic metal industry ceased. Fox sidelines this with the words 'He hasn't heard of the Roman Conquest and occupation.'
[32] *Ant.J.* XXXIX p. 298–299

XI

The Declining Years 1959–1967

Despite Aileen recording that her husband was 'visibly ageing' when they started their Wansdyke survey in 1955, he gave no indication to others that he needed to reduce his workload, or that he found life in Devon other than rewarding and attractive. His written output continued unabated and undiminished for the next four years, and even she admitted that 'his enthusiasm carried him up and over the chalk hills of Wiltshire' even to the 900 ft. summit of Tan Hill. He continued his work with the Royal Commissions, regularly attended meetings and lectures all over the country and was, to all appearances, physically and mentally active. At the end of March 1959, my parents and all the family had come to my wedding, a naval occasion in a small country Church near Penzance (Fig. 91). I had qualified as an Observer in the Fleet Air Arm in 1958 and was serving with my squadron onboard the Aircraft Carrier HMS *Victorious*. When the ship returned from the Mediterranean, her squadrons disembarked to their parent stations and I arrived at RNAS Culdrose in time to get married before the 5th April; thereby earning a handsome wedding present from the Inland Revenue. There was no noticeable

Figure 91: Charles and Jane's wedding, Penzance 1959

evidence of any decline on that occasion, but by the end of the year, when all three of his books had been published and the Wansdyke survey was complete, he seemed to lose interest in any new work and started to suffer from a short-term loss of memory.

Aileen refers to this period as the 'dark days of Cyril's decline' when he showed the 'early signs of Alzheimer's disease.'[1] This, she has assured me, was not a medical diagnosis but a convenient way for her to describe his symptoms. During that summer of 1959 he was particularly pleased to see Felicity, who had come over from Canada with her husband Patrick and their four children to meet all their British relations.

They stayed at the White Hart and after dinner in the Hotel I took my parents and Felicity home, leaving the others to talk until I got back. As my father got out of the front seat of the car he put his hand on the door pillar to steady himself. At the same time one of the two passengers got out from the back seat and shut the rear door trapping his fingers in the jamb. Although X-rays showed that nothing was broken the bruising was severe and the stress considerable.

This incident seemed to have no immediate effect, but over the ensuing seven years his ability to know what he was supposed to be doing, or to remember recent events and instructions gradually deteriorated, though his long-term memory for the past was unimpaired and his charm was still all embracing. Friends old and new engaging him in conversation on the 'old days', or probing his memory for the minutiae of his and his fellow archaeologist's work, had no reason to understand the problems that he caused for Aileen and his family. But the mental stress of his intensive activities over the previous forty years combined, almost certainly, with his move from the familiar surroundings and friends in Wales to Exeter, took their toll. Initially this took the form of forgetfulness – an irritant for Aileen, though of little immediate consequence. Indeed there was to be one more contribution from his pen for British Archaeology. Dr Geoffrey Bushnell, Curator of the Museum of Archaeology and Ethnology wrote to ask Fox if he would describe and comment on a Celtic bronze mirror that had recently been found and was subsequently acquired by the museum. His brief article[2] bears all the hallmarks of his acknowledged expertise and his letters of this period are similarly clear and free of any obvious sign of mental decline; there was certainly no indication of Alzheimer's disease to a layman.

However if by the end of 1960, when he reached his 78th birthday, there was no evidence that his penmanship had been noticeably affected, he was certainly aware of his forgetfulness and it was starting to prey on his mind. Writing to Arnold Taylor he said; 'I am sorry to subside into old age but I understand that's my place. I have had a good innings and good company. I much appreciated our friendship. Yours ever is the right phrase for both of us at the end of likely contacts.' He was also becoming increasingly concerned financially. Although the Royal Commissions covered most of his expenses on their behalf the work was becoming a burden and in December he wrote to the Secretaries to tender his resignation. Confirming this decision to Sir Goronwy Edwards, Chairman for the Wales and Monmouthshire Commission, he wrote 'It is hard to give up the periodical contact with old friends. But I am 78 and daunted by the coming responsibilities connected with the working party on top of the normal routine of Commissions. I am forgetful and sure I should get in a horrible muddle and it certainly would affect the reputation of the whole Commission.' In his reply the RCHM (England) Secretary wrote, 'I think of all the Commissioners you are the one to whom the Commission owes the most. You will be missed as much by the Investigating Staff of all ranks as by my Chairman and myself.' After 36 years as a 'particularly influential and knowledgeable Commissioner' it was with 'genuine regret' that the Minister of Works, Lord Salisbury, wrote on behalf of the Government to accept his resignation.

Shortly after Christmas this was followed by his resignation from the Exeter Diocesan Committee and the Council of the Friends of Exeter Cathedral. They were reluctantly accepted by Dean Knight, who wrote on their behalf expressing their 'very great gratitude for the help and advice, which you have always given with unfailing courtesy.' He also decided to inform the Chairman of the Executive Committee of the Athenaeum, that he could not justify the expense or luxury of a London Club that he was no longer using. The Secretary writing on his behalf replied 'Your friends are quite shaken by this news and hope that it is only a premonitory rumbling which will go with the East wind. There is no member whose appearances are greeted with more pleasure and your going would be felt on the Sofa as a personal blow. ... I beg you not to put your hint into execution. It would cause real sorrow in the Club and a sense of personal loss to all members.' But his mind was made up and he replied 'am breaking up. Forgive me if I don't alter my decision'.

Throughout this period in his late seventies he was still making his own arrangements, travelling by train, for visits to friends and relations; he went frequently to Oxford to stay with his sister Babs and her husband Bernard Gotch and to his brother Norman, who was now living in Wareham. In July 1961 he even accepted an invitation from Sir Henry Willink, to attend the Magdalene Feast and to stay for an extended weekend at The Lodge, though the letter is marked 'accepted with trepidation.' In addition he did make some attempt to work on his autobiography. This had been precipitated by a request in 1959 from Routledge & Kegan Paul, publishers of *Life and Death in the Bronze Age*, reinforced by a similar plea from Glyn Daniel and finally in 1960 by a demand from Mortimer Wheeler. Writing from the British Academy he told his friend that he needed to update the biographical notes of all Fellows for their obituary notices. This stimulated Fox into writing a series of short summaries of his early life, though none of them went beyond 1925. Wheeler expressed himself satisfied with the one that he received, as he was able to fill in the rest from his own knowledge

In December 1962 Aileen arranged to celebrate Cyril's eightieth birthday with dinner at the Royal Clarence Hotel in Exeter. For this auspicious occasion Felicity flew over from Canada, his sister Mary (Babs) came by train from Oxford, Roy and Julia Raglan drove down from Cefntilla and I came up from Cornwall. Aileen and my brothers Derek and George made up the party. It was a happy evening with Cyril in fine form. He had memorised and rehearsed his speech and spoke for at least five minutes without notes.

Unfortunately his loss of short-term memory accelerated from this time and as Aileen records 'it was increasingly difficult to leave Cyril alone and I had to ask for help from his relatives whilst I was away.' For these visits to relatives he would be put on a train, with a request to the guard to keep an eye on him and to make certain that he left at the appropriate station, where he would be met. For some journeys, like his visits to stay with my family in Cornwall, there were few problems; Penzance was the end of the line. However trips to Norman in Wareham or Penelope in the Wirral were a little more hazardous; they required a change of train. Penelope has vivid memories of a plaintive cry for help from the stationmaster at Crewe to come and collect an elderly gentleman, who didn't know where he was or where he was going, but had her address and telephone number in his pocket.

Having arrived was only the start of the problem for the relation with whom he was staying, for he became totally disorientated and was always asking how much longer he was staying in this 'hotel' before he was due to return home to 'Cardiff'. My family lost him in Penzance; he had supposedly gone to a newsagent to buy a paper and just disappeared. My father-in-law saved us. He was Chairman of the Penzance Bench and enlisted the help of the local police, who soon picked him up and returned him to the fold. His brother Norman had no such immediate call for assistance in Wareham; he lost him for hours when he just walked out of the house. He was eventually found, oblivious to the worry that he had caused, and equally oblivious to the reason that he had left the house in the first place (Fig. 92). However this loss of short-term memory and perceived inadequacy, together with his financial concerns, made him increasingly unhappy and unsettled.

In 1963 Fox tried to resign from the British Academy; he was convinced that he could no longer afford his membership dues. Although he had mentioned his financial worries to me and showed me his resignation letter, it cannot be traced by the Academy. As all papers for this period were destroyed in a fire, this is not of itself surprising. However from discussions with the Academy Secretary, it is clear that either his letter was destroyed, perhaps on instructions from Wheeler, or just not considered, as there is no record of his resignation in Academy minutes. He also attempted to resign his Honorary Fellowship of Magdalene and that evoked an equally cool response from Sir Henry Willink. The Master thanked him for his kind letter and wrote, 'but really we could not possibly think of accepting your suggestion. I do not feel that I have ever heard of an Honorary Fellow resigning. He costs the College nothing and one of the reasons for the election of Honorary Fellows is that the presence of their distinguished names is of benefit to the College. Far from benefiting the College by resignation you would – quite honestly – be doing the opposite.' He remained a Fellow of the British

Figure 92: Staying with his brother Norman at Wareham, Dorset 1966

Academy and an Honorary Fellow of Magdalene for the rest of his life.

In the same year Fox was presented with his own *Festschrift*. Entitled *Culture and Environment* this unusually large volume consisted of twenty essays by his closest friends and colleagues on subjects that were most dear to his heart. The introduction *Homage to Sir Cyril Fox* was provided by Sir Mortimer Wheeler and drew heavily on the biographical notes that he had so artfully sought some two years earlier. Fox's own gold blocked leather bound copy, signed by them all 'with affection', was read and re-read with delight and was a treasured possession for him and now for me. In reply to the congratulations from his sister Babs and her husband, two of over four hundred individuals and institutions contributing to this *Festschrift*, he wrote. 'It is quite astonishing to get such a number of notable papers (these goings on didn't leak out as far as I was concerned) and I am trying to write a thank you letter to my kind friends that is worthy of the kind and inspiring effort. Iorwerth Peate's reply to this letter of appreciation was generous and indicated that any differences between them were now forgotten. 'The contribution [*The Welsh Long House – A brief re-appraisal*] such as it was, was in gratitude for all that I learnt from you during our association in Cardiff'. The *Times Literary Supplement* (30 Jan. 64) considered the 'festschrift, dedicated to this doyen of the archaeological world in celebration of his eightieth birthday' to be 'a fine tribute to a fine scholar.' However 'the frontispiece, a drawing of Sir Cyril Fox by Evan Walters in 1937, while it brings out Fox's ruggedness, fails to convey to those who knew him at the height of his career the enthusiasm and excitement which radiated from him.'

The last three years of his life were a sad conclusion to a successful career and increasingly reflected his disorientation and inability to do anything constructive. Surprisingly he was still able to put thoughts on paper in letters to his intimates, or to converse unhesitatingly about times past. Towards the end of 1964 he wrote to Babs telling her that he had 'recovered from the burdensome contemplation of death which besets old age (inevitably I suppose) and a bout of sunshine and some long walks in these conditions have done wonders. … I have learnt of the death of my dear friend Roy – Lord Raglan. A heavy blow, he was much of an age with me … how difficult life is at times.' In the following year he wrote a heavily underlined note inside the front cover of his well-worn personal copy of *Pattern and Purpose* 'CF's Present (permanent) Address, 28 St Leonard's Road, Exeter' to remind himself that it was Exeter and not Cardiff that was his home. Tucked into the pages of the book was another note, marked 'Private' and 'Notes on myself.' It seemed to have been written at about the same time and described his plight. 'Mental change: rapid increase in forgetfulness – embarrassing my life. Start out with an errand: come back not done. Forget people's (friends') names. Unable to remember new names and my wife's friends. Fiddle around a whole morning in my office: nothing done at end. Forgetfulness … cannot remember what letters I have written or not written, posted or not posted. No matter: I have done all I wanted to do.' I believe that this last phrase is his most fitting summary of life; he had indeed done all and more than he could have conceived possible. He had enjoyed a rich and happy family life, divided only by the tragedy of 1932, and reached the pinnacle of his profession. He had no enemies and was held in the highest regard and with affection by all his friends and contemporaries. His life was complete.

In July 1966, shortly after returning to Exeter from the funeral of his mother-in-law, Alice Scott Henderson, at Walton-on-the-Hill, he had the first of several strokes. After a short stay in hospital he was transferred to the Cranborne Nursing Home in Exmouth. Aileen had found it extremely difficult and often irritating to cope with her husband in his declining years; she was certainly unable to care for him at home now that he was partially paralysed. He had a succession of visitors, mostly his family including Penelope who was able to see him on the day that he died, but it must have been a somewhat lonely last six months.

Amongst the last of his visitors were Glyn and Ruth Daniel, who recalled 'he was obviously very ill and his mind was in the past – the past of the '20s, '30s and '40s when he was active in Cambridge and Cardiff. We mentioned many names, some dead like Hector Chadwick, Louis Clarke, Sean O'Riordain, Lord Raglan, and some alive – Sir Thomas Kendrick, Tom Lethbridge, Maureen O'Reilly, Mortimer Wheeler, Stuart Piggott. All registered clearly in his mind and he said a kind appreciative sentence about each one. Then he said "Old friends – how fortunate I was to have so many friends." Cyril Fox was a modest man, and even at the end did not realise that he had had a lifetime of friends and admirers because he himself was always the most generous, most kind, most human friend to all of us. There are not many such men.'[3] A notable absentee was Wheeler, who Fox particularly asked to come, but in the opinion of Jacquetta Hawkes 'Rik evidently could not bear to see his friend with his precious vitality gone and never appeared.'[4]

Cyril Fox died shortly after his eighty-fourth birthday on 15th January 1967. His funeral was held in Exeter Cathedral: his ashes were scattered by the banks of the Exe, where he had so often enjoyed the sunlight on the water and the view of the city from afar. The Society of Antiquaries arranged his Memorial Service on 16th March at St James Piccadilly. The Church was crowded with friends, colleagues and representatives of every facet of his life. Stuart Piggott's address was a happy blend of his achievements and character, his scholarship and love of the English language, and his interest in his fellow man and craftsmanship. Interwoven throughout there were reminders of his charisma, his charm, enthusiasm and above all his sense of fun. It was a fitting conclusion to the life of an extraordinary man who had dominated British archaeology for over forty years and whose influence would continue for many years to come.

Notes

[1] A. Fox *Aileen – A Pioneering Archaeologist* p. 121, 127, 135 and 138
[2] A Celtic Mirror from Great Chesterford *Antiquity* XXIV p. 207–210
[3] *Antiquity* XLI p. 86–88
[4] J. Hawkes *Mortimer Wheeler, Adventurer in Archaeology* p. 350

Epitaph

Life's all getting and giving,
I've only myself to give
What shall I do for a living?
I've only one life to live
End it? I'll not find another
Spend it? But how shall I best?
Sure the wise plan is to live like a man
And Luck may look after the rest!
Rudyard Kipling

The wheel has turned full circle with Rudyard Kipling's lines an appropriate summary of life for one who, did indeed live like a Man and for whom luck stepped in on more than occasion to ensure fulfilment of his ambition. Yet he was a man on whom honour and eminence weighed lightly. He never lost the common touch, and his abiding interest in the achievements of his fellow man extended equally to the craftsmen of today, as to their Bronze or Iron Age forbears. Glyn Daniel described him as an inspiring companion, a loyal friend, a nice man; Christopher Hawkes said he was a genius; he called himself a man of yeoman stock. Whatever the description, his written words are all that now survive; how can they be judged? What is his place in the history of British archaeology? Will he be remembered, or will he be just another name in a research student's notebook?

The rapid advance of knowledge applies as much to archaeology as to any other science. It is tempting to judge the work and conclusions of archaeologists, such as Pitt-Rivers, Abercromby, Crawford, Fox or Wheeler in the light of information that is now available, rather than that which was evident at the time. Some assumptions that Fox made in his 1922 thesis, *Archaeology of the Cambridge Region*, such as settlement in forest land, were found to be in error in his own lifetime. The same applied to his contention in *The Personality of Britain* that invading cultural influences on native populations in the highland zone were less apparent than in the lowland zone. Today, the strict definition of these zones that he laid down, is also questioned. Many of the conclusions that Fox published in *Life and Death in the Bronze Age*, and to a lesser extent in *Pattern and Purpose*, were those that he made in the 1940s. He was well aware of advances in knowledge; criticism of his failure to revise his findings was certainly justified. His inclination to stay with his conclusions of the time, and a tendency to make up his mind before all evidence was gathered, seeking the support of colleagues for an established conclusion rather than an input to it, must also be accepted as a source of valid criticism.

Twenty years after his death Margaret Worthington commented on the short-comings of his survey of *Offa's Dyke* and the 'tone of the work, which leaves the reader in no doubt that everything that needs to be done, has been done and all the questions have been answered.' As she points out, Fox invariably assumed that an apparent gap had to be due to terrain or forest; 'the possibility of agricultural practices … as a means of destroying the Dyke was not considered. … In 1976 students from Manchester tested a gap in the dyke near Mold with a resistivity survey and were able to establish a line, which appeared to indicate the Dyke. Both they and Sir Cyril Fox would have done well to talk to the landowner who explained … that a previous owner (prior to 1860) had laid drains across the fields and flattened the dyke.'[1]
Peter Smith in his admirably clear and detailed introduction to the second edition of *Monmouthshire Houses*, indicates that Fox's readiness to assume that 'the earliest surviving structure that they had found encompassed the whole of the original house' is open to question. 'In the light of later work it seems likely that in many cases the smallest of these houses were fragments of larger houses.' In Smith's opinion, another very questionable conclusion is the allocation of lateral fireplace dwellings to the lowlands, whilst axial fireplaces are conjectured to be highland. 'In the light of a much broader knowledge of the evidence, it now seems arguable that the main alternative fireplace positions are most easily interpreted, not so much in terms of highland and lowland, but in terms of evolution … and some allowance must be made for preferences being dictated by social status.'[2]

Whilst all of these critical reviews are fair, indeed essential for a clear understanding of our island's heritage today, they are only examples of the advance in knowledge that has made many of the conclusions of yesterday's archaeologists open to question. However renowned, their work will rightly be subjected to intense scrutiny by succeeding generations keen to make their mark. It is unfortunate, that on occasions this can all too easily be achieved by using the knowledge of today to denigrate or destroy a reputation of the past. In addition there is a natural collapse of memory for all but a few singular people of any one profession. Asked to name a twentieth century archaeologist, the name that would come most readily to mind is Wheeler. Whilst no one would deny that he was a great archaeologist, he was essentially a showman, a celebrity, who grabbed the limelight for himself and as a by-product, brought archaeology to the notice of radio and television audiences. Others like Hawkes, Piggott and Fox were equally important in their day. Now, they are scarcely remembered, except by professional archaeologists, geographers and historians, or students or researchers seeking background information for their theses. But their day was that pioneering phase in the development of British archaeology; it was the link between Pitt-Rivers and Abercromby and the present highly specialised professional world. Who among the younger members of this world would be able to make fundamentally creative contributions alike to historical geography, prehistoric and Dark Age archaeology and vernacular architecture or, indeed, dare to try? This is what sets Fox apart from archaeologists of today and also from those of his own time, including Wheeler, each of whom achieved eminence in their own field, but none could match the totality of the wide ranging professional interests, creative scholarship and administrative talent that Fox dispensed.

Glyn Daniel's broadcast on the Welsh Home Service on 18th January 1967, encompassed all that this involved. 'During his reign [as Director of the National Museum of Wales] that fine museum grew and developed and flourished under his inspiring and inspired leadership. He lived up to the ideals of the museum and saw that it taught the Welsh about themselves and the world about Wales. And he managed to achieve what few but the really great in this world of museums do achieve, namely to run a very large museum efficiently, humanely and well, to take the proper part in Welsh cultural and academic life which the Director of a National Museum should do and yet to remain a creative scholar. For his 25 years saw an output of archaeological work – excavation reports, field surveys and general syntheses – which would have done credit to an archaeologist who had no museum to run. He had the ability to switch from the minutiae of museum administration to major issues of academic and museum policy and to his personal scholarship and writing with an ease and assurance which was the envy of most people.

His work as excavator of Bronze Age barrows and his work on the survey and description of Offa's Dyke will always be remembered as models of digging and field archaeology just as his books ... will long be remembered as stirring seminal works in general archaeology.'[3] To this Nowell Myres added 'his infectious enthusiasm for everything that interested him made him a brilliant and inspiring teacher both in public lecturing and informally. He had the supreme tutorial gift of thinking aloud in an exciting way and so involving listeners in the development of his own absorbing thoughts. His lecture at the 1932 Congress, afterwards published as *The Personality of Britain,* was the best public lecture both for subject and manner of delivery that I have ever heard. It was most memorable not only for the extraordinary effect it had on the audience at the time but on all subsequent archaeological thought about the early development of Britain.'[4]

These two passages sum up Fox's pivotal influence on British archaeology in the twentieth century. With the reports of his excavations in Cambridgeshire of Devil's

Dyke and Beacon Hill; with each of his major publications; *Archaeology of the Cambridge Region, The Personality of Britain, Offa's Dyke, A Find of the Early Iron Age in Anglesey, Monmouthshire Houses* and *Pattern and Purpose,* Fox determined the path of archaeological research and study in Britain. That is his lasting memorial.

> Lives of great men all remind us
> We can make our lives sublime
> And, departing, leave behind us
> Footprints in the sands of time
> *H. W. Longfellow*

Notes

[1] *Archaeology in Clwyd* 8 p. 14–16
[2] Fox and Raglan *Monmouthshire Houses* 2nd Ed. Introduction p. vi, viii
[3] *Antiquity* XLI 1967 p. 86–88
[4] Letter to the author 1986

Appendix I

THE ANCIENT FOX FAMILY OF SOUTHAMPTON – RECORDED FROM MID 17TH CENTURY

JOHN FOX (Ca.1640–1700) m.ELIZABETH (1664 – Tax Record)

- WILLIAM
- JOHN FOX (Ca.1674–1734) m.unknown (Ca.1700)
- MARY

JOHN b.7.1.1708 d.31.8.1719

EDWARD b.3.7.1713 d.6.1.1799

ELIZABETH

EDWARD FOX (1713-1799) m.ELIZABETH

- ELIZABTH b.21.11.1738
- ANNE b.18.4.1740 m.WILLIAM JOLIFFE
- SARAH b.6.11.1741 m.Ca.1761 SH.DICKERSON
- MARY b.26.3.1743 d.14.10.1748
- EDWARD b.31.7.1744 d.17.12.1786
- JOHN b.4.1.1745 d.8.3.1818
- WILLIAM b.22.12.1745 d.3.5.1748
- WILLIAM b.21.3.1749 d.7.12.1753
- CATHERINE b.2.11.1750 d.8.3.1818
- THOMAS b.11.6.1754
- WILLIAM b.21.5.1758

JOHN FOX (1745-1818) m.ELIZABETH

- J.J. ROUBY MD ==== Daughter name unknown
- MARY ELIZABETH m.JOHN FOX
- ELIZABETH SARAH b.10.8.1783 d.1822 m.THOMAS NICHOLS
- CHARLES b.6.5.1781 d.10.10.1848
- MARY ANNE b.17.1.1789 m.WILLIAM OKE

CHARLES FOX (1781–1848) m.MARY HAMMOND née PARSONS

- FREDERICK b.3.7.1825 d.9.12.1911
- MARY ELIZABETH m.Dr.DUSARTOY

The Fox family tilled the land in the Parishes of St Mary's and All Saints, Southampton. The registers of St Mary's were lost in a fire at the Rectory in 1706 and those of All Saints in the blitz in 1940. Details of the family prior to John Fox appear to have been lost.

The principal holdings throughout Eighteenth Century were in the Parish of St Mary's. This land lay to the south of St Mary's Church and included the land now occupied by Southampton Docks. It was lost, primarily through gambling, by Frederick Fox (1825–1911).

Mary Parsons was the sister of Capt. Jack Parsons (1791–1864) a Royal Naval Officer whose career ended as an Enforcement Officer on the South Coast. Her first husband was sometime Secretary to Capatin H. Nelson.

FREDERICK FOX (1825–1911) m.JANE; née ELGAR

He continued in RN service until his death and is believed by the family to have written the first biography of Nelson published shortly after Trafalgar.

Charles Frederick Fox went to Dorchester Grammar School where he met and became a lifelong friend of J.B. Clark. He joined the Southern Counties Bank at Chippenham becoming Manager at Ventnor, Newport Isle of Wight, and Winchester.

| WILLIAM SAVAGE WILSON | = CATHERINE ANNE b.22.6.1857 | CHARLES | ELIZABETH MARY b.13.1.1855 | LOUISA JANE b.4.3.1856 | CHARLES FREDERICK b.10.6.1859 d.17.9.1953 | LUCY b.20.3.1860 | ELLEN PARSONS b.17.1.1862 | GEORGE HAMMOND b.6.4.1864 |

CHARLES FREDERICK FOX (1859–1953) m.HENRIETTA MARIA née PAUL

| CATHERINE MARGARET b.20.3.1884 | FREDERICK b.19.3.1885 | OLIVE MARY b.20.3.1888 | GEORGE FOX b.26.1.1896 | CYRIL FRED b.16.12.1882 d.15.1.1967 Kt.1935 | NORMAN b.19.5.1884 m.LAURA C.I. BARNES | DOROTHY b.25.2.1887 m.Lt.Col.R.J. COLSON | MARY b.15.9.1890 m.BERNARD C. GOTCH |

CYRIL FRED FOX (1882–1967) m (1).OLIVE née CONGREVE-PRIDGEON m (2).AILEEN MARY née HENDERSON

| HELEN FELICITY b.3.4.1920 m.SYDNEY PATRICK REDGRAVE (1942) d.25.6.80 | PENELOPE b.26.11.1923 m.JOHN EAMES (1952) | CHARLES SCOTT b.29.7.1934 m.KATHLEEN JANE née ATKINSON (1959) | DEREK PARSONS b.28.9.1938 | GEORGE MANSON b.11.11.1943 |

GEORGE FOX WILSON m.SUSANNE née SHILTON

| Rev.FRANCIS FOX b.22.9.1946 | CHARLES b.2.2.1949 |

| VERONICA b.19.11.1944 | JULIA ELGAR b.9.7.1949 | JOCELYN PATRICK b.1.11.1950 | ROY FOX b.3.2.1956 | FLORIAN CONGREVE b.11.11.1954 | CLARE ELIZABETH b.1.11.1958 | LESLIE JANE b.2.1.1960 | VICTORIA ALICE b.24.11.1962 | PENELOPE ANNE 24.9.1964 |

Appendix II

AMGUEDDFA GENEDLAETHOL CYMRU
NATIONAL MUSEUM OF WALES

STRICTLY CONFIDENTIAL

Report of Directorship Committee

At its meetings on 26th March and 23rd April 1926 the Council appointed a Committee consisting of the President, the Vice-President, the Treasurer, Principal Trow (representing the Science Committee), Major F. Treharne James (representing the Art and Archaeology Committee, and the Director to consider the selection of candidates for the Directorship.

This Committee is, in the first place, of opinion that academic distinction is an essential qualification for such a post. In the second place, it has given careful consideration to the selection of candidates with special reference

(1)   to possible applicants outside the present staff of the Museum and
(2)   to members of the present staff of the Museum.

The results of these enquiries and deliberations are briefly as follows:-

(1)   The following authorities have been approached. The Director of the British Museum; the Universities of Oxford, Cambridge and London; the University College of Wales, Aberystwyth, the University College of North Wales, Bangor and the University College of South Wales and Monmouthshire, Cardiff. The reply from the British Museum was negative. The name of a scientist of distinction was suggested from Oxford but, on being approached informally, declined to stand. The College at Cardiff suggested two names. One of these gentlemen, after giving the matter careful consideration definitely declined whilst the other, who was also suggested by the College at Aberystwyth, has written a letter which will be read at the Council meeting. The other correspondence will likewise be placed before the Council at its meeting on the 25th instant.

The Committee further reconsidered the applications received in response to advertisement in 1924 together with certain names suggested by members of Council.

(2) The Committee considered carefully the qualifications of each of the five Keepers of Departments of the Museum on the basis of personal knowledge and of applications submitted either in 1924 or in 1926.

In consequence of these deliberations, the Committee submits to the Council the names of the two following gentlemen as well qualified to fill the office of Director with distinction.

Professor H. J. Fleure D.Sc. Professor of Geography with Anthropology at the University College of Wales, Aberystwyth; and

Cyril Fox Ph.D. Keeper of Archaeology in the National Museum of Wales and Lecturer in Archaeology at the University College of South Wales and Monmouthshire, Cardiff.

Professor Fleure has been closely associated with Wales throughout the greater part of his career. He was a student of University College, Aberystwyth and subsequently (!901–4) Fellow of the University College of Wales, whilst from 1903 to 1904 he was a Research Student in the University of Zurich. As Hon. Secretary of the Geographical Association he has been primarily responsible for the success of that organisation and he is Hon. Editor of the *Geographical Teacher*. His numerous publications include books and papers on Natural History (Marine Snails, etc), Geography, Anthropology and Archaeology. He is President-elect of Section H of the British Association for the Advancement of Science. His age is 48.

Dr Fox is a Doctor of Philosophy of Cambridge, where he formerly held the Kingsley Bye-Fellowship at Magdalene College. He was also Honours Lecturer in Western Europe Archaeology and Assistant to the Curator of the University of Archaeology and Ethnology. At one time he administered the Field Laboratories of the University of Cambridge (wherein post-graduate research workers carry out pathological and other investigations), and had considerable experience in general administrative duties including building contracts, control of staff, etc. He is now external examiner to the University of Ireland and a member of the Royal Commission on Ancient Monuments (Wales). His numerous and important publications include the *Archaeology of the Cambridge Region* and several papers dealing with Wales. His age is 43.

Cardiff
22nd June 1926

Appendix III

THE NATIONAL MUSEUM OF WALES
A BRIEF SKETCH OF ITS NATURE, FOUNDATION
AND EARLY HISTORY

by Douglas Bassett

'There shall be and there is hereby constituted and founded a Museum in the City of Cardiff with the name of "The National Museum of Wales".'

With these words, the first of the Charter of Incorporation granted by King Edward VII, the new 'body politic and corporate with perpetual succession and a common seal …' came into being. It was to be national in two senses: in receiving its main funding from the Government and in the broad sense of rendering service to the people of Wales but not in confining itself strictly to Welsh studies and Welsh concerns. It was to be both a national museum of Wales and a national museum for Wales.

The idea of a museum and library was discussed publicly and their creation demanded in the period of major awakening of a sense of Welsh nationhood, from the 1870s to the early years of the twentieth century. The two institutions came into being during the Edwardian 'high noon' or in Wales' 'Antonine age'. In a period characterised by considerable optimism, and when a number of other bodies were established the Museum, Library and University were often considered as the 'three badges of cultural and national distinctiveness'.[1]

The concepts were discussed at length on the floor of the House of Commons, in the meetings of the Honourable Society of Cymmrodorion held annually at the meetings of the National Eisteddfod, as well as in a number of Town and County Halls. A significant step in the process of establishing the new institutions was the Conference, arranged by the Welsh Members of Parliament in 1903, that included the Chairmen of the County Councils, the Principals of the University and of its three constituent colleges, and the Chairman and Chief Executive of the Central Board of Education.

This was followed by the preparation of draft plans and by an approach to the Government regarding financial support. Sir Isambard Owen, senior deputy

Chancellor of the University, and joint 'architect' of the initial scheme for a federal university, prepared the draft plan for the Museum. Sir Isambard's careful consideration involved study visits to several institutions, including the national museums and galleries in Dublin and Edinburgh.

Because of the differences of opinion regarding the site or sites of the proposed buildings, and particularly in the absence of a nominated capital of Wales, the Government established a special committee of the Privy Council to consider the matter. On the basis of memoranda submitted by the four competing towns – Aberystwyth, Caernarfon, Cardiff and Swansea – the committee proposed that the Museum should be placed 'in the largest centre of population'– in Cardiff, whereas the Library, its sister institution, should be placed in the 'more healthy and tranquil atmosphere of Aberystwyth.'

*   *   *

The promises made by Cardiff Borough Council in its Memorandum to the Privy Council and fulfilled in *Cardiff Corporation Act 1909* included the following: the prime site of some four acres immediately adjacent to the newly constructed Town (later City) Hall, as part of the 'front row' of the first intentionally planned civic centre in Britain, in Cathays Park; the contents of the Municipal Museum (renamed the Welsh Museum of Natural History, Science and Art in 1901); £7000 in public subscription; and the product of a rate of one halfpenny in the pound (worth approximately half of the Government's first annual grant-in-aid).

Following the decision to site the Museum in Cardiff, the City Council erected a Gallery within the City Hall suitable to house temporary exhibitions during the first stages of construction of the new Museum building. It provided accommodation for the meetings of the Museum's Court and Council as well as providing a number of other services. Furthermore the Cardiff Naturalists' Society, which had founded Cardiff's museum and fostered it throughout its 45 year history, forged a special link with the new institution: it made it one of its rules that all objects of interest found by its members would be deposited in the National Museum.

*   *   *

The Charter of Incorporation, besides bringing the Museum into being, described the means by which it was to be governed and administered. It made provision for the following: a Court of Governors as 'the supreme governing body' and constituted so as to represent all parts of and all appropriate interests in the Principality; a Council, to act as the executive body; and a Director, as Chief Administrative Officer. It also designated the President, Vice-President (or President-elect) and Treasurer as the Museum's 'Officers'. The composition of the Court of Governors was based largely on that of the University of Wales, created in 1893 with 100 members in order to reflect the 'popular' origin of the institution. In the words of one of the University's historians: 'the fundamental feature of the University's Court (unlike that of any other University in Britain) and the frame of its claim upon the interest of our countrymen at large, is that it commits the supreme power without reservation in the hands of a large elective body, very largely composed of the people themselves'.[2]

The Museum Court initially included representatives of the bodies involved in the movement towards the establishment of the institution – the House of Commons, the County Councils, the University and its colleges, etc, as well as nine members appointed by the Lord President of the Council. Two Supplemental Charters, in 1911 and 1925, were granted in order to make the Court more representative. Four additional categories of membership were added: the main regional and national societies and organisations in Wales; the Affiliated Museum Scheme; the Lord Lieutenants of the thirteen counties and the four major museums and galleries in London.

The Court attempted to be 'national' in other ways. From the beginning the President, who served a five-year term, was chosen alternately from North and South Wales. From 1910 it appointed 'correspondents' in the various counties, a scheme that functioned for two decades. It held its Spring meeting in a different town every year – alternately in North and South Wales – in order to 'lay before the inhabitants of the locality concerned a statement regarding the work of the National Museum with a view to interesting them of its progress'. On each occasion the members were welcomed formally by the Mayor. The local press reported on the proceedings as well as on the content of a public lecture given by a senior member of the Museum on the previous evening under the chairmanship of the President. The Court was therefore materially different from the Boards of Trustees of the other national museums in size, representation and in the nature of some of its activities. It differed also because, through its Council and Standing Committees, it was responsible for: members of staff who were not Civil Servants and who were appointed without any reference to the Civil Service Commission; the building and maintenance programmes, which were undertaken without any assistance from the Ministry of Works; and for publishing of books and catalogues without recourse to His Majesty's Stationery Office.

The Court, through its Council, was responsible for all aspects of the Museum's work until September 1939 when normal meetings of the Council were temporarily suspended and an Emergency Committee, with plenary powers, was appointed. The three-man Committee, under the chairmanship of the immediate Past President, Ivor Windsor Clive, Second Earl Plymouth, continued to deal with urgent matters after normal meetings were resumed. Among them was the problem associated with Dr Iorwerth C. Peate, which occasioned the only dissension between Court and Council in the Museum's ninety-five year history.

The Museum differed from its counterparts in London and Edinburgh in another significant way: the range of its collections and its disciplines was much wider. In the

AMGUEDDFA GENEDLAETHOL CYMRU

Figure 93: Architect's diagrammatic view of the proposed entrance or main hall of the Museum as conceived in 1911. The figure on the balcony stands outside the Council Room (National Museum of Wales)

words of the Charter, the object of the Museum 'shall be mainly and primarily the complete illustration of the geology mineralogy zoology botany ethnography archaeology art history and special industries and the collection preservation and maintenance of objects and things of usefulness or interest connected therewith'. And further the collection of all objects and things 'whether connected or not with Wales', which would help in attaining the purposes of the various educational bodies in Wales. Stated in another way, the Museum was designed to fulfil the functions performed in Scotland, for example, by the four state-aided bodies, the Royal Scottish Museum, the National Gallery of Scotland, the Scottish National Portrait Gallery and the Museum of Antiquities of Scotland, all in Edinburgh.

In spite of serious financial difficulties, the Museum became progressively more distinctive. In 1920 it organised a conference of the educational bodies in Wales in order to define its role in formal education. The result was the first official working relationship in the country between the Ministry of Education and a national museum, and the establishment on a small scale of a loan service to Welsh schools. In 1923, at a time when 'one of the peculiarities of the present museum system in England, Northern Ireland and Scotland' was 'the almost entire absence of any form of co-operation'[3] an Affiliation Scheme was launched involving both the National and local museums, under the Museum Director as Senior Officer and the Museum Secretary as administrator. Apart from the long-standing scheme of loans and purchase grants operated by the Victoria and Albert Museum, this scheme was the first direct recognised relationship between national and local museums. By 1930 all but one of the small museums in Wales had joined the scheme and were participating in its annual Summer School in museum procedures and techniques. In 1928 the first Museum Guide in the Welsh language was issued; in 1932 lectures to Secondary Schools throughout Wales were inaugurated on a county basis and in 1937 a film was produced by the Museum on its work in the context of developments in Wales. Concurrently with these developments, two outstations were acquired, in 1920 the purpose built 'Turner House' Art Gallery at Penarth, and in 1930 the long-established Caerleon Antiquarian Museum in Monmouthshire, thus initiating a tradition that would continue for the next half century.

* * *

The design of the new building in Cathay's Park received more than the usual attention. This was partly because it was generally realised that designing museums was difficult and partly because of the expertise and experience of the first Director Dr William Evans Hoyle.[4] Before drawing up the list of requirements for the building and compiling the *Conditions and instructions to architects* (1910) the Museum Council required the Director to study forty or so museums and galleries in North Germany and Scandinavia. It appointed three senior London-based architects to advise in the initial stages and to adjudicate the 130 sets of plans attracted by the open competition. It then set a precedent by appointing two museum experts, one from London and the other from Dresden, to assess the winning plans from a technical and administrative stand point. Finally it required the Director and the senior partner of the winning architectural firm, A. Dunbar Smith, to make another study tour of European museums before finalising their detailed plans. In the original plan the first floor was continuous throughout the south face of the structure and the dome appreciably lower than in the actual building. Following a suggestion by one of the technical advisers, Dr F. A. Bather of the Natural History Museum, London, it was decided to open the structure up and thus transform the central octagon of the entrance hall, with headroom of 28 feet, to one of 85 feet roofed by the dome; and to accommodate the Council Room, Library and Director's suite, originally placed centrally on the first floor, on a new second floor (as illustrated).

The resulting design was highly praised both from an architectural aspect and as a scientifically planned museum. The building, which harmonised with the City Hall, was dignified and nobly proportioned, strikingly individual and yet based upon a fine classical tradition. The essential elements of its internal design were clearly expressed in its external form. The most comprehensive critique of the suitability of the building as a museum was the one commissioned in 1925 by the Carnegie Trust from the eminent American museologist Benjamin Ives Gilman of the Museum of Fine Art, Boston, USA. He drew attention to the incorporation of essential museum features, including a number of the latest ideas – as in the lighting and heating. He paid particular attention to the fact that, unlike most other major museums, virtually as much space was allocated to the study, reference and reserve collections as to the public galleries. He considered that the most important idea embodied in the design was that of the division of varied collections into departments structurally more or less separate from one another – citing the English psychologist Stanley Jevons' contention that the treatment of large museums as a congeries of small ones was a *sine qua non* of their essential success.

Gilman, who considered that the new Museum building 'stands almost alone among great museums as an example of intelligent planning' not only brought the Museum to the attention of the profession in a most complimentary way but he also unintentionally provided the authorities with an ideal quotation for use in publicity and promotion. 'The study of this admirable design awakens a vivid wish. It is greatly to be hoped that some man of ability and opportunity, who has found in the hills and streams of Wales and in the qualities of its people factors of a great fortune, will one day repay the debt by completing so highly intelligent a plan, and endowing the country with a museum not only thoroughly modern at its conception, but promising to remain modern through a long future.'[5]

The construction of the building was a slow process for three reasons; the time taken to design the structure, the disruptive effect of the War, and the difficulty in raising the money necessary to match 'on a pound for pound basis' the capital grants from the Government. The first contract, for the foundations and sub-structure of one third of the proposed building, was awarded in July 1911 and completed in time for the laying of the Foundation Stone by HM King George V in June 1912. The second contract, for the first part of the superstructure, was awarded in 1913 with work commencing in 1914. Because of the effects of the War, progress was slow and construction halted in 1916. Under the adverse conditions of the immediate post-war years, when construction re-started, a special effort was made to respond to strong public demand to open a small portion of the building. This was achieved in October 1922, but only by raising a large loan from the bank. The financial situation worsened in the early years of the period characterised by one historian as the 'locust years', until in 1924 a major donation led to the organisation of a second major public appeal for money partly sponsored by the Lord Mayor of the City. By 1926 the Museum Council felt that 'the time was ripe for the formal opening although the space available for exhibition purposes was still disproportionate to the magnitude and importance of the collections.' The part of the building opened by HM King George V in 1927 was still not as large as the one originally envisaged by the Council as the minimum accommodation needed 'to start the Museum on its career as a national museum.' Under normal circumstances this 'minimum development' would probably have been complete by 1915 or 1916.

In 1928 therefore, despite the general financial situation in the country as a whole, the Museum sought and, rather ironically, received assistance from the Treasury, because of the exceptional level of unemployment in South Wales at the time. With substantial support from a small group of benefactors, it was possible to erect the superstructure on the remainder of the substructure erected in 1911 including the major part of the east wing with its 440-seater Lecture Theatre. The significance of the erection of this major extension was threefold: it provided approximately twice the gallery space and additional 'storage:' it added a much-needed gallery for temporary exhibitions above the Lecture Hall auditorium; and it created, in the Lecture Theatre, the basis for a wide diversity of new working relationships with other bodies.

The attempts initiated in 1937, to raise money to construct the companion west wing – this time targeted at the Welsh-American communities – did not succeed. As a result the building remained, as it was in 1932, until the second half of the 1960s; and throughout the greater part of Cyril Fox's directorship.[6]

*   *   *

It was almost certainly a coincidence that the major advances at Cardiff between 1926 and 1932 took place during a period of particular interest in the development of museums and galleries in Britain generally. Two events of considerable significance were: the appointment in July 1927 of a Royal Commission on National Museums and Galleries – in itself a clear indication that the subject had become a matter of public concern; and the Conference organised in 1926 by the Carnegie United Kingdom Trustees, which led to a general inquiry into the non-national public museums of the British Isles.[7] The subject that received the greatest public attention, was the absence of 'anything that can be called a Folk Museum in Britain' and the proposal to create an 'English [Folk] Museum.' The matters were discussed in detail by a specially convened committee, containing representatives of six of the country's leading cultural and scientific societies, and by the 'Folk Museum Committee' jointly established by the First Commissioner of the Office of Works and the President of the Board of Education. The financial crisis of 1931 meant however that none of the recommendations made by either committee received proper attention and none were acted upon. It was to be another eighteen years before the discussions were restarted and proposals made. In the meantime the only institution to make a sustained effort to create a representative national collection and to foster this new discipline was the National Museum of Wales in its Department of Folk Culture and Industries. This Department, which was 'to provide the people of Wales with a source, hitherto untapped, of self-knowledge' was the first of its kind in Britain and in the wording of the period 'in the Empire.'

*   *   *

The first of the Museum's departments were established between 1914 and 1919. The subjects were the ones most widely represented in British museums at the time – Art, Archaeology, Botany, Geology and Zoology. The ethnographic and mineralogical collections, mentioned in the Charter, were incorporated with archaeology and geology respectively. No attempt appears to have been made to establish a Department of Industry. One surprising aspect of the work of the departments in the early years is the level of success achieved in spite of the continuing financial difficulties and the space problems arising from the protracted building programme. It was not until the early 1930s that anything approaching adequate space was available in order to carry out the range of activities implicit in the Charter.

In contrast to the state of torpor and the lack of attention to pastoral work maintained by Mortimer Wheeler, and cited in the main text of the present study, the record portrays a different picture. Members of staff, particularly in the three Natural History departments, were able to forge links with individual collectors, University staff, academic and amateur societies, commercial firms, Government and civic agencies in England as well as in Wales. In part because of such contacts they were able to provide a variety of advisory, identification and information services, based largely on the collections, to the specialist, the professional, the student and the 'man on the street'.[8]

Notes

[1] They included; a separate Welsh Department within the Board of Education (1907); the South Wales District of the Workers' Educational Association (1907); the Royal Commission on Ancient Monuments (1908); and, a little later, the Glamorgan School of Mines, Treforest, and a separate Advisory Board for Wales of the Ancient Monuments Board. Following the deliberations of the Royal Commission on University Education in Wales, the distinctive University of Wales Board of Celtic Studies (1919) and the Press Board (1922) were established.

[2] Principal T. F. Roberts, cited in Williams J. Gwynn 1993 The *University Movement in Wales* [A history of the University of Wales Vol. I], Cardiff, University of Wales Press.

[3] Quotation from Sir Henry Miers' report – see Note 6. See also Lee, A. H. 1937, Museum Lectures in Secondary Schools, *Mus.Journ.* 36 pp 507–09; Lee, A. H. 1937, A film of the National Museum of Wales, *Mus.Journ.* 37 pp. 414-16

[4] During his term as Director of the Manchester Museum, Evans Hoyle was recognised as an authority on the planning, construction and general principles of museums, with experience in the USA and continental Europe. He was an influential figure in the Museums Association.

[5] Gilman's critique, dealing with twenty-one aspects of the Museum's plan and building, was published in the American Association of Museums journal *Museum Work*, 1926 pp. 34–46.

[6] The only part of the sub-structure (erected in 1911–12) not covered by 1932 was that for the proposed Natural History Pavilion immediately behind the entrance hall and which provided a very adequate foundation for the temporary building erected at Cyril Fox's suggestion in 1926 to house the 'Bygones Collection'.

[7] Miers, Henry A. 1928, *A report on the public museums of the British Isles (other than National Museums) to the Carnegie United Kingdom Trustees, Edinburgh,* Constable. *Royal Commission on national museums and galleries* Reports 1928, 1929, 1930, HMSO. At this time, and in spite of its Charter, the National Museum of Wales was not considered a 'national' museum either by the Royal Commission or the Carnegie United Kingdom Trustees; nor was it included in the remit of the Standing Commission on Museums and Galleries, created in 1931 to advise on the, or the Committee of Directors of National Museums and Galleries established in 1932. These omissions were not remedied until after Cyril Fox's retirement.

[8] Each department had a specialist library, in addition to the Museum's main Library, and also a reception area for visitors. Further details are given in Part IV of D. A. Bassett's The Making of a National Museum (*Transactions of the Honourable Society of Cymmrodorion,* 1992), which outlines the history or the natural history departments.

Bibliography

Part I – Cyril Fox

(Excludes Notes, Miscellanies and Reviews – for a complete list see L. J. Lloyd's contribution to *Culture and the Environment* Chapter XXI) (The date of reading, if known, is shown in brackets)

1922

Anglo-Saxon Monumental Sculpture in the Cambridge District (14.02.21), *Camb.Ant.* XXIII 15–45

1923

The Archaeology of the Cambridge Region, Cambridge University Press, xxv, 360. [See also 1948]
Excavations in the Cambridgeshire Dykes: I. Preliminary excavations : Excavations at Worstead Street; II (with W. M. Palmer) The Fleam Dyke (24.10.21), *Camb.Ant.* XXIV 21–53

1924

Objects from the Settlement at Abington Pigotts, Cambridgeshire (12.11.24), *Proc.Pre.E.Ang.* IV 211–32
(with W. M. Palmer) Excavations in the Cambridgeshire Dykes: III The Fleam Dyke second report: Excavations in 1922 (4.12.22), *Camb.Ant.* XXV 21–36
Excavations at Foxton, Cambridgeshire, in 1922 (4.12.22), *Camb.Ant.* XXV 37–46
(with L. Cobbett) The Saxon Church of Great Paxton, Huntingdonshire (29.01.23), *Camb.Ant.* XXV 50–77
An unusual Beaker from Huntingdonshire, *Ant.J.* IV 131–3
A Jug of the Anglo-Saxon period, *Ant.J.* IV 371–3
(with W. M. Palmer) Shudy Camps, Castle Camp and Waltons Park, *Cambridge Chronicle*
(with L. C. G. Clarke) Excavations in Bulstrode Camp, *Records of Bucks* XI 283–8

1925

On two Beakers of the early Bronze Age recently discovered in South Wales; with a record of the distribution of Beaker pottery in England and Wales, *Arch.Camb.* LXXX 1–31
On a Burial Place of Dwellers in the upper Taf valley, near Whitland, Carmarthenshire, *Arch.Camb.* LXXX 275–88
(with Earl Cawdor) The Beacon Hill Barrow, Barton Mills, Suffolk (19.05.23), *Camb.Ant.* XXVI 19–65

Excavations in the Cambridgeshire Dykes, IV. The Devil's Dyke: Excavations in 1923 and 1924 (26.5.24), *Camb.Ant.* XXVI 90–129

A late Celtic Bronze Age Mirror from Wales, *Ant.J.* V 244–57

The Shefford Beaker, circa 1800 B.C. *Beds.Hist.* IX 1–4

Note on four Sepulchral Vessels of the Bronze Age from North Wales, *Arch.Camb.* LXXX 177–96

1926

(with W. M. Palmer) Excavations in the Cambridgeshire Dykes V. Bran or Heydon Ditch first report (9.3.24), *Camb.Ant.* XXVII 16–35

A Bronze Age Barrow on Kilpaison Burrows, Rhoscrowther, Pembrokeshire, *Arch.Camb.* LXXXI 1–35

The Ysceifiog Circle and Barrow, Flintshire, *Arch.Camb.* LXXXI 48–85

Offa's Dyke: A Field Survey. First report: Offa's Dyke in Northern Flintshire, *Arch.Camb.* LXXI 133–79

(with T. C. Lethbridge) The La Tene and Romano-British Cemetery, Guilden Morden, Cambridgeshire, *Camb.Ant.* XXVII 49–63

A 'Dug-out' Canoe from South Wales (17.12.25), *Ant.J.* VI 121–51

1927

An 'Encrusted' Urn of the Bronze Age from Wales; with notes on the origin and distribution of the type, *Ant.J.* VII 115–33

A Settlement of the Early Iron Age (La Tene I. Sub-period) on Merthyr Mawr Warren, Glamorgan, *Arch.Camb.* LXXXII 44–62 [Reprinted separately by the National Museum of Wales (1927)]

A La Tene I Brooch from Wales with notes of the typology and distribution of these brooches elsewhere in Britain, *Arch.Camb.* LXXXII 67–112

Offa's Dyke: A Field Survey. Second report: Offa's Dyke from Coed Talwrn (Treuddyn Parish) Flintshire, to Plas Power Park (Bersham Parish), Denbighshire, *Arch.Camb.* LXXXII 232–68

The National Museum of Wales [written evidence] in *Oral evidence memoranda and Appendices of the Interim Report. Royal Commission on National Museums and Galleries.* 278–9

1928

(with W. F. Grimes) Corston Beacon: an early Bronze Age Cairn in South Pembrokeshire, *Arch.Camb.*LXXXIII 137–74

Offa's Dyke: A Field Survey. Third report: Offa's Dyke from Plas Power Park (Bersham Parish), Denbighshire, to the River Vyrnwy on the boundary between Llanymynech (Shropshire) and Carreghefa (Montgomeryshire) Parishes, *Arch.Camb.* LXXXIII 33–110

The Beaupre Porch, Glamorgan, *Cardiff Nat.* LIX 15–18

The Early Iron Age in England and Wales [summary of a paper read 19.2.28], *Camb.Ant.* XXX 52–3

(with G. R. Wolsely) The Early Iron Age site at Findon Park, Sussex, *Ant.J.* VIII 449–60

1929

(with D. W. Phillips) Offa's Dyke: A field survey. Fourth report. Offa's Dyke in Mongomeryshire, *Arch.Camb.* LXXXIV 1–60

Dykes, *Antiquity* III 135–54

1930

Three Questions and an Answer – The Preservation of Ancient Wales (7.28). *CPRW* [Reprinted from *The Welsh Housing and Development Year Book* 1930 75–8]

(with D. W. Phillips) Offa's Dyke: A Field Survey: Fifth report. Offa's Dyke in the Mountain Zone, *Arch.Camb.* LXXXV 1–73

1931

Affiliation: from the point of view of a parent institution (Cardiff Conf. Jun 1930) *Mus.Journ.* 30 343–52

(with D. W. Phillips) Offa's Dyke: A Field Survey. Sixth report: Offa's Dyke in the Wye Valley, *Arch.Camb.* LXXXVI 1–74

Sleds, Carts and Waggons, *Antiquity* V 185–99

1932

The Personality of Britain: its influence on inhabitant and invader in prehistoric and early historic times, Cardiff, National Museum of Wales. Further editions 1933, 1938, 1943 (Revised), Reprint 1959

Contributions (Sections II and V) of *A Handbook of the Prehistoric Archaeology of Britain*, Oxford

A Survey of McGill University Museums, McGill University, Montreal 37 pp

Saxon Grave-Slab at Balsham, Cambridgeshire, *Camb.Ant.* XXXII 1 p

1933

(with C. A. R. Radford and G. C. Dunning) Kidwelly Castle, Carmarthenshire; including a survey of the Polychrome Pottery found there and elsewhere in Britain (14.4.32), *Arch.* LXXXIII 93–125

The Archaeological Collections of the National Museum of Wales. Cambrian Archaeological Association Presidential address, *Arch.Camb.* LXXXVIII 153–84 [Reprinted as *A short account of the Archaeological Collection;* Cardiff, National Museum of Wales 1934]

The distribution of Man in East Anglia, c.2300 BC – 50 AD: a contribution to the prehistory of the region. Prehistoric Society of East Anglia Presidential address, *Proc.Pre.E.Ang.* VII 149–64

An appreciation of Dunbar Smith FRIBA, *Journ. RIBA,* December 1933

1934

Open-Air Museums, Museums Association Presidential address, *Mus.Journ.* 34 109–21

A Folk Museum for Britain [broadcast lecture on West Regional Programme], *Listener* 1 Aug. 1934

Wat's Dyke; A Field Survey, *Arch.Camb.* LXXXIX 205–78

(with Aileen Fox) Forts and Farms on Margam Mountain, Glamorgan, *Antiquity* VIII 395–413

(with Aileen Fox) Field Survey of Glamorgan [Reports 1934–39] *BBCS* VII–IX

1936

Caer Dynnaf, Llanblethian. A Hill Fort of Early Iron Age type in the Vale of Glamorgan *Arch.Camb.* XCI 20–24

1937

The new Cambridge and County Folk Museum (3.11.36), *Mus.Journ.* 36

The National Museum of Wales; pp 97–107 in *The Book of Cardiff*, Oxford University Press

Peasant Crofts in North Pembrokeshire, *Antiquity* XI 427–40

1938

Illustrated regional guide to Ancient Monuments, Vol. IV, South Wales and Monmouthshire, HM Office of
   Works, HMSO. Second edition 1949.
Two Bronze Age Cairns in South Wales: Simondston and Pond Cairns, Coity Higher Parish,
   Bridgend, *Arch.* LXXXVII 129–80
Two Bronze Age Cairns near Bridgend, Glamorgan, *Man* Jun. 1938 90–91
The Western Frontier of Mercia in the VIIIth Century, *Yorkshire Celtic Studies* I 3–10

1939

(with H. A. Hyde) A Second Cauldron and an Iron Sword from the Llyn Fawr Hoard, Rhigos,
   Glamorgan, (26.1.39), *Ant.J.* XIX 446–48
The Socketed Bronze Sickles of the British Isles, with specific reference to an unpublished specimen
   from Norwich, *Prehist.Soc.* 1939 222–48
(with Aileen Fox) Tor Llawdd, on Mynydd y Gwair, Llangyfelach, Glamorgan, *BBCS IX 308–72*

1940

A Croft in the Upper Nedd Valley, Ystradfellte, Brecknockshire, *Antiquity* XIV 363–76
The Distribution of Currency Bars, *Antiquity* XIV 427–33
The Re-erection of Maen Madoc, Ystradfellte, Brecknockshire, *Arch.Camb.* XCV 210–16

1941

(with Aileen Fox) The Golden Mile Barrow, in Colwinston Parish, Glamorgan, *Arch.Camb.* XCVI
   185–92
Stake Circles in Turf Barrows: a record of excavation in Glamorgan 1939–1940, *Ant.J.* XXI 97–127
'The Boundary Line of Cymru': The Sir John Rhys Memorial Lecture 1940 (30.10.40), *Br.Acad.*
   XXVI 28 pp
A datable 'Ritual Barrow' in Glamorganshire [Six Wells 271'], *Antiquity* XV 142–61
The Non-socketed Bronze Sickles of Britain, *Arch.Camb.* XCVI 136–62
*A Country House of the Elizabethan Period in Wales. Six Wells, Llantwit Major, Glamorgan. Measured and
   drawn by the Ancient Monuments branch of His Majesty's Ministry of Works and Buildings,* Cardiff,
   National Museum of Wales 28 pp

1942

Some South Pembrokeshire Cottages, *Antiquity* XVI 307–19
A Palstave from Llanbister, Radnorshire, *Arch.Camb.* XCVII

1943

A Beaker Barrow, enlarged in the Middle Bronze Age, at South Hill, Talbenny, Pembrokeshire
   [with a note on plant remains by H. A. Hyde] (18.11.42), *Arch.J.* XCIX 1–32
The Dominic Inscribed Slab, Llangwyryfon, Cardiganshire [with epigraphy by Ifor Williams,
   R. A. S. Macalister and V. E. Nash-Williams], *Arch.Camb.* XCVII 205–12
A Bronze Age Barrow (Sutton 268) in Llandow Parish, Glamorganshire (31.10.40), *Arch.* LXXXIX
   89–125
Museum and Art Gallery Service in Wales and Monmouthshire, Cardiff, National Museum of Wales 20 pp

1944

An Early Iron Age Discovery in Anglesey, *Arch.Camb.* XCVIII 134–38 Reprinted in *The Transactions of the Anglesey Antiquarian Society and Field Club* 1944; Welsh translation by I. C. Peate *Y Llenor* 1944, 81–4

1945

Anniversary Address: Society of Antiquaries of London (23.4.45), *Ant.J.* XXV 107=16

A Shield Boss of the Early Iron Age from Anglesey with ornament applied by chasing tools, *Arch.Camb.* XCVIII 199–220

A Find of the Early Iron Age from Llyn Cerrig Bach, Anglesey. Interim Report. Cardiff, National Museum of Wales 72 pp

1946

Field Archaeology in South Wales 1939–45; Personal Reflections and Record, *BBCS* XII 52–56

Anniversary Address: Society of Antiquaries of London (2.5.46), *Ant.J.* XXVI 109–17

Linear Earthwork: Methods of Field Survey, *Ant.J.* XXVI 175–79

A Find of the Early Iron Age from Llyn Cerrig Bach, Anglesey. Cardiff, National Museum of Wales 98 pp

1947

An Open-work Bronze Disc in the Ashmolean Museum, *Ant.J.* XXVII 1–6

Anniversary Address: Society of Antiquaries of London (23.4.47), *Ant.J.* XXVII 113–19

Reflections on *The Archaeology of the Cambridge Region, Cambridge Historical Journal* IX 21 pp

1948

Anniversary Address: Society of Antiquaries of London (23.4.48), *Ant.J.* XXVIII 115–22

(with M. R. Hull) The Incised Ornament on the Celtic Mirror from Colchester, Essex, *Ant.J.* XXVIII 123–36

Celtic Mirror Handles in Britain, with special reference to the Colchester Handle, *Arch.Camb.* C 24–44

The Archaeology of the Cambridge Region, 1923, reissued with an Appendix; Reflections on *Archaeology of the Cambridge Region,* Cambridge University Press

1949

A Bronze Pole-Sheath from the Charioteer's Barrow, Arras, Yorkshire, *Ant.J.* XXIX 81–83

Anniversary Address: Society of Antiquaries of London (28.4.49), *Ant.J.* XXIX 137–44

1950

Burial Ritual & Custom in the Bronze Age, pp 51–74 in *Early Cultures of North-West Europe* (H. M. Chadwick Memorial Studies). Edited by Bruce Dickens, Cambridge University Press

Somerset from a South Wales viewpoint: Somersetshire Archaeological and Natural History Society Presidential Address, *Som.Arch.* XCV 53–62

Two Celtic Bronzes from Lough Gur, Limerick, Ireland, *Ant.J.* XXX 190–92

1951

(with Lord Raglan) *Monmouthshire Houses: a study in building techniques and smaller house plans in the 15th to 17th Centuries. Part I. Mediaeval Houses,* Cardiff, National Museum of Wales 114 pp. 2nd Edition with Introduction by Peter Smith (1993) Merton Priory Press and National Museum of Wales

The Study of early Celtic Metalwork in Britain (10.8.51), *The Advancement of Science* No. 50 10 pp
Round Chimneyed Farm-houses, pp 124–43 in *Aspects of Archaeology in Britain and beyond:* essays presented to O. G. S. Crawford. Edited W. F. Grimes, London
Three 'Rounded-Gable' Houses in Carmarthenshire, *Arch.Camb.* CI 106–12
A group of Bronzes of the Early Iron Age in Yeovil Museum, *Som.Arch.Nat.* XCVI 108–11

1952

Triskeles, Palmettes and Horse Brooches, *Prehist.Soc.* 1952 47–54
The design by Miss D. Marion Grant for the East Window of the Lady Chapel, *Friends of Exeter Cathedral 22nd Annual Report,* 13–16

1953

(with Lord Raglan) *Monmouthshire Houses: a study in building techniques and smaller house plans in the 15th to 17th Centuries. Part II. Sub-Mediaeval Houses,* Cardiff, National Museum of Wales 135 pp. 2nd Edition with Introduction by Peter Smith (1993) Merton Priory Press and National Museum of Wales
The Siting of the Monastery of St. Mary & St. Peter in Exeter, *Friends of Exeter Cathedral 23rd Annual Report,* 23–28

1954

(with Lord Raglan) *Monmouthshire Houses: a study in building techniques and smaller house plans in the 15th to 17th Centuries. Part III. Renaissance Houses,* Cardiff, National Museum of Wales 178 pp. 2nd Edition with Introduction by Peter Smith (1993) Merton Priory Press and National Museum of Wales

1955

Offa's Dyke, a field study of the Western frontier works of Mercia in the 7th and 8th Centuries, British Academy, Oxford University Press

1956

The Cleaning of the Image-Wall and Porches of the West Front, *Friends of Exeter Cathedral 26th Annual Report,* 19–23
The Siting of the Monastery of St. Mary and St. Peter in Exeter, pp. 202–17 in *Dark Age Britain:* essays presented to E. T. Leeds. Edited D. B. Harden. London

1958

Pattern and Purpose, a survey of Early Celtic Art in Britain, Cardiff, National Museum of Wales 160 pp

1959

Life and Death in the Bronze Age: an archaeologist's fieldwork, London, Routledge 193 pp

1960

A Celtic Miror from Great Chesterford, *Antiquity* XXXIV 207–10
(with Aileen Fox) Wansdyke Reconsidered, *Arch.J.* CXV 1–48

Part II – A Selection of other Sources and References

Ashbee, Paul (1960). *The Bronze Age Round Barrow in Britain,* Phoenix House, London

Bassett, Douglas A. (1982–84, 1992), *The Making of a National Museum,* Parts I–IV [A prehistory and history of the National Museum of Wales], Transactions of the Honourable Society of Cymmrodorion, London

Brassley, Paul, Lambert, Anthony and Saunders, Philip (editors) (1988), *Accounts of the Reverend John Crakanthorp of Fowlmere, 1692–1710,* Cambridgeshire Records Society

Chainey, Graham (1952). *A Literary History of Cambridge,* Pevensey Press, London

Crawford, O. G. S. (1953), *Archaeology in the Field,* Phoenix House, London

Daniel, Glyn E. (1950), *A Hundred Years of Archaeology,* Duckworth, London

Daniel, Glyn E. (1960), *A Hundred and Fifty Years of Archaeology,* Duckworth, London

Daniel, Glyn E. (1986), *Some Small Harvest,* Thames and Hudson, London

Daniel, Glyn E. as Editor of *Antiquity* 1927–1967

Evans, E. Estyn (1973), *The Personality of Wales,* BBC Wales, Cardiff

Foster, I. L. L. and Alcock, L. (editors) (1963), *Culture & Environment: Essays in honour of Sir Cyril Fox,* Routledge & Kegan Paul, London

Fox, Aileen (1964*), South West England* [series *Ancient Peoples and Places*], Thames and Hudson, London

Fox, Aileen (2000), *Aileen – A Pioneering Archaeologist,* Gracewing, Leominster

Hawkes, Jacquetta (1982), *Mortimer Wheeler, Adventurer in Archaeology,* Weidenfeld and Nicholson, London

Lees-Milne, James (1977), *Prophesying Peace,* Chatto & Windus, London

Lloyd, L. J. (1963), Bibliography of the published work of Sir Cyril Fox, pp. 503–12 in *Culture and Environment. Essays in honour of Sir Cyril Fox,* Edited by Foster I. L. and Alcock L. Routledge & Kegan Paul, London

Myres, Sir Henry A. (1928), *A report on the public museums of the British Isles (other than National Museums) to the Carnegie United Kingdom Trustees,* T and A Constable, Edinburgh

National Museum of Wales (1920–1948), Annual Reports.

National Museum of Wales (1927), *Formal Opening of the Museum by His Majesty King George V. accompanied by Her Majesty Queen Mary on Thursday, the 21st April, 1927. Programme of the Ceremony.* 22 pp

National Museum of Wales (1937), *A matter of great interest to Welsh-Americans. An appeal for funds to erect Welsh-American galleries.* 22 pp

National Museum of Wales (1943), *Museum and Art Gallery Service in Wales and Monmouthshire: a Memoramdum embodying recommendations for post-war development, prepared by the Council of the National Museum for submission to the Welsh Reconstruction Advisory Council.* 20 pp

National Museum of Wales (1944), A *Proposal for a National Museum Schools Service, a Memorandum prepared for the Welsh Department of the Ministry of Education at the request of the Permanent Secretary.* 12 pp

National Museum of Wales (1993), *Wales in Miniature* [a short history of the Museum], 34 pp

Peate, Iorwerth C. (1929), *Guide to the collection of Welsh Bygones. A descriptive account of old-fashioned life in Wales, together with a Catalogue of the objects exhibited.* [Edited with a Preface and Introduction by Cyril Fox], National Museum of Wales and the Press Board University of Wales. xvi + 148 pp

Peate, Iorwerth C. (1940), *The Welsh House: a study in folk culture,* The Honourable Society of Cymmrodorion, London. xviii + 232 pp. 2nd Edition (1944) Brython Press, Liverpool. 3rd Edition (1946)

Peate, Iorwerth C. (1976), *Rhwng dau fyd: darn o hunangofiant,* [Between two worlds: A fragment of autobiography], Gwasg Gee, Dinbych 200 pp. Ailargraffiad (1980) (Aberystwyth). (Translation arr. D. A. Bassett)

Sauer, Carl O. (1941), The Personality of Mexico, *American Geographical Reiew* July 1941

Scott-Fox, Charles (1993), Joseph Benwell Clark [series *Dorset Worthies* No. 20], Dorset Natural History and Archaeological Society. 4 pp.

Smith, Peter (1988), *Houses of the Welsh Countryside,* HMSO

Smith, Peter (1993) Introduction to the Second Edition pp iv–xxviii in Cyril Fox and Lord Raglan *Monmouthshire Houses: a study in building techniques and smaller house plans in the 15th to 17th Centuries.* Merton Priory Press and National Museum of Wales

Stevens, Catrin (1986), *Iorwerth C. Peate* [series *Writers of Wales*], University of Wales Press on behalf of the Welsh Arts Council

Subbaro, B. (1956), *The Personality of India,* Baroda

Summers, Roger (1960), *The Personality of Rhodesia,* Proceedings of the American Philosophical Society, Philadelphia

Wheeler, Sir Mortimer (1955), *Still Digging: Interleaves from an Antiquary's notebook,* Michael Joseph, London

Part III – Unpublished Material

1. Minutes of the Court and Council of the National Museum of Wales 1920–1948
2. Letters and written records from the Cyril Fox family archive, held by the author, together with correspondence with the author and taped interviews with eminent archaeologists of his day – all of whom are now deceased. The references in the manuscript 'letter to the author' reflects the invaluable assistance provided so willingly by his friends and colleagues. Following publication of this volume it is intended to offer this archive on permanent loan to the National Library of Wales.

Index